ONE LANGUAGE ~
SOURCE OF ALL TONGUES
BY
ARNOLD D. WADLER

The AMERICAN PRESS
FOR ART AND SCIENCE

NEW YORK 28

412
W 123

Copyright, 1948

ARNOLD D. WADLER, NEW YORK CITY 28.

Copyright Under the Articles of the Copyright Convention of the Pan-American Republics and the United States.

Dedicated to

RUDOLPH STEINER

CONTENTS

EXPLANATIONS.

(1) *Transcription of Words of Foreign Languages.*
Words of tongues, such as French, German, Spanish, Italian, etc., which use the same alphabet as English, are quoted as they are written or printed in their own orthography. Japanese words are quoted as they are written in *Rôma Jikai* (Latin alphabet).
The principle of transcription of Rôma-Jikai is as follows: the *consonants* are written and pronounced as in English. The *vowels* are pronounced as in almost all European tongues:

A	as in FAR
E	as in NET, or as A in FATE, LATE
I	as in FISH, or in NEED
O	as in SORRY, or in CORN
U	as in ROOM

This is the same principle which is used in Webster's Dictionaries. It is used in this book for words of those tongues which are *not* written in the Latin alphabet, but in any other system of writing, be it ideographs, syllables or an alphabet, e.g. Greek, Russian, Chinese, Hebrew, Babylonian, Egyptian, etc.

(2) *Numbers added to Chinese Words.*
They mark the numbers contained in *Giles, Chinese-English Dictionary.* This dictionary is of a particular value for the purpose of this book, for it quotes in almost all cases not only the form of the words as contained in the different Chinese dialects (Shanghai, Canton, Foochow, Hakka, etc.), but also the related words in Annamese, Korean and Japanese. The latter often show the consonants which were dropped in the decadent Mandarin dialect.

(3) *American Indian Vernaculars.*
These include words of tongues such as Mexican, Peruvian, Brazilian, and Chilean.

Mexican	=	Nahuatl
Peruvian	=	Quichua
Brazilian	=	Tupi
Chilean	=	Araucan

We shall keep in mind the fact that there are still other dialects spoken in Mexico, Peru (e.g. Aymara), Chile and Brazil (Guarani, Bororo, etc.). The names of these additional dialects are given. Thus the terms *Mexican, Peruvian, Brazilian, Chilean* refer to the main dialects spoken in these countries.

ABOUT THE AUTHOR

THIS BOOK is the outcome of studies of the common origin of all Languages extended over nearly thirty years. From his boyhood the author was attracted by this question and prepared himself for its solution by studying ancient and modern tongues, trying to master at least one idiom as representative of every linguistic family: Germanic, Romance, Slavic, Semitic, Chinese, African and the pre-Columbian vernaculars of America, Mexican, Peruvian, Maya and so on.

He gained the impression that human tongues, beneath the surface of their present and historical diversity, actually form a unity as a result of their descent from a common source. This possibility was opposed to some degree by many of his teachers and other scholars, but their objections did not convince the author.

In 1919 a little booklet fell into his hands, published by the late Professor Dr. Herman Beckh of Berlin University, a pupil of the great scholar Dr. Rudolf Steiner. In this booklet Professor Beckh compared words of different language families: Indo-European, Semitic, Tibetan and American, in accordance with Rudolf Steiner's teaching, "There was once actually a common primeval tongue upon earth, and all languages, modern or ancient, are but dialects of this single mother-tongue of all mankind."

From that moment the author concentrated his research by studying as many grammars and vocabularies of various idioms as were accessible to him, collecting the necessary material, and methodically arranging the words on the plan of an *Etymological Dictionary of Human Speech*. He chose such a word as *Man* and grouped around it all words of other languages which were related to it. This was merely raw-material however; it had to be completed by information and explanation gained from related fields of knowledge: Anthropology, Ethnology, Mythology, History and Prehistory, Natural Science etc. A large brown brief-case contained this unique collection of files, enriched by new notes from day to day.

In 1933 the critical world situation compelled the author to leave his legal practice in Berlin, and go to Switzerland and thence to Paris, where he continued working on his subject. As the fruit of his studies, in 1935-37 he published three books in Switzerland: *The Tower of Babel* (DER TURM VON BABEL), *Germanic Prehistory* (GERMANISCHE URZEIT) and *The Aryan Riddle* (DAS RÄTSEL DER INDOGERMANEN).

This occurred in a time when the deepest materialism of our modern age overshadowed Central Europe. The books found a warm response in the free press of the countries around Germany: Switzerland, Netherlands, Austria, Czechoslovakia, Scandinavia. Even some German papers published friendly reviews. In 1937 a Berlin paper admitted that "Wadler's Tower of Babel is a meritorious advance into the field of totalitarian linguistics." Official circles however tried to suppress the book, and even its advertisement in a scientific review was not permitted. Nevertheless almost eighty percent of all three volumes sold in Germany.

The story of this present work however involves still more adventures. After the fall of France in 1940 the author, who had been in the service of the French Government as a translator from six languages, had to leave Paris suddenly. He confided his treasure, still contained in the brown brief-case, to a French Red Cross nurse, and went to the Basque country and later to Marseilles. Cut from all his friends by the establishment of an occupied zone, he did not even know where his precious linguistic material was hidden, and the result of a lifetime of effort seemed lost. Early in September he finally obtained the visas for Spain and Portugal. The Portuguese Consul gave him a hint to leave Marseilles immediately, for the Spanish border would be closed at any hour, but at the very moment of departure the author received a letter from Switzerland telling him that his brown brief-case awaited him in Périgueux near Bordeaux.

Should he abandon his material and escape to the Atlantic,

or risk his freedom and life, and save the brown brief-case? The author went to Périgueux. Back in Marseilles he learned that the Spanish border had been closed, but fortunately, in a few days, it was reopened. The author climbed over the Pyrénées, went to Lisbon, and later sailed to the United States. On the last day of 1940 he landed with his precious brief-case in New York.

Years of continued research followed, particularly extended to pre-Columbian languages and civilisations. In 1942, at the start of a lecture tour from coast to coast, the author was invited by The Indian Office in Washington to visit the Indian Country. In New Mexico and Arizona, with the aid of the United States Reservations Authorities, he made interesting studies of Indian life, speech and religion. Since that time he has continued lecturing and teaching.

* * *

The book now submitted to the public is not a reproduction of the three books formerly published in Europe, which should have been completed by a fourth volume dealing with pre-Columbian America. "One Language — Source of All Tongues" though including a few fundamental points contained in the former books, is an entirely new and independent work in which the stress is placed upon America. Ancient America is recognized as the key to the problem of a common primeval tongue, of the origin of mankind and of our civilisation. The material is greatly enriched, the method of investigation widely improved and the presentation simplified and clarified. It is hoped that the wealth of material now submitted for the first time will convince every unbiased reader.

PAUL MARSHALL ALLEN

The Scudder Collver School
New York City

AUTHOR'S NOTE

I wish to thank the subscribers whose generous contributions made the publication of this book possible at this time.

I owe particular gratitude to my friend and editor, Paul Marshall Allen, for his excellent cooperation in bringing this material to the English-speaking world for the first time.

DR. ARNOLD D. WADLER

New York City,
October, 1948

CHAPTER ONE

THE TOWER OF BABEL

LANGUAGE IS Man's loftiest expression in the Universe. United with the light of his thinking, it is the spiritual rainbow-bridge that links him with those regions of the Cosmos which we seek far above the valley of our earthly existence.

As the Thought, the Logos, is the Sun, the Lux, which enlightens our whole World, the Tongue of Man is the Song which permeates it with celestial harmonies. From the innocent stammering of the infant to the loftiest descriptions of Man's experiences in the Universe, human speech is one of the deepest world enigmas.

Where was human speech born? Who engendered it? The origin of Man's voice, of human Speech is shrouded in darkness, in the silent dawn of the world's unfolding, of Man's descent into earthly life. Human memory is too short to penetrate those earliest waves of existence; our knowledge is too weak to reach those distant spheres. Whatever we know about the origins of human speech, we owe to myths and to legends, not to history. Conscious history is silent about the morning-tide of our earth-existence.

If we wish to learn anything about our past, we must recognize that the span of time not covered by history is far longer than the historic epoch of recorded events. Therefore it is necessary to study traditions, myths, legends and holy books in place of other records if we wish to penetrate the first epochs of humanity. These may not always be reliable or well preserved. Their language may be strange and alien to us, difficult to understand. Yet we must try to learn and to understand them. For it is true as *Wilhelm Wundt* stressed in his Psychology of Nations (*"Völker-Psychologie"*), that myths, legends and holy books are the form of history of the early epochs of mankind.

I

The Bible is one of those books which contains very ancient wisdom. Its Cosmology goes back to an epoch when the art of writing had not yet been invented, and mythological and religious contents were transmitted orally from generation to generation. Much was lost and much was altered and distorted later, when scribes sat down to preserve all these traditions in records. Yet, what immense treasures of knowledge and wisdom have been saved from destruction and oblivion in the course of all ages!

The Bible describes the creation of heaven, earth, nature and man by the *El-ohim,* in Old Greek, *Hel-ioi* (the sun-spirits). They blew the breath of life and of speech into Adam's body, into Man, their highest earthly creation, thus conveying to him the charm of language. It is he, Man, who gave all the other creatures, animals and plants and minerals, their names. The Bible further tells us that there was in the beginning upon earth one language consisting of a single name for a given object. The human family still lived together, and most of the continents were not yet peopled.

In a grand tableau the Biblical story attributes the loss of that primeval tongue to the moral decay of humanity. It is expressed in a symbol, the erection of a tower "whose top was to reach unto heaven", the tower of Babel. Still another feature is very remarkable. The Bible mentions the building and foundation of cities, the use of bricks which were burnt thoroughly, and of slime instead of mortar. We shall see later that the story of the Tower of Babel suggests the stone age. The whole undertaking was considered as a rebellion against the divine beings in later accounts. Thus God descended, destroyed the tower by a thunderstorm, and confused the original tongue "so that they were unable to understand one another." They fled from that place and dispersed into the four quarters of the earth. This was the beginning of the peopling of the continents.

Modern science regards these Biblical accounts with scepticism. Thus in the Age of Enlightenment many scholars merely mocked at the story of the Deluge. However in the course of the Nineteenth Century, a change of attitude developed. The Western world became more and more acquainted with the myths and traditions of the different nations. Scholars began to study ancient and modern folklore, fairy tales, legends, myths. The more they studied, the more they were amazed. For the record of a Flood, of a Deluge, of a water catastrophe had been preserved by almost all the peoples of the world, civilized and primitive, from China, across Asia and Europe, to the West Coast of America. Then science admitted that such a catastrophe actually happened at a certain epoch. Whether we call it the ice-age or the flood, does not matter.

Strangely enough, most modern students, even those who accept the Biblical teachings, are convinced that the story of the Tower of Babel in Genesis is entirely isolated in literature. True, there are cuneiform texts which describe a tower, a *zikkurat* (monument), erected in Babylon. But that is not the point. There were many towers built in Mesopotamia as in various other parts of the ancient world. Yet what matters here is not the building itself but the primeval tongue and its destiny. No cuneiform tablet speaks of this common language nor does any Egyptian hieroglyphic text present any clue to its existence.

Yet, the story of the primeval tongue is not only preserved in the Bible, it is found all over the world, in the Eastern and in the Western hemispheres. Starting in the Far East, from China, and wandering West, to America, we are faced with remnants of this account in the literature of many nations. In the Far East, the old tradition of the *Chinese* people teaches that there was an age called the Golden Age, under the reign of the primeval Emperor *Shin Hoang*, the age of Harmony and of the Great Unity, when religion, law and speech were still united all over the world. That great ruler, a personality of exceptional virtue and talents, was still capable of directing the so-called six Ki or powers, namely stillness and motion, light and darkness, rain and wind, as he was endowed with other faculties of higher beings. Shin Hoang, we are told, was able to show how the various tongues of the world are related to the original speech of humanity. In the book "Li Ki" (Six Powers) it is reported that, when the common tongue split into different branches, the Universe had deviated from its right way, the Tao.

Hindu wisdom contains a symbolic description of the splitting up of the primeval tongue into various vernaculars. The Vata or fig tree was the symbol of the original language. An ancient Hindu legend contained in *Niclas Müller's* Faith and Knowledge of the Hindus,* relates that in the beginning that marvelous, giant tree overshadowed the first generations of mankind, protecting them against the wild elements. That tree was the link which united all members of humanity. It grew to heaven, in full brightness and splendor. However, misled by their haughtiness the people tried to turn the proud Vata tree into a Jacob's ladder.

To punish their arrogance, the Gods hit the ambitious tree with their thunderbolts, cutting off its branches and dispersing them all over the earth. Out of these branches twenty-one new Vata-trees grew. Unfortunately Niclas Müller does not mention the source of this Hindu legend. Two of its features connect it with the story of the Tower of Babel: the wish to turn the Vata tree into a staircase to heaven, and the moral rebellion against the divine world. We find similar features in Greek and Norse mythology, such as the attempt of the giants to storm Mount Olympus, and the Germanic Asas (German: die Asen) to conquer Walhalla. In the Teutonic tongues, *AS-a* means *giant*, powerful and in Hebrew, *AZ* means "strong, powerful".

Some vestiges of the Biblical account of the Tower of Babel are found in an *Old Persian* legend. According to this tradition there was but one language on earth in the beginning, the language spoken by all mankind. Later Ahriman, the spirit of Evil, split this language into thirty different tongues. This confusion of speech took place under the reign of king Tahmuraz.

In his book *Isis and Osiris* Plutarch stresses that at the

_____
*Niklas Müller, Glauben und Wissen der Hindu.

end of time the whole Earth will become homogeneous, there will be no death, but one eternal life, one kingdom in which all mankind will live a blessed life, using but one common tongue. Since in antique eschatology (description of the end of the world) the final period closely resembles the initial epoch, we can deduce from this picture that in the beginning too there was but one common speech of all mankind.

Upon leaving Asia and passing to Europe we find few reminiscences of the story of Babel. Greek mythology must have known something about this tradition, but in Greek literature no record of it has survived. Only in a Roman legend we encounter some reflex of the lost Greek wisdom. The *Roman* mythologist Hyginus relates in his *Fables* a story according to which in bygone epochs men did not as yet know either cities or laws. They lived under the rule of Jupiter and all used one and the same tongue. Then all at once Hermes (Mercury) started interpreting (Greek: *HERME-neuo*) the common language, thus separating humanity into nations. Discord arose among the mortals. Cut to the heart Jupiter then gave the reign of humanity to a mortal man, king Phoroneus. Thus divine rulership was replaced by human.

This legend again reminds us of a very ancient common tradition of mankind. Hermes-Mercury is linked with the origin of speech and of writing in most mythologies of the Old World. Thus in Egypt it is Hermes-Thoth (Mercury) who is the god of speech and the inventor of hieroglyphic writing. In Norse mythology Wotan or Woden is identical with Mercury (Anglo-Saxon *WEDNES-dey=Mercury's day*). In Scandinavia too Odhin-Wotan was the god of speech and poetry and the creator of the Runic alphabet.

In the Baltic countries it is among *Esthonians* that the tradition of a common language has been kept alive. An Esthonian legend relates that in ancient times humanity had common dwelling places and a common tongue, but their numbers increased so much that their home-land became too small. So the Ancient of Days wished them to spread over the earth, and he allotted to each nation a particular home.

But in order to estrange them still more from one another
he decided to bestow upon each nation particular inclina-
tions, customs, an individual name and a special language.
On a certain day each nation was to appear once again before
him. He put a kettle filled with water upon the hearth, let
the water bubble and buzz, and assigned to each approaching
tribe its language, character and name, according to the seething and hissing of the water.

While all the other nations did not appear until later in
the day to receive their vernacular according to the buzzing
of the boiling water, the Esthonians, slim, smart and jolly,
were already a long time on the spot, before the water in the
kettle had even started to boil. In order not to keep them
waiting, the Ancient of Days assigned to them his own tongue.

In Western Europe there is a very slight trace of the common original tongue preserved in some *Irish* legends; that
tongue was called by the Celtic people *Gortigheam.*

But the ancient tradition of a common origin of languages
extended beyond the boundaries of the Old World across the
Atlantic. The myths and legends of many American Indian
tribes contain an echo of the Biblical account, yet that tradition is particularly alive among the Maya tribes. In the holy
book of the Quiché tribe of *Guatemala,* called the *Popol
Buh* (Maya *Buh*=German *Buch*=*book*) we find passages describing the existence of a common tongue and its sudden
confusion. These descriptions are so alive and so like the
Biblical report that some scholars upon reading them were
convinced that some Spanish missionary intent upon introducing Christianity to Guatemala was their real author.

In several of its passages, particularly in chapters thirty-
one and thirty-three, we hear of the primeval tongue: "Thus
spake there those who gazed at the rising of the sun. All had
but one language." ... "This happened after they had arrived
in Tulan, before moving West. Here the tongue of those
tribes was changed. Their speech became different. All that
they had heard and grasped when departing from Tulan had
become incomprehensible to them. Here they separated. Some

of them moved East. Many came to this place (to Guatemala)."

There is a most tragic tone in the description which the Popol Buh gives of that moment when the tribes that migrated West suddenly became aware of the confusion of their tongue (Chapter 35 C) : ". . . and the heart of the clans was crying. For the tongue of the Balam Quiché, Balam Aqhab, Mahukutah and Iki Balam had already turned different . . . . Alas, alas, we have forsaken our speech! Why did we do this? Now we are lost! How were we deluded? One was our tongue when we departed from Tulan, one the country where we were born. This was not a good deed, said the tribes sitting all together under the trees and bushes . . .".

Thus we see that many nations and tribes in various continents and countries, in the New and the Old World, had guarded a faint reminiscence of the fact that once in the beginning mankind had dwelt together in a common homeland and had spoken one and the same tongue. That distant land shrouded in the mist of oblivion was the cradle of humanity and of our entire civilisation.

Our knowledge of the past is but piece-work, a mosaic containing many gaps. One nation contributed this corner, others another part of the picture. Some nations appear not to have made any gift at all. While the Quiché Indians of Guatemala have borne in mind for thousands of years the memory of the primeval tongue, the great civilized nations of the Near East, the Egyptians and the people of Hellas seem not to have known anything about a common primeval tongue of all humanity.

Or did they forfeit recollection of it?

CHAPTER TWO

ON THE ORIGIN OF SPEECH

WHILE THE Hebrew people had received information on the original language from the myth of the Tower of Babel and their holy books, neither the ancient Sumerians, the Babylonians, Phoenicians or Arabs seem to have obtained that knowledge or to have preserved it in their literature. So it is also with the Egyptians and Greeks.

Why this silence? If — as we seek to prove — all civilisation of mankind stems from the same source, is it likely that nations leading in culture should be lacking such an important tradition? The reason why no knowledge of a once existing primeval tongue had been transmitted by Sumerians, Babylonians, or Egyptians is due to the *change in man's consciousness* in different epochs.

Human consciousness develops as well as the soul and spirit of every individual. Time and space exert their influence upon it, and the consciousness of the twentieth century is certainly not the same as that of the sixth or fifth millennium B.C., nor is the consciousness of the Greek nation in the age of Socrates and Plato like that of the contemporary Mayan, Mexican or Peruvian tribes or of the Bantu clans in the first Christian centuries. Even the human consciousness in different continents was not alike in the same epoch.

Yet, despite all these different characteristics we can speak of a general human consciousness and trace its growth and evolution. When we obtain a kind of bird's-eye view of this development, we can divide the whole into four periods:

(1) The Mythological Age
(2) The Religious Age
(3) The Philosophical Age
(4) The Naturalistic Age.

Since the Fifteenth Century we have been living in the epoch of Natural Science, while before this period the leading nations of mankind had lived in a kind of Philosophical Age. This was the case in Egypt, the cradle — or one of the cradles — of the art of writing, and particularly in Greece, in the classical epoch of Philosophy and Art.

We search the Nile Valley in vain for an hieroglyphic report on the Confusion of Tongues. The Mythological Age had vanished, and the Age of Thinking had started there. In this Age of Thinking Egyptian Pharaohs, formerly priest-kings guarding the hidden initiation wisdom, did not care about any myths, but dealt with primeval speech on the basis of knowledge.

In his book on History *Herodotus* tells how the Pharaoh *Psamtik* sought to discover which human language was the most ancient. He ordered two infant boys to be taken from their mothers' breasts and confided to the care of one of his shepherds. They were to be brought up in complete solitude in a desert cave, out of contact with any other human beings, and the king's shepherd was strictly forbidden to utter even a sound in their presence. After a year or two the two babies would stammer their first words. The shepherd was to watch for this moment, keep their first words in mind and report them to the Pharaoh.

A year passed, then several months. Day after day the shepherd went to the cave where the infants lived, brought them food and drink, took care of them and watched for the moment to pick up their first sounds. Day after day — silence, not the slightest trace of conscious, articulate speech. Finally however, one day when the shepherd approached the cave somewhat later than usual, the poor little boys, driven by hunger, came walking toward him, outstretching their little arms and screaming in imploring tones *"Bekos, Bekos"*! Amazed about what he had heard, the king's shepherd guarded his secret and did not tell the Pharaoh about it. The following day the same thing happened. Again the two infants came running toward their guardian, begging *"Bekos, Bekos"*!

Now the shepherd was certain he had fulfilled his task, so he went and reported the story to the Pharaoh. The king turned to his wise men and asked them to tell him in which language the word *Bekos* occurred and what it meant. After a short investigation the wise men of Egypt reported that *Bekos* was a Phrygian word, and that it meant *bread*. "And thus" declared Herodotus, the father of History, "Psamtik was convinced that Phrygian was the oldest tongue, and the Phrygians the oldest people."

This experiment of the 'enlightened' Pharaoh Psamtik was repeated in the Thirteenth Century by the Emperor Frederick II. The result of his effort was more tragic: both infants died after having been separated from their mothers. In the Sixteenth Century, *Laurent Joubert,* a French scholar, published in Avignon a book "Public question: Which language would a child talk that never before heard anyone talking?" (*Quel langage parlerait un enfant qui n'aurait jamais ouy parler?*) .

At the beginning of the Nineteenth Century the mysterious case of *Caspar Hauser* stirred Germany and Europe, the strange story of a presumed German prince who had been kept in a basement up to the age of sixteen out of contact with any other human being, without education, without learning any language. Again appeared the old question of the original tongue, and many scholars, naturalists and others, look at this problem even nowadays in a similar way as did the Egyptian Pharaoh Psamtik some three thousand years ago.

After all, is there a natural tongue which every human being, deprived of any contact with other human beings from the very first moment of his life, would produce automatically, without being taught it? This is the question, and we must say that the whole modern experimental approach to the problem marks a high degree of ignorance about the inner nature of speech. Psamtik was as wrong as Herodotus, as was the scholarly Emperor Frederick II, and quite a number of people in the Nineteenth Century, the Naturalistic Age, who dreamt of a natural primeval tongue, produced automatically by some physical impulse.

Language is a social phenomenon. No human being would consciously use any word without starting first — as all infants do — stammering and babbling certain articulate sounds which are composed of elements of every tongue. No infant is able to utter out of itself the vocabulary of any vernacular, to turn baby-talk into sensible words and sentences, without being helped step by step by his mother, his father, his nurse and his entire surroundings. It is by dialogues, and not by monologues that we learn even our own mother-tongue. As human beings we are endowed with speech organs and a general talent of speaking, but not with the power of learning any particular language by ourselves, without any intercourse with another human being. There is no such thing as a "natural tongue".

Herodotus' story as well as Psamtik's whole experiment are thus of very doubtful value. We can investigate it by studying the word *Bekos* allegedly uttered by the two Egyptian infants. It means *bread* or — in a wider sense — *food*. *Bekos* sounds similar to such Greek words as *TAUR-os* (bull), *THE-os* (God), *ANTHROP-os* (man). Yet what is particularly Greek in this Phrygian word *Bek-os* is but the ending *-os*. The root or stem of the word is *BEK-* (bread). Thus *Bek-os* means what is *BAK-ed*. This word is not exclusively Phrygian. Its roots can be found in the English-speaking parts of the earth, in German dialects, as *BECK* (baker), in Russian, *PEK-aty* (to bake), *PEK-lo* (hell), from its hellish fire, "the bakery" of the sinning souls. We could quote many other vernaculars where relatives of the Phrygian word *BEK-os* can be encountered.

Old Egyptian wisdom had entirely fallen into decay when Psamtik undertook his experiment. What he sought for was the lost primeval tongue of all mankind, but his power of imagination was as insufficient as his knowledge. Psamtik lived in the twilight between an age of faith and an epoch of science, he did not as yet come into the daylight of true knowledge. There is but one scientific method by which one can find the way back to the primeval speech: *the oracle of language itself.*

As a matter of fact Psamtik's experiment had only one feature in common with the Philosophical Age: he established a problem. But the way he attempted to solve it was a method adequate only to the Age of Natural Science. This was quite different in *Hellas* where the best thinkers devoted their greatest efforts to discuss and to solve the question of the origin of speech in a true philosophical way. There is no other country where such an importance was attributed to this problem as in classical Hellas. We can say without exaggeration that the question of the origin of speech was the focus of Greek philosophy. Almost all the great thinkers: Heraclitus, Democritus, the Sophists, Socrates, Plato and Aristotle partook in its discussion.

The questions that occupied their minds were basic problems of speech. What was the nature of the words, what were their elements, how did speech originate? Did language come down from heavens as a gift of the Gods? Had it been fashioned on earth as man's invention? How did speech begin, develop and to what degree did mankind take part in its creation?

All antiquity, judging from the myths and legends, considered human speech a gift of Gods, and believed in particular deities of speech. In *India* it was *Brahma* or *Brihaspati* (the lord of prayer) who created language; in *Babylonia* the *fish-like god Oannes;* in *Egypt—Thoth-Hermes*, in *Rome Janus*, and among the *Germanic tribes Odin-Wotan* or his son *Bragi*, the *deity of poetry.* When the Mythological and Religious Ages came to an end, and the Philosophical Epoch started, two contrasting opinions existed regarding the origin of speech. Two opposing groups of philosophers were passionately struggling against one another: the adherents of *Physis* (nature) and those of *Thesis* (convention)!

What was the idea underlying *Physis* and *Thesis?* Both words did not express the same concept in Hellas in the last millennium B.C. which they express in our present time. To Heraclitus and Pythagoras, to Socrates and Plato, Physis was not yet the mechanical, automatic, abstract and empty nature as it is thought to have been. To the great thinkers of Hellas a cosmological conception such as the theory of Kant and Laplace where matter develops out of itself in obedience to abstract natural laws, was simply unthinkable. Creation without a creative spirit, a creative personality, a creative plan and idea, in one word without a *conscious creator* was senseless. To those great thinkers of humanity, nature was still identical with the Divine Nature, was a manifestation of God. As Emerson expressed it: "Behind nature, within nature, there is God"!

The great thinkers of Greece still had an inkling of the innate, deeper laws active in the life of language. According to them, nothing in the word is accidental. The sounds used in the shaping of words fulfill a certain natural and thus also divine mission. In Plato's dialogue, *Cratylus*, both Socrates and Plato tried to establish even the sense of each sound, the consonants and the vowels. It was Socrates' first attempt to penetrate into the difficult field of etymology and semantics. Here Socrates did not trust himself and decried his efforts as foolish and even ridiculous. As a matter of fact these studies of Socrates and Plato were ingenious, but unsuccessful.

These two philosophers were the most important champions of *Physis*, while on the other hand Democritus and later, Aristotle were fervent defenders of *Thesis*. Thesis is the theory that speech was not a creation of God, or the result of an innate human faculty, but merely a deliberate human invention. There is no actual reason why a word should designate this and not the other thing. The only reason for our linking a certain sense with certain sounds is the result of a convention created by families, tribes, peoples and nations.

Democritus had four reasons for adhering to the prinicple of Thesis. It is nothing but the result of convention that we call the sweet — sweet, the bitter — bitter, the cold — cold and the warm — warm. We could just as well use different names for each of these qualities. Speech owes its origin to chance, to mere convention. Why? Here Democritus quotes the *four* reasons for his conviction. First, the *Homonyms*, different

words consisting of the same sounds but having another meaning. Thus the word *S-O-L-E* can designate a *fish*, a *part of
the foot*, of a *shoe*, or — *alone*. We could add SOUL also although it is spelt differently. Secondly, the *Synonyms*, words
consisting of different sounds, but having the same or a similar meaning, such as *to beat, to strike, to blow, to hit, to rap,
to flog* and so on. Third, *the change of names*. Was not Theo-
phrastus first called Tyrtamus? Did the change of his name in
any way alter his personality? Did not Plato himself adopt a
new name? Was he not first called Aristocles? Did this change
transmute his nature? Finally, the *Anomalies* in speech, the
lack of regular analogies. Why do we form the noun *knowledge* from the verb *to know*, but never create *throwledge* from
to throw?

These arguments of Democritus' sound very plausible. Are
we not all familiar with the unfortunate irregularity of all
tongues, with the crux of irregular verbs? However of far
greater importance was the critique exerted against Plato's
and Socrates' ideas on speech by Plato's own pupil, the great
Aristotle. Why did he oppose his great teacher? Why did he
act like a horse who, to use an expression of Rudolf Steiner,
kicks his own trainer? Why did he adhere to Thesis? With
much more ingenuity than any other thinker Aristotle stressed
and explained the purely conventional origin and character
of speech. "Nothing in speech stems from nature!" he said in
De interpretatione (chapter 2). Sounds alone, even when articulate, are not yet language. To turn simple sounds into
elements of speech, we must connect with them a certain
meaning, a thought."

"How do we proceed in this task? By Physis? By Thesis?
According to nature, or by mere convention? Were sound
and sense linked with each other according to the principles
of Physis, then of course all nations would by necessity use
the same tongue! Sound and sound groups are but expressions
of thoughts or sensations. All nations, all human beings nourish in their hearts and minds the same sentiments and ideas.
Were the words no mere symbols, were they to correspond
essentially and inwardly with our thoughts and feelings, were

they identical with them, then, of course, all nations, all men ought to express the same sentiments and ideas in the same way! This, however, is not the case. Not only do various tongues possess different sounds, but entirely different words and forms of speech as well. Consequently language must have originated in every nation in a different way. "Words" Aristotle continues (chapter 4) "are but sounds which by arbitrary convention are linked with a certain meaning."

This was the last word of Antiquity about the origin of speech, at the beginning of the Christian Era. This sharp opposition of Aristotle toward Plato was by no means his only diversion. It is in three essential questions that he turned against his teacher: the descent of Man, the origin of speech, and the Lost Continent of Atlantis. Aristotle's adverse criticism unfortunately discredited some of Plato's ideas concerning the whole problem of Atlantis. In a certain sense we may say that Aristotle's opposition to Plato paved the way to the modern naturalistic world-conception.

What was the tragic mistake of Aristotle? His arguments and conclusions were logically correct and convincing, yet nevertheless wrong. We may already doubt his assertion that all nations and all human beings nourish in their hearts and minds the same sentiments and ideas. Their very spiritual and soul diversity brings about the most frequent and important variations in speech. It is because all mortals have to experience death and yet have an entirely different attitude toward this inevitable occurrence in man's life, that different people express their idea of death in entirely different ways using different vowels and different consonants.

However let us suppose that Aristotle was right in saying that feelings and thoughts are alike, but that every nation uses different words for the same sentiments and ideas. Yes, the languages are different today, but *was this always the case*? Is their diversity due to their original nature, or to their later development? Had the father of Logic put this inevitable question, he would have been led to the great problem of evolution, and he would have found the Ariadne thread to lead him out of the labyrinth.

CHAPTER THREE

UNITY OF SPEECH IN ASIA AND EUROPE

WITH THE opening of the Christian Era the ancient civilisations with their Oriental culture had fulfilled their life, fallen into decay and vanished from the stage of world history. The Babylonian, Egyptian, Phoenician and Persian Empires collapsed, their records were buried beneath the soil of the Near East, a few centuries passed and there was no priest, no scribe, no student in the whole world able to read and to understand any text written in hieroglyphs or cuneiforms! Darkness shrouded the millennia of the Ancient Ages. The languages of those great nations disappeared and were superseded by the speech of conquerors and newcomers.

The new era, the epoch of Christianity, brought about a deep change of humanity. It is in full agreement with historical truth that mankind started officially a new calendar era from the incarnation of Christ upon earth. For about at the moment when the three crosses were set up on Golgotha an event of greatest historic importance occurred. This was *the Migration of Peoples.*

It was neither the first nor the last of those mysterious waves of transplantation which were to change the whole surface of the earth. Many groups of Asiatic, particularly of Turanian tribes pressed Westward: Mongols, Huns, Finno-Ugrians, Slavic, Germanic and Celtic clans. Some of them settled in the western parts of Asia, some wandered into Europe, pushing forward to the South, the West, the North. The whole aspect of the earth changed. The old nations, the founders and leaders of ancient civilisations, were removed from the scene or became silent, while young, powerful tribes who had lived for long millennia in silence, now began to play a leading part in the chorus of mankind.

These new tribes, such as the Slavs, Teutons, Celts, were illiterate yet uncorrupted, destined to become the great leading nations of the future. Their former connection with Asia and the Asiatic tribes is established by the affinity of language. The Germanic clans, Scandinavians, Anglo-Saxons, Germans and Dutch, must have been neighbors of the Finno-Ugrian tribes, particularly of the Hungarians, from their very first appearance on the stage of history. The story of Attila, King of the Huns, is contained in both the Edda and the Nibelungenlied. The relations of the Huns with the Teutons do not date from the time when they met in Europe; they go back as far as to Asia and to a very remote epoch of antiquity, millennia before Christ. Further new waves of migration followed during the whole First Millennium A.D.

Language is one of the most reliable witnesses of all these movements. Up to the time of the Migration of Peoples it is the classical tongues, Greek and Latin, which characterize Europe. Suddenly with the young nations' coming to the fore, new implements are introduced and new words begin to replace or to supersede classical names. We may mention here a few of them: *trumpet, drum, song, stamp* and even such an outstanding word as *self*.

(1) *Northern words coming to the fore after the Peoples' Migration*

English	German	Latin	Greek
trump-et	Tromp-ete	tub-a	salp-inx
drum	Tromm-el	tymp-anum	tymp-anon
song	Sang	cant-us	ôd-e
stamp	Stemp-el	sig-illum	sphrag-is
self	selb	ips-e	aut-os

Hundreds of such new terms penetrated into most European tongues in the course of the following centuries; many of them became predominant expressions of modern languages.

When Europe accepted the Christian faith the story of the Tower of Babel became a corner-stone of European civilisation and knowledge. No one doubted its reality, neither laymen nor scholars; it became the common property of the

European mind. Thus, the tradition of a primeval tongue spread over the western part of the earth during the Middle Ages. Later the struggle between faith and science began, and from that time also the attacks against the Bible were instigated. During all those centuries the legend of the Tower of Babel was only an object of faith. Every faithful Christian had to accept it, but none was able to prove it, to turn it into a matter of knowledge.

Many attempts were made indeed to prove the reality of the Biblical myth. Many people looked for vestiges of the lost original speech. All kinds of phantastic comparisons were made, distorting some words until they *looked* similar to others, in order to prove the truth of the legend. All in vain. In the Eighteenth Century, the Age of Enlightenment, the French Encyclopedists merely mocked at the idea of a common origin of language. "Viewed from the standpoint of philosophy and apart from all good suggestions one can draw from the holy books, . . . is not the idea of a primeval tongue just a pleasant vagary? What should we think of a man who would wish to explore which was the primeval cry of all animals and how it came about in the course of many, many centuries that sheep started bleating, cats mewing, pigeons cooing and birds chirping? They all understand one another very well in their tongues, nay much better than we ourselves . . . Each species has its own vernacular and that of the Eskimo and Algonquin was not the language of Peru. *There never has been such a thing as an original tongue,* or an original alphabet, as little as there has ever existed any primeval oak or original plant."

This assertion was the result of extreme carelessness, for which scholar would seriously call the different nations and tribes — *species,* in spite of their different tongues? Further it was a mark of complete ignorance. There are numerous words which the Eskimo of Alaska and of Greenland (also the Algonquin) have in common with Peruvians and other South American tribes.

(2) Words common to Eskimo and South American dialects.

Eskimo	kennek (mountain sheep)	Peruvian	guanac-o (mtn. sheep)
″	luk-luk (brent-goose)	″	lleca-lleca (heron)
″	app-a (father)	Caribbean	ap-e (father)
″	coon-ea (woman)	Brazilian	cun-a (woman)

It was rather preposterous of the Encyclopedists of the Eighteenth Century to make such an objection, since even to-day, almost two centuries later, we are far from being able to definitely state the relationship of American Indian vernaculars; and yet we know that the Athabascan language family extends from South America to Alaska.

Still more ironical was Voltaire's attitude. To him, Etymology was a discipline where consonants counted little, and vowels nothing at all. At the beginning of the Nineteenth Century the French philosophers who had belittled the primeval tongue and made fun of etymology received a drastic answer from destiny. About 1803 a Danish scholar, Rask, and about 1816 a German student, Franz Bopp, pointed out that the ancient holy tongues of India and Persia, Sanskrit and Avestan, were closely related to most languages of Europe, Greek and Latin, the Germanic, Celtic and Slavic dialects. Later on more vernaculars were added to this group of tongues, Lithuanian, Lettish and Albanian in Europe, Armenian, Hittite and Tokharian in Asia. Some German students called this family of tongues *Indo-Germanic,* pointing to its geographical extension from India to the Atlantic with England considered a Germanic country. French scholars preferred to call it *Indo-European.* Here a list of its members:

(3) List of languages forming the Indo-European Family.

European branch	Asiatic branch
Old and Modern Greek	Sanskrit
Latin	Avestan, Old Persian, Persian
French, Italian and all	The daughter tongues of
Romance vernaculars	Sanskrit and Avestan
English, German and the	Armenian
Teutonic tongues	Hittite
Celtic, Irish, Scottish,	Tokharian
Welsh, Cymric, Cornic	
Russian, Polish and the	
other Slavic dialects	
Lithuanian, Lettish	
Albanian	

This list is not at all complete, since there are a few Indo-European vernaculars spoken today in the Caucasus Mountains, probably one of the central cross-roads of the migration of peoples into Europe.

As a matter of fact, Bopp's discovery was not at all new. Since the great voyages to India several European residents of that fabulous country had reported to Europe that Sanskrit words were identical with Latin or other European terms. It was not at all difficult to recognize in Sanskrit *TRA-ya* (3) the English word *THREE,* or in Indian *SARP-a* (snake) the English word *SERP-ent* or the Latin *SERP-ens,* just as it was easy to connect *DEV-a* (god) with Latin *DIV-us* (god) and with *DIV-ine.* Such harmonies of words, as they were called, have been recognized by several European scholars since the early Middle Ages. What was new in Bopp's study was the evidence that not only did the vocabulary prove them related, but also their *conjugation,* their structural character.

(4) *Identical Conjugation in Sanskrit and in Old Greek.*

Sanskrit	*Old Greek*
DA-DA-mi (I have given)	DI-DO-mi (I give)
DA-DA-si (thou hast given)	DI-DO-s (thou givest)
DA-DA-ti (he has given)	DI-DO-ti (he gives)

This new approach to the problem gave all the results obtained from that moment on an entirely different character: community of grammar could certainly not be the effect of an accident, but of true genealogical relationship, of common descent, destiny and life. Such coincidences were more reliable and acceptable. They were not the result of guesswork or wishful thinking, but of scientific facts. Philologists — particularly in Germany — stressed more and more the scientific character of the new method of investigation, underrating perhaps the pioneer work of the past and overrating the few common features of grammatical structure which had been discovered between a part of the members of the Indo-European family.

Then came Jacob Grimm, who with his brother Wilhelm,

had edited the beautiful German fairy tales. He pointed to another scientific feature of relationship between the vernaculars of the newly discovered group: he established the well-known *Grimm's Law of sound-shifting*. What is this famous Law? When we compare the consonants of Sanskrit, Avestan, Greek, Latin, Celtic and Slavic words on the one hand with the corresponding consonants of the most ancient forms of the Germanic words, we discover a sort of change which Grimm and his adherents consider *regular*.

We find in Sanskrit, *DAS-a* (ten), in *Greek, DEK-a*, in Latin, *DEC-em,* in Russian, *DES-ety*. But in the Teutonic vernaculars we find in Gothic, *TAIH-un* (lO) in Anglo-Saxon, *TEN* or *TYN*, in English, *TEN*. Here the initial D is changed into T. Such changes occur in each of these tongues. Yet the Germanic languages are much more affected by them than the other members of the Indo-European circle: not only have they moved ahead and away from all the other cousin-tongues, but they moved *twice*. They show *two* subsequent phases of sound-shifting. D was changed into T, according to Jacob Grimm, when all the Germanic tribes still formed a unit and spoke the same language, primeval or common Germanic. Then came a period when High German, of which modern German is a part, moved away from its sister-tongues, from Gothic, Anglo-Saxon, Old Norse. Instead of *TEN* we find *ZEHN* in German; *T* shifted to Z *(TS)*.

(5) *Illustration of Grimm's Law of Sound-Shifting.*

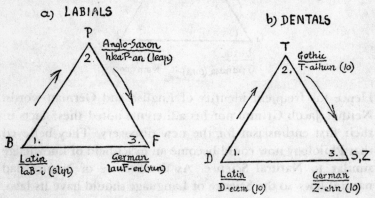

c) LARYNGALS

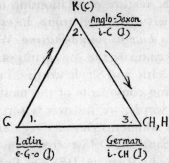

Though it is not always easy to find correct examples of Grimm's sound-shifting we have this example for the laryngal sounds: Latin, *EG-o* (I), Anglo-Saxon IC (I) and German *ICH* (I). Here, sound-shifting is still wholly at work. In another instance, however, Latin, *GRAN-um* (grain, corn) a switch from *G* to *K* (*C*) took place in Anglo-Saxon, *CORN*, but there is no second movement from Anglo-Saxon to High-German, *KORN* (corn).

(6)   *Grimm's Law not at work. No second sound-shifting from Anglo-Saxon to German.*

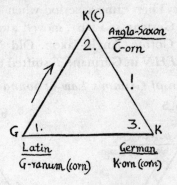

Hence the frequent identity of English and German words. Neither Jacob Grimm nor his adherents noted these facts in their first enthusiasm for the new discovery. They believed that Philology now could become an exact field of knowledge similar to Natural Science. As the Science of Nature had natural laws, so the Science of Language should have its laws, hence sound-shifting rules became phonetic laws and were considered the backbone of modern Philology.

Grimm himself gave the impulse toward this trend by mechanizing his Law rigidly, all too rigidly. He took each group of consonants of the three spheres of articulation, labials (B, P, F), dentals (D, T, TH-S-Z) and laryngals (G. K, CH-H), arranged them, and compared them with the wheels of a moving car: whenever one of the wheels reaches the spot where another wheel was before, that other one already has moved to a new place. The same is true in sound-shifting, if we observe the changes in three different periods.

(7) *The three periods of sound-shifting.*

	Labials	Dentals	Laryngals
I. *Indo-European*	B P F	D T S	G K H
II. *Germanic*	P F B	T S D	K H G
III. *High German*	F B P	S D T	H G K

An Indo-European B appears in Germanic as a P and in High German as an F; an Indo-European P shifts in Germanic to F and in High German back to B, and so on. This phonetic scheme was considered sacrosanct, a law! Some of Grimm's followers, the so-called 'Young Grammarian' school of Vienna University did not admit any exception to Grimm's Law.

There was a certain secret note in this singular enthusiasm of German philologists for Grimm's Law to which unfortunately Anglo-Saxon, French, Italian and other students did not pay enough attention. In the first decades after the discovery of Grimm's law, German philologists developed a sort of odd and unpleasant patriotism, considering sound-shifting in a political rather than in an objective, scientific way. The phonetic changes so frequent in the Germanic tongues were not considered merely as linguistic phenomena, but as characteristic features of the Teutonic tribes and a basis for their vital strength, foreshadowing the great role which these peoples would soon play in history. Instead of becoming aware of the obvious insufficiency of Grimm's Law which centered all phonetic evolution of the Indo-European Family exclusively around the Teutonic tribes, instead of checking and correcting this manifest one-sidedness, Grimm and his adherents made a virtue of it, extending its importance and transforming it into the touchstone of linguistic relationship. For them there could be no relationship without fixed and firm laws of sound-shifting! This idea was adopted by students of other linguistic families such as Semitologists. Today the science of language still adheres to these incorrect viewpoints.

In order that we may avoid any sort of injustice, let us look in an unbiased way at the whole question. If we replace the term *law* — which is far too rigid — and call sound-shifting merely an innate tendency in the life of speech, then of course we shall find another, a better way to explain these phenomena, and obtain the right appreciation of the value of these changes which are encountered in almost all languages.

Let us compare English with German, to start with, since English represents the *second* and German the *third* and last period of sound-shifting. Here we must admit that Grimm was right to a great extent. English *TEN* becomes in German *ZEHN*, English *TWO* turns into *ZWO, ZWEI*.

(8) *Grimm's law at work in shifting from English to German.*

English	German
TEN	ZEHN
TO	ZU
TWO	ZWO
TEAR	ZERR-en
TWIG	ZWEIG
TWELVE	ZWOELF
TAP	ZAPF-en
TAME	ZAHM

We could quote many more instances where Grimm's law is actually at work and the English *T* corresponds with the German Z (*TS*). Yet even here we cannot speak of a law without exception, for *T* should — as a matter of fact — shift to *S*, as the English *THAT* becomes *DAS* in German, the English *WATER* turns into WASSER. Again we are amazed how frequently English *TH* shifts into *D* in German, so that many students are inclined to believe this to be a regular change.

(9) *Transition from English TH to German D.*

English	German
THAT	DAS
THIS	DIES
THIN	DUENN
THICK	DICK
THORN	DORN
THANK	DANK
THING	DING

Yet the English *THEY* jumps out of the rule and appears in German as *SIE !* *THRIVE* corresponds with German *TREIB-en, THRIFT* with *TRIFT*. Further, despite such frequent regular transmutations every teacher who knows both English and German will admit that there are numberless instances where — opposite to what the Young Grammarians taught — Grimm's Law does not function at all, so that English and German words show identical consonants.

(10) *Cases with no sound-shifting between English and German.*

English	German
COM-e	KOMM-e
FISH	FISCH
DAM	DAMM
BLOOM	BLUM-e
COAL	KOHL-e
SEA	SEE
PELT	PELZ

Doubtless some may deny that *PELT* and *PELZ* are Teutonic words, and may derive them from the Latin PELL-is. However there is partly a change in the transition of the final -*T* into Z (Pelt-Pelz). This is a very frequent occurrence, because many words not only in English and German, but in all other dialects of the Indo-European group partly do and partly do not change their consonants at all. Let us take the word *HEART* as an example.

(11) *Indo-European words where sound-shifting only works in part.*

Sanskrit	Anglo-Saxon	German
HARD (heart)	HEORT-e (heart)	HERZ (heart)

Here are examples of the three stages of sound-shifting in an Indo-European, a Teutonic and a High German word. The

H of the Sanskrit *HARD* is supposed — according to Grimm's Law — to shift in Anglo-Saxon into *G*, and in German, to *K* (List 7), but the *H* does not change at all. On the other hand the final consonant is obedient to Grimm, and the Sanskrit *D* correctly transmutes into the Anglo-Saxon *T* and the German *Z*.

We could cite many more irregularities or exceptions, such as the important and very ancient word to *HAV-e*.

(12) *No sound-shifting in the word to HAV-e*

Latin	*Anglo-Saxon*	*German*
HAB-eo (have)	HABB-an (to have)	HAB-en (to have)

None of the consonants shifts here, neither the initial *H* nor the final *B*. However a staunch adherent of Grimm could well object that to HAV-e is not encountered either in East-India or in Hellas. It appears in Latin and is restricted to the Teutonic vernaculars. It may be a late-comer in speech, hence the lack of sound-shifting. This is not at all true. The word goes back to very remote epochs. We could choose another example, the personal pronoun *THOU*, German *DU*: Latin *TU*, Sanskrit *TVA-m* (thou) with an initial *T*, Anglo-Saxon *THU* (thou) with a *TH*, and High German *DU* with a *D* — *T*, then *TH*, then *D*. The moment, we start from the *Greek* instead of the *Latin* tongue, from *SY* (thou), the whole picture is different.

(13) *The ancient word THOU in Indo-European tongues.*

GRIMM'S LAW AT WORK   GRIMM'S LAW NOT AT WORK

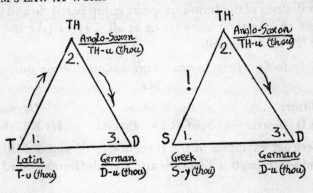

The sequence *S-TH-D* starting from Greek *SY* (thou) does not fit at all into Grimm's Law. Again we encounter other examples such as the Latin *DOM-o* (I tame), Anglo-Saxon *TAM* (tame), German *ZAHM* (tame), a sequence of *D-T-Z*, and here we must admit that there is something true in Grimm's observation. Then we take two English words with the same consonants, *better* and *bitter*, and observe how they change in German.

(14) *Transition from English better and bitter to German.*

GRIMM'S LAW AT WORK		GRIMM'S LAW NOT AT WORK
English	better	bitter
German	besser	bitter

Such instances are very frequent in the transition from English to German, and extend through many members of the Indo-European circle. Perhaps in 40% or 50% of examples we see sound-shifting at work in Germanic vernaculars. In a greater number of instances however there is no change of consonants at all.

(15) *Change of consonants and their stability.*

English	German
SHIP	SCHIFF
LIP	LIPP-e
RIB	RIPP-e
RUB	REIB-on
SIB	SIPP-e
CLAD	KLEID

Why do we stress all these details? Why do we devote this effort to show that Grimm's conception of sound-shifting is not correct? Because this theory plays an extraordinary role in linguistics and some other fields as well. Professor Max Müller of Oxford considered the establishment of Grimm's Law the starting point of Philology as a science. He says in his *Lectures*: "Mere guesses, however plausible, are completely discarded from the province of scientific etymology. What etymology professes to teach is no longer merely that one word is derived from another, but how to prove, step by step, that one word was regularly and necessarily changed into another." And this exaggeration reached its climax when he continued: "Etymology is indeed a science in which identity or even similarity whether of sound or meaning is of no importance whatever. Sound etymology has nothing to do with sound" (Lectures, II, 259).

Other scholars such as the American *William Dwight Whitney,* pointed to some of these mistakes, yet still refrained from criticizing the great Grimm. In his essay *Darwinism and Language* (*North American Review,* 1874, pp. 61-68) Whitney wrote on Max Müller: "It is never entirely easy to reduce to a skeleton of logical statement a discussion as carried on by Müller, because he is careless of logical sequence and connection. . . ."

Yet Whitney unfortunately never dared extend his criticism to Grimm and his "law". This has been done by a great Austrian scholar, *Hugo Schuchardt* of Graz University, fellow of the Austrian Academy. In an essay published in 1925 by this institute (Philosophic-Historical Section, vol. 202, essay 4, page 4) he fiercely attacked the Young Grammarian theory.

We shall see that nothing will be detracted from the scientific character of linguistic research by checking and improving Grimm's "law", or by considering it as a rule with possible exceptions. Words change their sound and sense in the course of their life. Without realizing this fact it would be impossible to recognize any relationship between two words, once they appear transformed according to the peculiar style of each vernacular. The tragic mistake of Grimm and Max Müller consisted in overrating their mother-tongue and in not extending their field of investigation beyond the all too narrow boundaries of the Indo-European Family. They were convinced that the study of German and a few related tongues would solve all the problems of the science of language. The whole misconception of an "Aryan" race exclusive of some leading nations of antiquity and of the Near East can be traced to this grave error.

CHAPTER FOUR

THE BEGINNINGS OF ENGLISH

WHEN AND where was the first English word or the first English sentence uttered? No answer. We do not know anything about the origin of nations and their tongues; their beginnings are shrouded in darkness. History does not tell anything about the start of the Chinese, the Bantu, the Egyptians or the Peruvians.

It was easy to establish a theory such as that of Thesis, a conventional origin of human speech. But how did such a convention occur? According to a Roman tradition quoted by Vitruvius in his work on architecture, a speechless horde of primitive savages once gathered in a forest during a thunderstorm. Suddenly a thunderbolt hit a tree under which they had taken refuge, setting it afire. Panic-stricken, the horde dispersed, then, little by little, attracted by the warmth of the flaming wood, gathered around it and thus learned the use of fire. Then they began to give a name to every thing by a sort of common silent consent.

What a strange phantasy of rationalistic thinking! What a strange gathering of primitive, mute aldermen, a kind of Anglo-Saxon *Witenagemot,* solemn, yet taciturn. A Parliament that creates a language! The word Parliament stems from French, from PARL-er (to speak), for it consists of people who speak and even speak up. A speechless Parliament is an obvious contradiction, but a speechless Parliament that creates a language is a miracle!

Sounds do not spring into life by themselves: they are produced by man, by animals, and by the elements of Nature. The changes of articulate sounds linked with sense are due to definite reasons. Modern linguistics began to recognize this fact: hence the establishment of the so-called 'sub-stratum idea.' According to this conception sounds change by passing from mouth to mouth. Each individual has more or less his own way of articulation, of pronunciation.

Foreigners who settle in English-speaking countries have in the beginning great difficulties in pronouncing the TH, and very often mispronounce it. Let us take such a word as *BREATH,* containing a *TH.* BREATH, the breath of life, has one kind of *TH.* Let us pass to the verb to *BREATH-e:* a second sort of *TH,* once (in Anglo-Saxon) even written with a different letter. Yet what is the organ of breathing? *BREAST!* This is the same as German *BRUST.* Hence: we use the same mispronunciation — if we intend to call it so — as the Germans who pronounce *S* instead of a *TH.* How do we name a windy spot where the breath of air is running fast? *BREEZ-y!* Here we use a kind of "wrong" pronunciation and probably used it in France and in England long before the American continent was discovered.

(16) *Sound-shifting within the same language.*

to BREATH-e   BREEZ-e   BREATH   BREAST

The population of Great Britain is not homogeneous. The British Isles were conquered by foreign tribes repeatedly, and their former inhabitants mixed with the newcomers. Thus we see that the pronunciation changes and the sounds begin to "shift" when a language passes from one nation or tribe to another. A country is conquered, and whether vanquishers or vanquished take up another tongue or a number of its words, these are spelled in a different way. In the remote epoch of exogamy, when young people were obliged by customs or religious laws to marry outside their tribes, there were even different dialects or words used by different sexes: men and women expressed their ideas and feelings in a different way.

Thus sound-changes are often a mark of migrations or of other transformations of peoples. Had Jacob Grimm known this fact, he would have realized that the frequent transmutations of the Germanic tongues are presumably due to the fact that foreign tribes took up the language once spoken by the ancestors of the Teutons, perhaps in Asia or in some other part of the world.

Thus we see that we must distinguish between the individuality of each nation and the individuality of its language. English is not exclusively a branch of the Germanic group, or a section of the Indo-European or "Aryan" primeval tongue. If the idea of a unique common mother-tongue of all mankind is to be proved, then there never were "primeval tongues" of Aryans, Semites, Egyptians, or American Indians! All the little brooks and streams of speech flowed down from one and the same source, without any interference. Their transformation and present character is due to their evolution. It is simply not true that Italian, French, Spanish, Romanian are Romance tongues or daughters of Old Latin. The *cod-fish* e.g. is called *MORUE* in French, but *BACALL-ao* in Spanish and Portuguese. The French name stems from Latin, but the Spanish and Portuguese name is peculiar of the Iberian Peninsula.

We must try to work back to the beginnings of English by understanding its geographical location and surroundings. We must study the harbors where words and whole tongues could arrive and leave. Celtic people and Romans, Anglo-Saxons and Vikings, Normans and others thus landed on the British Isles. The Atlantic opened the door over-seas, the Channel was another door to the European continent, to Holland, Belgium and Germany, to France, Spain and the Mediterranean basin, finally to all the four quarters of the world. The British Empire is the best evidence of the truth of such a conception.

To find our way back to the origin of English we must first study its composition, its different layers or strata. The usual way of looking at English as a mixture consisting chiefly of Indo-European ingredients will not yield fully satisfactory results. When we open any etymological dictionary of English such as Skeat, or when we trace the source of words in Webster, we find many, many words designated "Etymology unknown", or "Origin obscure or dubious." *The Indo-European or "Aryan" tongues cannot be used as the only key to the past of English.*

The last conquest of the British Isles took place in 1066, by the Normans, after the battle of Hastings. It was almost the same time that Vikings from Scandinavia landed on the northeastern coasts of America. The Normans were also Vikings who had conquered a part of France (Normandy) a few centuries before. These conquerors had given up their own Teutonic tongue and had accepted the French language. Now they carried French into the British Isles, transforming pure Anglo-Saxon into a mixed language, half Germanic, half Roman, into English.

Before the Normans, Danish warriors had conquered England, introducing some hundred Danish words to the Isles. The most decisive event in the formation of English took place in 446 A.D., when Germanic tribes left their homes in Germany and Denmark on the shores of the Baltic and landed in England under their mythical leaders *Hengist* and *Horsa* ("stallion" and "horse"). This was the first time that such Germanic words as

God, sea, shield, spear, shaft, Ethel

were uttered on British soil!

Or were they not exclusively Teutonic?

The earliest date in recorded history which we can find in our search for the beginnings of the English language is the year 55 B.C. when the Romans occupied part of England. In that pre-Christian epoch, the language or languages spoken on British soil were hardly altered by the Roman conquest. Scotland remained untouched by that event.

Who lived on the Isles before the Romans arrived? Celtic people, Scottish, Welsh, Kymric and Cornic tribes, and the Irish people of Erin. All these groups were related with one another by blood and language. They were also akin to the Celtic people on the European continent, particularly to the Celts of Brittany. In addition there were Celtic people spread over Central and Southern Europe and in a good part of Asia. We must begin to realize an important fact: *Celtic* as a name was not used in early antiquity for a nation alone, but was the general designation of a great part of humanity of the oldest continents. The Galatians in Asia Minor, the Kaldu on the shores of Lake Van in Armenia, and the Chaldaeans of Mesopotamia as well as other tribes had something in common with the Druidic Celts who lived once in a great portion of the Old World and were called Galat-oi (Celts, Galatians) by the Greek historians.

When did these Celtic tribes, including the Gauls, arrive in Europe? When did they penetrate to the British Isles? Many scholars believe that the Celtic invasion took place in about the Sixth Century B.C. Thus the Celts would appear to be the oldest inhabitants of England. However, for two reasons this date cannot be correct. First, the Celtic tribes are not merely a branch of the Asiatic "Aryans" who migrated to the West as late as the Sixth Century B.C., as little as the Celtic vernaculars are merely members of the Indo-European Family. Had the Celts moved from Asia to Europe about the Sixth Century B.C., the Babylonian, Egyptian, Hittite or Hebrew priests, scribes or historians would certainly have inscribed in historic records such a gigantic migration from East to West. Such an event presumably would not have escaped their attention.

Second, the Celtic tribes very early had closer relations with the *Iberians,* the ancestors of the *Basque* people, the oldest inhabitants of the Iberian Peninsula. These Iberians were so closely allied with the Celtic people that the historians of classical antiquity spoke of so-called Celt-Iberians as a mixture of Celtic and Hiberian tribes. Celtic people must have lived in Western Europe long before the Sixth Century B.C. There are English scholars, anthropologists, linguists, who assert that Celts must have settled in England several millennia before Christ. Those students who — all too hastily — incorporated the Celtic dialects into the Indo-European Family could perhaps go back to about 2500 B.C. the period when the alleged Indo-European mother-tongue split into an Eastern and a Western branch.

If we go back to the year 2500 B.C. as the time when Celtic people reached the European shores of the Atlantic, this would not tell us what tribes lived in the British Isles before the Celtic Conquest and which tongue was first spoken there. Roman writers speak of the *Picts* and the *Caledonians* as the earliest known inhabitants of England. Certain features of their description remind us of the American Indians. It is probably from their custom of tattooing themselves that they were called Pict*s* (Latin *PICTI=painted, tattooed*). The name of their relatives, the Caledonians of Scotland, is strikingly assonant to Celts, Kaldu, Chaldaeans, Galatians.

How can our mention of the *Picts* help us to shed some light upon the beginnings of English? There are about 300 Pictish inscriptions preserved, written in Ogham, an alphabet used in the Middle Ages by Irish monks. According to the British Encyclopedia ("Pictish") "no attempt to interpret those inscriptions as any form of Celtic has produced anything but bosh." The reason for this is simple. *Pictish is no Indo-European or "Aryan" vernacular at all,* or students would have easily recognized it. The British Isles were presumably not peopled with "Aryans" in the earlier epochs. *English did not start as an Indo-European dialect, either Celtic or Germanic.* Only by its evolution did it obtain an Indo-European character.

Yet what else could Pictish be? By a study of the Indo-European tongues we cannot solve this problem. Only from the viewpoint of the community of speech does the solution become possible. Again let us draw attention to those ancestors of the Basques, the *Hiberians.* Some old form of that most ancient European vernacular may have been the idiom first spoken in Britain and Ireland.

Are any Basque words to be found in English? There are more than we imagine. There are English words which hardly can be connected with any European linguistic group except with Basque, such as the common word *KEY.*

(17) *The word-stem KEY in English and in Basque.*

English	Anglo-Saxon	Old Frisian	Basque
Key	Caeg, Caeg-e	Kai, Kei (key)	Gak-o (key)

With only the exception of Old Frisian the word *KEY* is

not encountered in any other of the Germanic or Indo-European vernaculars except in English and in Basque. Through

(18) *The word for key in other Indo-European tongues.*

German	Latin	French	Old Greek	Russian
Schluessel	Clav-is	Clef	Kleis	Klyuch

Basque, as often happens in ancient idioms, we are able to discover the original meaning of *KEY*, Anglo-Saxon *CAEG-e*. Basque, *KHAK-o* means a hook, and a key was originally a sort of hook.

There are words such as *LAND* common to the whole Teutonic circle and to some Celtic vernaculars, lacking in all the other Indo-European tongues, but found in Basque. *Land* is a very old word found in country names such as Eng*land*, Scot*land*, Ire*land*, Ice*land*, Green*land*, Hol*land*, Fin*land*, Switzer*land*, most of them countries located in the vicinity of the

(19) *The word-stem LAND in the Germanic group.*

Anglo-Saxon	English, Dutch, German	Old Norse,	Gothic	Swedish
Land, Lond	Land	Land		Land

Hybernian or Hiberian region of the European west-coast. The word is lacking however in Latin, Greek and Slavic, in India, Persia and Armenia, as well as in the other parts of the Old World. Only in French do we find *Land-e* (heath, moor) presumably borrowed from some Celtic or Germanic dialect. Finally, we meet the word in Celtic vernaculars and in Basque.

(20) *The word-stem LAND in Celtic dialects and in Basque.*

Basque	Irish	Welsh	Breton	French
Lann	Lann	Llann	Lann, Lan	Land-e
(land)	(land, church)	(open place)	(land)	(heath)

We shall find many other connections between Basque and English; *this is but the first superficial result of our new method of investigation.*

Words are keys to the mysteries of the past. The word *Land* can open still other doors. English students both of anthropology and linguistics, expressed the opinion that the first invaders may have landed in the British Isles as early as about 7000 B.C. Who were these invaders who penetrated France and Spain in so remote epochs? Were they perhaps the same people who left us masterworks such as the ceiling-paintings of the Franco-Cantabrian caves, those of Altamira in Spain and Trois Frères in Southern France? Whence did they come, from the West, East or North? Let us apply our new method and seek for the answer. Let us take the word *Land* and see where there may be further links. In Gaulish we discover *Land-a* (land) just as in Basque the form *Land-a* (land). The shorter form, *LAN* can be found across the Atlantic, in Mexican: *LAN* (land, country, place), preserved in country names such as Tu-*lan,* Azt-*lan,* Tlapal-*lan.*

(21) *The word-stem LAND, LAN in Indo-European,*
Basque, American.

Mexican	*Basque*	*Breton*	*English*	*Gaulish*	*Welsh*
Lan	Land-a	Lan (n)	Land,	Land-a	Llann
(land)	(land)	(territory)	Lane	(land)	(yard)

We realize here from the first example of a word extending across the Atlantic to the New World that even if an Indo-European word is found in part or in all "Aryan" idioms, this does not by any means prove its Indo-European nature or origin. To shut our eyes to the overwhelming fact that such words are by no means exclusively Indo-European or "Aryan", but can be found in all parts of the world, does not only represent a kind of scientific insufficiency, but a falsification of scientific conclusions. Most of the conclusions drawn from the mere observation of the Indo-European horizon are simply erroneous, worthless. There can be no doubt whatever about the necessity of extending the linguistic search as far as possible, over all continents and at least to all of the linguistic families. Only then will modern science be able to answer numberless questions which remained unanswered and problematic during the Nineteenth Century and represent a burdensome legacy and undesirable weight upon our present age.

In this chapter we have been able only to briefly consider the beginnings of English. We shall have to learn much more about this problem. Some light has been shed on it by taking into consideration the Basque tongue as representing an early language possibly spoken in the British Isles. Now let us find out if the Basque or Hiberian people were really in close touch with the British Isles and with other parts of Europe in remote epochs of history.

CHAPTER FIVE

PEOPLE AND PLACE NAMES OF ANTIQUITY

IN THE course of the Nineteenth Century many scholars realized that names of places, rivers and mountains, countries and nations as they were mentioned by writers of antiquity could be of a great help in studying the unrecorded part of ancient history. Why is the Atlantic Ocean called *Atlantic?* Why is a chain of mountains in North Africa, near the Atlantic, named *Atlas?* Do these two names have anything to do with one another?

Why is the western continent of the Old World, the region where the sun sets, called *Europe?* On the west coast of Africa there is a negro tribe and its country both called *Yoruba. Ereb* in Hebrew means *evening, sunset, west.* Europe means the Occident. Is Yoruba related to Europe? does it mean the same?

Such names from a remote antiquity, an epoch without hieroglyphs or wedge-writing, without characters or letters, without scribes, historians or records are not only mysterious and attractive, interesting in the best sense of the word, but most informing at the same time. If we listen to their whispered tales, we can uncover old secrets of the Universe, of unrecorded history. The first fact which we learn is the reappearance of such enigmatic names in different periods and in different parts of the world. One hears a name and later its echo resounds from quite a different quarter of the earth, and one must ask immediately, What does this echo mean?

In 1939, the author of this book was travelling across Brittany visiting many old places, studying menhirs, dolmen, galgals and stone-henges, walking across those hundreds of obelisks, the *alignements* of the ancient Druidic mystery centre of Carnac. These circles of at least eleven hundred pointed stones were the ruins of what was once a gigantic calendar built up from the wisdom of the stars in the vicinity of the

38

Atlantic shore, thousands of years before the Christian Era . . .

Easter-time is approaching, the festival of the goddess *Eostre,* in German *Ostara,* the deity of beauty, of growth, of the spring, the festival of *Beal,* the Celtic sun-god. There are no books, no records as yet to indicate the precise date of starting the solemn Spring ceremonies. Yet on this day, at a certain hour a procession advances slowly and solemnly, approaching the sanctuary, at its head the high-priest, the Pen-Tyarn, followed by dozens of Druidic priests, the so-called Tyarns. Suddenly the procession stops. They have reached one of the menhirs from which the Pen-Tyarn can gaze across the rows of stones to the shore of the ocean. There the sun is rising at a certain point, visible across another obelisk. This is the right date, and the High-Priest gives the signal to start the celebration . . .

From the coast we went up to the Archaeological Museum whose director at that time was Zachary Le Rozic, a widely known scholar, son of an old Breton family. He is the author of a Breton Dictionary and of many pamphlets dealing with Celtic and Druidic excavations. We started to speak about the name *Carnac.* "Were you ever impressed by the similarity of those names of ancient Mystery Centres, *Carnac* in Brittany and *Karnak* in Old Egypt, near Thebes? Did you ever wonder that an ancient sanctuary of the Orient and a Druidic mystery place, have the same names? Does it not seem to you that they must have some connection with one another?"

"Well" he answered, "We suspected such a relation long ago . . . Yet . . . if we only could get any evidence."

"Evidence? The best is that of language. Look for more such names and study their meaning. Compare, compare, and use your imagination! Brittany and Egypt are not the only regions where we encounter this name. There are two more localities in the Celtic part of the British Isles, called *Carnock,* one of them in Scotland (in the Rosshire County) and the other near Edinburgh and the Firth of Forth. We also find a town called *Karnak* in Turkistan, and another *Karnak* in

India. The East and the West, three continents, have places called. *Karnak.*"

(22) *The name of the Druidic centre Carnac in 3 continents.*

Europe, Brittany	Carnac
Scotland, N. England	Carnock
Africa, Egypt	Karnak
Asia, India	Karnak

"That is not all. Do you know what the name *Carn-ac* or *Karn-ak* means? -ac or -ak is an ending used in remote epochs in many languages. Are there not many names of localities in south-western France ending in -ac, such as *Cogn-ac, Luss-ac, Berger-ac?* Then take *Carn:* in Welsh and in Gaelic it means a *cairn, a heap of stones* piled up in a conical way. *Karn* in Egypt means the same: Arabic *Karn* is a heap of stones and -ak in Egyptian Karn-ak is an ending."

Le Rozic was amazed, yet these relationships are really far more important and frequent than we imagine. There are many more links in this word-chain:

(23) *Karn-ak and Carn-ac are derived from Carn (cairn).*

Europe, English	Cairn	
Gaelic, Welsh	Carn	(cairn)
Greek	Kran-aos	(rocky)
Asia, Arabic	Karn	(cairn)
Hebrew	Keren	(peak)

We now begin to understand that many other names of ancient geography belong to the same group: the city of *Kern-e* or *Cyren-e* in North Africa, *Acron* of the Philistines in Palestine, the mountainous province of *Akarn-ania* in Hellas, *Ca-rin-thia* and the *Carn-ic Alps* in one of the greatest mountain chains of the world, and many others.

Now we return to the Basques, and to the evidence of their connection with the people of the British Isles. Let us keep in mind that the Basques today have survived in the territory of the Pyrénées Mountains on the Hispano-French border. Their tongue is the most ancient witness of unrecorded European history, related with Egyptian and North-African languages on the one hand and with the dialects of the Caucasus on the other. The grammatical structure of their venerable speech is strikingly similar to American Indian idioms. Connections with the West — across the Atlantic — and to the East with African and Asiatic (Caucasus) tongues. The Basque people are descendants of the Hiberian nation which gave Spain and Portugal the name of the Hiberian peninsula and had founded and carried on the so-called Hybernian Mystery Centres for thousands of years in the lands extending along the shores of the Atlantic Ocean in Western Europe from Hiberia to the Hebrides and doubtless beyond.

Were the Basques always compressed in that narrow corner which is called the Basque country today, or did they once extend far beyond it, and in which direction? With what other nations were they then in contact? In Latin and in Spanish their name is *Vascon-es*. Vasco da Gama was of Basque descent, as we can judge from his name. The French province extending north of the Pyrénées on the shores of the Atlantic is called *Gascogne* or **Guascogne* which again means the *land of the Basques*. Thus we arrive almost as far as Bordeaux in reconstructing the ancient home of the oldest nation of Europe. This conclusion, drawn from linguistic facts, is easily supported by archaeological evidence: the Franco-Cantabrian caves, which, like the American Indian *Kivas* and many caves in early epochs, were Mystery Centres and religious gathering places. More geographical evidence is offered by the name of the *Biscayan* or *Viscayan Gulf*, marking the extension of the territory once peopled by the Basques up to the northwestern tip of Brittany and France, to the English Channel. Here the Basques must have come into contact with the most ancient natives of England at a time long before the Celtic invasion from the East. We could call this region the western contact-zone.

Yet there is an eastern contact-zone as well which again can be proved by language. There was a time when the Basques extended over all France, before even the Gauls had arrived from the Orient. The mountain-chain which separates France and Germany, the *Vosges,* was called in Latin *Voseg-us Mons* (Vosges mountain), and in modern German die *Vogesen.* Yet in the oldest German records such as the

Walthari-Lied (Walther's song) this barrier was still named *Wasgen-Wald* or Wasgen Forest. This old name *Wasgen-* is so assonant to *Vascon-es* that we cannot but see in it the name of the Basques. *Wasgen-Wald is literally Basque Forest.* The Basques without any doubt once extended as far as Germany and probably deep into Central Europe. This was in an epoch long before the landing of the Celts, the Romans, the Anglo-Saxons in the British Isles.

(24) *The name Basque extending from Spain to Germany.*

Latin, Spanish	Vasc-ones	(Basques)
France	*Guasc-ogne	(Gascogne)
France, England	Visc-ayan Gulf	(Biscayan Gulf)
German	Wasg-enwald	(Basque Forest)

Thus we realize that when the Roman writers spoke of cross-breeds such as the Hibero-Pictish tribes in England, there are reasons to believe that such a population actually dwelt in England in a remote antiquity. This connection between Hi-berians as ancestors of the Basques or of other West-European tribes and the early inhabitants of the British Isles, is proved by other factors, particularly the extension of the name *Hi-beria* (Spain) and *Hybernia* (Ireland, Scotland). In the vicinity of Carnac there is the little town of *Quiberon,* again a very ancient mystery place.

The name of the Hiberians or Hybernians sounds very similar to that of the Hebrews, just as similar as that of the Chaldaeans to Caledonians and Celts. Is not *Quiberon* assonant to *Hebron* in Palestine, one of the oldest sanctuaries of the Holy Land? What does the name *Hebrew* mean? Are the Egyptians right in calling the Hebrews *Habiru* (allies) from *Habir* (a person initiated in a mystery or in mystery wisdom)? There are old traditions according to which the He-brew people actually were connected with Hybernia and Hy-bernian Mystery Centres. Hebron in Palestine is tied with Quiberon by some mystical link.

What is amazing in the reappearance of these names in different parts of the Old World — and they are mostly restricted to it — is the fact that the more we dive into this problem the more astounding parellelisms we encounter. We know that the Angles, Jutes and Saxons before conquering the British Isles, lived in Northern Germany and Southern Scandinavia and migrated West in the year 446 A.D. Before them the Celtic peoples crossed Europe on their way west to England. Did they leave any traces of their former homes or the route of their migrations? On the Lake of Constance we find a city called *Lind-au*, and in its vicinity another town named *Bregenz* or in Latin, *Brigantia*. Farther East in the Bavarian Alps we find a third town, *Kempten* (Latin and Celtic, *Campodunum*).

We shift to the British Isles and there we encounter again the little town *Lind-um* (Lincoln), then in its neighborhood a Celtic tribe *Brigant-es*, so assonant to *Brigantia* (*Bregenz*), and not far away *Cambodunum* (Slack, Central England). There is still another city, *Brigantia*, in the West in Spain, the town of *Braganza* surrounded by legends and myths. Are these names evidences left behind by Celtic tribes on their way East, or were their migrations directed West?

This world-wide extension of old names of peoples and

(25) *Lindau, Bregenz, Kempten in Germany and their echo in England.*

Germany	England
Lind-au	Lind-um (Lincoln)
Bregenz (Brigantia)	Brigantes (a tribe)
Kempten (Campodunum)	Cambodunum (Slack)

tribes is a most informing clue of the Past. While modern scholars have tried to bring forward the idea that the Indo-Europeans are the representatives of primeval European Man, we find here real traces of that man through his traditional use of names.

The three tribal settlements of Lindau, Bregenz and Kempten still exist in the neighborhood of the Lake of Constance. During the Roman Epoch this lake bore the name *Lacus Venetus, Wendish Lake*. Why was it called *Venetus*? Is not *Venetia* the Latin name for *Venice*, and also the name of the whole province surrounding that old city? Were not the old tribes living in the vicinity of Berlin in the Spreewald, called *Wends, die Wenden?* Who were these Wendish people whose names we so often encounter in ancient history, in legends and in tales? Homer in his Odyssey mentions the *Enet-oi* (*Henet-oi*) who lived in Paphlagonia on the Black Sea (Asia Minor) as neighbors of the Galatians, the Celts. Herodotus speaks of the Illyrian *Veneti* (*Wends*) in the Balkans, and Tacitus speaks of the *Veneti* as living in a region adjoining the Finnish people.

The home of the Wends now restricted to the vicinity of Berlin extended much farther in bygone epochs. As we find the tradition of a drowned settlement of humanity represented as a submerged town in old tales, e.g. *Ker Ys* in Brittany, German legends tell us of the submersion of *Vineta,* seat of the ancient tribe, *Venadi or Venedi,* Old German *Winida,* Anglo-Saxon *Winedas,* Old Norse, *Vind-r.* The Baltic Sea itself was called in Greek *Venedikos Kolpos,* or *Wendish Gulf.*

While scholars in the Nineteenth Century suggested that the Indo-Europeans did not live in the neighborhood of an ocean, since they had no common word for *Sea,* and merely one name — *Nav-is* — for a boat, *nevertheless* we must conclude from the dwelling places of the Wendish people that they certainly lived near lakes and sea-shores and must have been bold sailors. We find them scattered around the Black Sea, the Adriatic and Baltic, and — the link with England and Western Europe — on the coast of the Atlantic. *Veneti,* or Breton, *Guened* or *Guenez,* was the name of the Celtic tribes of Brittany, and *Vindo-* or *Venta* appears in names of many English towns: *Venta Belgarum* (Winchester), *Windo-mora* (Ebchester), *Venta* (Caerwent), *Banna-Venta* (Norton), *Venta Icenorum* (Caistor by Norwich). All of these were ancient *Wendish* settlements, just as *Vindo-bona,* Vienna, the present capital of Austria.

We can connect all these names with the little town in Normandy called *Vendes,* and with *Vannes* in Brittany (Breton *Guened*), as well as with the name of the *Vendée* province in France, near Gascogne (the Basque province), well known in the French Revolution. In Germany we can add the *Vandals,* Latin *Vandali* who gave their name to the Spanish *Andalusian (Vandalusian)* province and presumably to the North African tribe of the *Wandala.* Further we can connect the name of the Alpine province *Vindelicia,* the land of the *Wendels,* of the Bavarian Mount *Wendel-stein* (Wendel's Rock) and the legendary name of the ocean *Wendel-meer* (Wendels' or Wendish Sea) with this whole chain. This last is probably one of the oldest names of the Atlantic used in ancient German poems for the sea which separated the earthly from the spirit world, as in Greek mythology the river *Styx* (silence) separated the Netherworld from the upper realm.

Still the list of related names is by far not yet exhausted. Once there lived on Teneriffe, in the Canary Islands, an old tribe called the *Guanche,* whose language and civilisation were suppressed by the Spanish conquerors in the Fifteenth Century. Only about one hundred words of that ancient tongue are preserved and one of them, *Guanath* (people) corresponds with the name *Guanche* and with *Gent-iles,* Latin *Gent-es* (people). Is it not interesting that a nation expresses an idea of representing all mankind by calling itself "human being", and not just a small section of humanity? Thus the name of the *Manchu* also means *human beings* as well does that of the African *Bantu* tribe. In the Araucan Indian vernacular of Chile, *Uento* again means "man, a human being."

(26) *The name Wends an old name of Primitive Man.*

English	Wend	
Latin	Venet-i	(Wends)
Greek	Enet-oi	(Wends)
Africa	Bantu	(men)
Asia	Manch-u	(men)
America, Chile	Uent-o	(man)
Guanche	Guanath	(people)

We shall not as yet draw any conclusions from the language links which we discover in connecting Europe and America. As a matter of fact we find in Europe further language affinities which are important. In his chronicle (about 1100

A.D.) Adam von Bremen calls the Finnish people *Finnedi,* and Herman Wirth in his *Ura Linda Chronicle* (1933) calls one of the mothers of the three races, the yellow race, *Finda.* Though the *Ura Linda Chronicle* is a forged record, we cannot condemn all of its content, and the name *Finda* no doubt is based upon truth. For a long time anthropologists have realized that in olden times members of the yellow race, such as the Lapps in northern Scandinavia, the Mongol tribes in northern Siberia and the Eskimo groups in northern America were previously inhabitants of France, Scandinavia and other regions. We find such names as *Finnedaelen* (valley of the Finns) as far south as Denmark.

Further examples of names of old tribes which we find in different parts of the world may be of interest, particularly the name of Scotland and Scythia. Let us start with the ancient name contained in *Car-diff, Car-lyle, Caer-leon* and in the Breton legend of *Ker Ys.* The word *Car, Caer, Ker* means *town* and *house,* just as villa and village actually mean *dwelling place, home.* In Gypsy English *Ker* is *house,* in Breton *Kear, Ker,* house, town. Then comes a wide gap extending over all Central, Southern and Eastern Europe and a part of Asia. The word *Ker, Car* does not occur in German, Dutch, Scandinavian, in Latin or the Romance tongues, in Greek, in Slavic, in Sanskrit or in Old Persian. It reappears in Asia and Africa in the Semitic group: Hebrew *Kar-ya* (village), *Kir* (town), then in the Ural-Altaic family so close to the Mongols, in Zyryan *Kar* (village) and again in Chile, in the Araucan *Kar-a* (town). There is also a parallel Hebrew word (H)IR (town) whose echo we find in Basque (H)IR-i (town).

(27) *The word Car, Caer (town, house) in*
different continents.

America, Chile	Europe, Breton	Asia, Hebrew	Zyryan	Africa
Car-a (town)	Ker (town)	Kir (town)	Kar (town)	Car-thage

This one word thoroughly observed and rightly understood could reverse the whole Indo-European conception of the true nature of such modern languages as English, French, German, Russian and Spanish. What we discover in them as common property largely belongs to a recent stratum of their vocabulary and structure. In addition numberless words are related to old vernaculars, belonging to very ancient epochs and strata of speech. These are scattered all over the world. We discover them not only in Basque, Hebrew or other Asiatic and African vernaculars, but in America. For example, we have seen that *Caer,* contained in English town-names, and in Breton, is not encountered in Sanskrit, Latin, Greek, German or French, but in the Araucan dialect of Chile. It is the *age* of such words which allows us to connect them with other tongues and not the "genealogical" relationship of the nations and tribes that speak them.

There is hardly another word which is as significant in a language as the term *Self.* Peoples, tribes may borrow words from other nations or languages, but not a word like *self.* According to the opinions of certain linguistic specialists, *once* the relationship between the different members of the Indo-European or "Aryan" family has become established, their words must show some relationship. This, however, does not apply to the word *Self,* the expression of man's personality.

(28) *Different words for Self in the Indo-European tongues.*

English	German	Latin	Italian	Greek	Slavic	Sanskrit
Self	Selb	Ipse	Medesimo	Autos	Sam	Sva

When we compare the different terms for *Self* in various branches of the Indo-European group, it seems as though each branch had created its speech independently. Each of the Germanic, Romance or Slavic sections uses entirely different words for *Self,* words which are not found outside the "Aryan" circle. The Germanic word *Self, Selb,* is encountered outside the Indo-European group, in two vernaculars: in the inscription of Canevoi (Italy), written in a Venetian (Wendic) dialect, SSELBOI-SSELBOI (self, same) and also in the Far East, in Manchu, SILB-a, *the same name.* We must realize that primitive speech used the picture of a name for the personality, the *Self*.

(29) *The word Self in Germanic, Venetian (Wendic), Manchurian.*

English	Old German	Venetian, Italy	Manchurian
Self	Selb-o	Sselboi-Sselboi	Silb-a (same name)

Again we must draw attention to the wide gap between Germany and Italy where links of this word-chain are found, and the Far East. In that vast territory extending over thousands of miles, no trace of the word *Self* is to be found. Such gaps are particularly significant, for they show that the relationship between such languages must go back to a very remote antiquity.

There is an obvious relationship between the name *Scythians,* or *Skythoi* in Greek, and the words *Scot* and *Scottish.* The Egyptians called the Scythians Shat-iyu (Asiatics), the Babylonians, *Ishkuz-a* or *Ashguz-a,* and the Hebrews either *Ashkuz* or *Ashkenaz.* Who were those mysterious Scythians of antiquity?

(30) *The Scotch and the Skythoi of Old.*

English	Greek	Egyptian
Scot, Scotch	Skyth-oi	Shat-iyu

Babylonian	Hebreew
Ishkuz-a	Ashkuz, Ashkenaz

It seems that in an ancient epoch all the tribes of the northern part of the earth were called *Scot* or *Skyth,* for their countries were in the shadow or darkness a great part of the year (Greek skot-os=darkness). This explains the relationship between the Egyptian word *Shat-iyu* and *Shad-ow,* German *Schatt-en.* As the Babylonian and Hebrew word *Ashkuz* corresponds with *Scot* and *Skyth,* so is Ashkenaz related to *Scandza* or *Scanzia,* the old name of Scandinavia. *Ashkenaz* is mentioned several times in the Old Testament.

An important fact to which attention must be drawn concerns the constant movement of the dwelling places of the Scythians toward the East. Herodotus (IV, 8) tells this tale:

When Hercules drove away the cattle of Geryones, he came to the land now peopled by the Scythians which then was an uninhabited country. Geryones dwelt outside the Pontos, the Mediterranean Sea, on the island which the Greeks called Erytheia near Gadeira which lies on the ocean beyond the Pillars of Hercules. Doubtless this island must have been located amidst the Atlantic. The Scots originated from the Scythians and the western border-line of this mysterious nation extended, about the First Millennium before Christ as far as the Atlantic, or even farther West.

A few centuries later when the Phoenician Pytheas of Marseilles sailed to the British Isles and the North Sea, he described the Scythians as living on the Rhine, close neighbors of the Celts. The Germans were not yet mentioned in that remote time, but the Scythian tribes had been pushed back from the Atlantic to the Rhine. Then in the Sixth Century A.D., when Jordanes wrote his story of the Gothic tribes, the Scythians lived still farther East, on the Vistula River, and the Germans on the Rhine. At that time no classical historian knew very much about the dark continent which extended in the north of Europe and Asia. They did not know whence the Germans and the Scythians had come, nor did they have any inkling about Indo-Europeans and the relationship of their tongues. Greek and Roman scholars knew very few foreign languages nor did they realize that Latin and Greek are intimately related. Jordanes believed that the primitive peoples had come from Scandinavia; thus he called that peninsula "a factory of tribes" (officina gentium), and Tacitus later on named it "the womb of nations" (vagina gentium) . . . .

Western Europe with its Druidic religion and its belief in reincarnation seems to have been one of the great centres from which human civilisation streamed into the world. Whence came the people who founded the Hybernian Mystery Schools? Perhaps in dark ages without memory there was a migration from the West to Hybernia, to the entire west coast of Europe. Those mysterious harbingers of a new age may have landed in the Basque country of antiquity, extending from the Hiberian peninsula to the Hebrides and Orkneys. They may have worshiped their gods in those strange Franco-Cantabrian caves, the Kivas of Western Europe whose walls they covered with marvelous master-works of art. Then they may have extended Eastward, to the center of Asia, in two waves of migration, one northward across the European continent, the other to the south across North Africa and Palestine.

There are two different groups of that primitive Franco-Cantabrian art, the northern style in France and other European countries, and the southern style (called Capsien) which spread from southern Spain into Africa and on toward the Orient. We see in one of these paintings a medicine-man disguised as a deer performing hunt dances before the tribe. Does this not remind us of the American Indian deer-dances of the West?

The connection of such hunt ceremonies in various quarters of the world may appear strange, but their relationship is beyond doubt. In early ages when Man was predominantly a hunter who lived and depended upon game, hunt dances were part of a religious enactment by which man implored the God of hunting for a successful chase.

But what is amazing is another fact. In Old Mexico, the Aztec goddess of hunting was called *Mish-coatl*, and in Nicaragua the god of hunting — *Maz-at*. *Mash-atl* means *deer* in Mexican, and in Sumerian, the oldest recorded tongue, *Mash* meant *antelope*. These names are identical with Algonquin *Moos-e* (deer), and Lappish *Mees-e* (reindeer).

(31) *Mexican Mash-atl (deer) same as Sumerian Mash
         (antelope).*

America, Mexican   **Western Asia, Sumerian**
Mash-atl (deer)   Mash (antelope)

It is a strange coincidence that the deer is called with the same name in pre-Columbian Mexico as in Sumerian, a language recorded as early as some 7000 years ago and which ceased to be spoken some 5000 years ago. Where and when could the ancestors of the Mexicans and Sumerians have met to choose the same word as a name for the deer, or is this coincidence merely accidental? Then let us examine another "accident", another name for the deer, Babylonian *Turakh-u*, ibex, capricorn. Again its echo is found in America, in Peruvian *Tarukh-a*, deer, and in North Africa, in Tuareg *Turik* (antelope).

(32) *Babylonian Turakhu (ibex) in America and Africa.*

American, Peru	Africa, Tuareg	Asia, Babylonia
Tarukh-a (deer)	Turik (antelope)	Turakh-u (ibex)

Again we see a pre-Columbian American word, used by hunters as a term for deer, for game, far away in Babylonia. We could enlarge this list by many more names of animals, characterizing the age of hunting. Why do we find them in the Old World mostly in the Orient, in Babylonia, Egypt, Palestine, but not so frequently in Europe? Here we touch one of the most important problems of our subject. It is a principle of modern linguists in comparing various tongues to go back to the oldest available idioms, words, or forms of speech. Which tongues are the oldest? Those which first were recorded in *writing*. The coordination of writing with speech is of such a deep importance for our research that it cannot be exaggerated.

This leads us back to the Franco-Cantabrian region with its caves, their ceiling-paintings, the medicine-man performing a hunt-dance. In one of those caves at Mas d'Azil in southern France, as in Spain, Portugal and England, pebbles were found covered with mysterious geometrical signs and decorations partly similar to letters of our alphabet.

(33) *Pebbles found in Mas d'Azil and otherwhere.*

The French archaeologist Piette dated them as far back as 12000 to 8000 *B.C.* This is a very important and significant estimate, for it corresponds with the epoch of the Franco-Cantabrian cave-paintings and the appearance in western and south-western Europe of that people who introduced this art of the stone-age, and it corresponds with the epoch of the Flood. Piette considered these signs painted in red and black as *magic symbols*. Other scholars believed them to represent numbers, syllables or letters. Were they actually letters, or rather symbols? We must now pass to a study of *writing*, for without knowing its development it is impossible to rightly understand the evolution of speech.

CHAPTER SIX

THE ORIGIN OF WRITING
IN PICTURE — CONSCIOUSNESS

Language was a product of an entirely different consciousness than is ours today. It did not arise out of abstract thinking, since primeval Man had first to develop this faculty in the course of thousands and thousands of years. Those who doubt this should study the evolution of writing, since the art of writing can be called the shadow of speech.

Writing developed far later than speech. Thus the span of unrecorded time is so much longer than the period recorded by historical documents. Primeval man did not need writing. His extraordinary power of memory took the place of hieroglyphs, cuneiforms and letters in the beginning. Behind every word, there was something different from an abstract idea. Ideas were not merely thoughts in the beginning of human life on earth. Every student of Greek knows that *ID-ea* is the same as the Latin VID-eo (I see), that ideas originally were *visions, images* which were connected with *sounds*. The English word to *WIT* is the same word-stem, and a *wit-ness* is a man who saw what happened. Every witness was in the beginning an *eye-witness,* to whom an event in the past was not dark, but *white*. Thus in German also *Ich weiss* means I know, and *weiss* means *white*.

Writing did not start from single sounds, from letters, from any alphabet, but from words as a whole. The first attempts of writing had nothing at all in common with our present alphabets, nor with language directly, but were used to support, as in poetry had rhythm, alliteration and rhyme, the failing memory. Later on, more tangible devices were required for this purpose: *knots* for instance.

In his *History of the Alphabet* C. Isaac Taylor speaks of the Peruvian *Quipus* (knots). These consisted of a main cord

53

to which at given distances were fastened thinner cords of different colors, each cord being knotted in various ways for special purposes, each color having its own significance. Red strands stood for soldiers, yellow for gold, white for silver, green for corn and so on, while a single knot meant ten, two single knots meant twenty, double knots one hundred, two double knots, two hundred. The use of knots, Taylor continues, is older than that of writing. It extends over all five continents. We find them used in Africa among the tribes of the west coast and in Egypt, then in the region extending from Melanesia to Formosa, in China, in Australia, in Scotland and in Germany.

Shi King, a sacred book of the Chinese, relates the use of knotted cords prior to the invention of writing. Lao Tse in his *Tao Teu King* mentions such Chinese Quipus, and legends speak of the tying of knots in strings as early as 2800 B. C., when Fo Hi invented the 8 symbols: heaven, balance, water, earthquake, wood, sacrifice, boundary and earth.

(34) *China. The Eight Symbols of Fo Hi. (About* 2800 *B.C.).*

1. HEAVEN =====   5. BALANCE ==≡

2. WATER ==≡   6. EARTH-QUAKE =≡=

3. WOOD ≡=≡   7. SACRIFICE ==≡=

4. EARTH ≡ ≡   8. BOUNDARY =≡≡

Heaven, water, wood and earth probably are symbolic expressions for the spirit, the soul, the plants and the mineral kingdom, and the other symbols, balance of mind, earthquake or inner thunderstorm of the passionate soul, sacrifice and boundary are closely connected with them.

Even today country people in Germany make knots in their handkerchiefs to recall certain items when they go to town shopping, to help their memory.

Plato tells of an ancient Egyptian legend dealing with the invention of hieroglyphs by Thoth-Hermes. "When Thamuz was king of all Upper Egypt . . . there came to him Thoth, the inventor of letters . . . and said: This art, o king, will make the Egyptians wiser and improve their memories, for it has been found to be a recipe both for memory and for wisdom."

"Most ingenious Thoth! replied Thamuz, one man can invent arts, but only another can judge whether they are to be baneful or beneficial to the user. Now you are the father of letters, and from predisposition say the opposite of what you should. For this art will put forgetfulness in the souls of the learners through disuse of the memory inasmuch as they will trust to external records, nudges from others, and will not of themselves keep their memories alert from within. Wherefore you have found a recipe not for memory, but for prompting. You give your disciples the semblance of wisdom but not the reality, and they, having become great but undisciplined readers will seem wonderfully wise, but will be for the most part lacking in judgment and tiresome to be with because of their learned pretensions" (Phaedrus, 274/5) .

Most nations, however, who aided the advancement of civilisation enjoyed the art of writing and considered those who had invented or adapted it, those great teachers of mankind, as higher beings or Gods. The Egyptians ascribed the invention of hieroglyphs to Hermes-Thoth, the Germans to Odin-Wotan, the Teutonic Hermes. The Edda depicts in *Havamal*, in Odin's song (Othins ljothr) a scene where Odin hung for nine holy nights on the tree of life, as an initiation, and on that occasion "took up" the runic writing, typical of the Germanic tribes.

Odin's Song.

"I ween that I hung
Hung there for nights full nine.
With the spear I was wounded
To Odhin, myself to myself
On the tree that none
What root beneath it runs.

On the windy tree

And offered I was

May ever know

None made me happy
And there below I looked.
I took up the runes
And forthwith back I fell.

With loaf or horn

Shrieking I took them

Nine mighty songs
Of Bolthorn, Bestla's father.
And a drink I got
Poured out from Othroerir.

I got from the son

Of the goodly mead

Then began I to thrive
I grew and well I was.
Each word led me on
Each deed to another deed."

And wisdom to get,

To another word,

These runes were still in use in Germany and particularly in Scandinavia until the Fourteenth Century and partly even later. Tacitus in his *Germania* says that these runic letters were magic letters, and that priests and initiated people would take beech twigs, carve runic letters on them, put them on a linen cloth, shake them and then pick three of them. From these three beech sticks they would prophesy the future. Strangely enough, Mexican mythology describes the invention of writing by the use of tree twigs as a symbol of letters or elements of writing. A mystical bird, called *Tuli,* flying over the country dropped twigs containing magic signs. The initiated priests took up the twigs and used the signs.

At the beginning of writing there were no letters, but only pictures, and the writers were artists. A few examples will make this clear. We start with instances taken from Chinese, not from Egyptian hieroglyphs or Sumerian and Babylonian 'Wedge-Writing' (cuneiforms). Why do we choose Chinese characters? We do this because Chinese ideographs are still in practical use today in China and in Japan, and also because a retrospect observation of the form of Chinese characters shows clearly the deep change in human consciousness which occurred within a few thousand years. This transformation is visible in Chinese as in almost no other kind of picture writing.

We might enter a lecture hall and write this sign on the

blackboard: (35)

If our audience has not studied Chinese writing at any time, they would be unable to read it. However, if this character is written precisely as it was originally, its meaning is unmistakably clear.

The same holds good for this character too:
As it is written here, no one can read

(37)

it who is not particularly trained. However, if we go back some two thousand or fifteen hundred years before the Christian Era, we find that this same character was written thus:

(38)

This is another modern character:

(39)

Its original picture form shows immediately what it represents:

(40)

Thus everyone understands the picture, while the modern character is quite a puzzle. The same applies to another sign:

(41)

When we go back to the ancient form of this sign we realize that it is something similar to a *goat*.

(42)

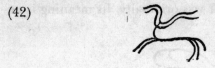

(43)      Is this a house, a plant or an animal?

At the time when the Ten Commandments were announced on Mount Sinai, this character was written as follows:

(44)

It is not as capricious as a jumping goat, walks somewhat shyly on its four legs, has an oval for a head, has two distinct antlers: a *deer*!

Yet what about this character?   (45)

Instantly we recognize, when we pass to the original picture, an animal which lives in the water, and yet can live on earth as well: a *turtle*.

(46)

Thus writing in its beginning was a kind of imitation, a representation of the universe by vision, by images. There were pictures for everything visible as well as invisible to our sense organs. There were pictures for the elements, fire, water, earth and metals, for the heaven, the sun, moon and stars, for mountains and fields, for rain and sunshine, light and darkness, morning and evening, a living man and a corpse, for mother and father, infant, son and daughter. Little by little even the most complex ideas such as sacrifice, protection, a prisoner, a hermit, love, tears, singing and so on could be represented by images.

(47) *Original Chinese Pictures and Decadent Characters.*

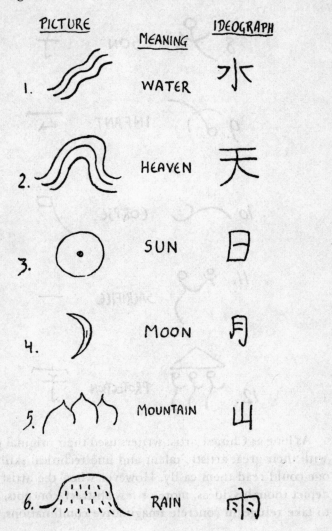

PICTURE	MEANING	IDEOGRAPH
7.	MAN	人
8.	SON	子
9.	INFANT	厷
10.	CORPSE	尸
11.	SACRIFICE	一
12.	PROTECTION	宇

As long as Chinese artist-writers used their original pictures with their great artistic talent and fine technical skill, everyone could read them easily. However when the artist had to depict thoughts, ideas, more or less abstract concepts, he had to take refuge in concrete imaginative combinations, and in symbols. The signs were no longer direct representations of things, but became mere allusions.

The sun was represented by a circle with a point in its midst as it was in Sumerian and Egyptian picture writing, in Maya inscriptions, and as it still is today in Astronomy.

(48) *The Picture of the Sun One of the Oldest Symbols.*

The moon was generally depicted in crescent form. Water was painted as three waves, a mountain as three peaks like the prongs of a trident, and the heaven was pictured by three spheres. Protection appeared in a *symbolic* form: three persons under a roof, while two women under the same roof expressed quarrel and discord. Light was represented by a *combination*: sun and moon, and the morning was shown by the sun rising above the horizon. Love was symbolized by a compound sign consisting of mother and child, the same symbol as the Madonna of the Catholic Church. A hermit was characterized by a man living in the solitude of mountains, a prisoner as a man surrounded by a fence, tears as water pouring down from an eye, and singing by a mouth and a bird. All these symbolic representations were still so imaginative, vivid, artistic and natural that a glance at them sufficed to keep them in mind forever. Further, they were easy to learn and to reproduce.

(49) *Compound and Symbolic Chinese Signs.*

PICTURE   IDEOGRAPH

MEANING

1. HERMIT   仙

2. PRISONER   囚

3. TEARS   泪

4. SINGING   鳴

5. — DISCORD   姦

6. — LOVE   好

7. LIGHT   明

These signs are interesting from several viewpoints. Many of them were so absolutely natural — the representation of tears for example — that not only the Chinese, but the Egyptians and the Maya used them. Was this the result of a tradition or of an independent parallel imagination?

(50) *Tears, Crying Pictured in a Similar Way in 3 Continents.*

AMERICA, MAYA   AFRICA, EGYPT   ASIA, CHINA

A study of the method behind this picture-writing can be of a great help in the field of Semantics (origin and development of the meaning of words). We shall see that the idea of protection in Latin was phonetically circumscribed in the same way as it was imaginatively in Chinese picture-writing. Language and writing use the same principles of expression in the field of phonetics and imagery.

As time passed this artistic, creative power of expression gradually declined, the form of the pictures became more and more abstract, more enigmatic, until the time came that not only the reader, but even the scribe himself did not know the original significance of these more and more complex characters, often consisting of as many as twenty five different strokes. The drawings turned into *ideographs,* and their meaning had to be learned. Thus from six to twenty years were required to learn and read these signs. The counting of the numbers of strokes and lines became more important for the art of writing and reading than an understanding of their original meaning, their image.

Chinese writing no longer represents the original form of the pictures as it did some two to three thousand years ago. It is a decadent form of writing where true images were replaced by conventional abbreviations, abstract characters, a number of strokes. The bridge between things and their representation has been destroyed. We shall see that what happened in the field of writing, happened in other branches of human activity as well as a result of a change in human consciousness.

Out of a picture-consciousness there had evolved in a quite natural way a creative picture-writing appealing to every man's comprehension without regard to nation or race. What had been lost in the spoken language, the former unity of mankind, seemed to be partly retained by this kind of writing whose uniting force has not as yet been entirely lost even though it fell into decay and became abstract ideography.

Classical Chinese is restricted to a comparatively small zone surrounding Peiping (old Pekin). In the other parts of the gigantic Chinese empire the vernaculars spoken particularly on the Eastern and Southern coasts (Canton, Hakka, Shang-hai and so on) are so different from the Mandarin-Tongue that they could well be considered different idioms. Yet Chinese people, whatever their dialect, can read the character *Shan* (mountain):

(51)

Whether they spell it *Shan* or *San* or otherwise, they all use their particular word meaning mountain. The same would be true of any other nation. If representatives of various linguistic groups were to learn Chinese ideographic writing and were to read the character   , what would they do?

(52) *How Different Nations Would Spell the Sign:*

English	Mountain
Spanish	Sierra
German	Berg
Greek	Oros
Slavic	Gora
Arabic	Gebel
Chinese	Shan

Their words would sound different, showing the effect of the Confusion of Tongues, but the meaning of all these different words, English, Spanish, German, Chinese, would remain the same, and a pale shadow of the original picture which still lies at the bottom of the sounds would be visible as a sort of silhouette. In the present, decadent forms of abstract ideographs there is still a living spark of that great fire whose light and warmth once guarded the original unity of mankind.

(53) *Symbolic Use of Pictures and Words in Egyptian Hieroglyphs.*

Arm (limb, symbol of force)   Arm (weapon)   Arm-y (power)

The *Egyptian hieroglyphs* enter history about 7000 to 6000 years ago, in the fifth millennium before Christ, in an amazingly perfect artistic form. They are sometimes similar to the Chinese pictures — since picture-writing shows many common features in different quarters of the earth — yet, they are different from them. We may say that the oldest Chinese pictures, though more recent than the Egyptian hieroglyphs, show great artistic boldness, courage and enthusiasm. The Egyptian drawings are beautiful, more regular and certainly more consciously designed than the primitive characters of China, yet the basic ideas are often the same in both.

(54) *Some Egyptian Hieroglyphs.*

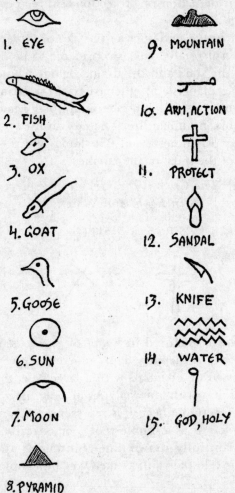

1. EYE

2. FISH

3. OX

4. GOAT

5. GOOSE

6. SUN

7. MOON

8. PYRAMID

9. MOUNTAIN

10. ARM, ACTION

11. PROTECT

12. SANDAL

13. KNIFE

14. WATER

15. GOD, HOLY

The images behind the Egyptian hieroglyphs are often the same as in the spoken language in depicting an abstract idea. For instance, an arm is used for a limb, for power, for a tool, for a weapon, or for an army.

The sun is represented as a circle with a point inside, the moon as a crescent. Animals are sometimes depicted completely as in the original Chinese pictures and later only characterized by their heads. Such abstract ideas as *help, protection* and so on were expressed in a much deeper, more inner way in Egypt than in China. The Chinese passed to a sort of naturalism in their depiction of protection as three persons taking refuge under a roof.

In Egypt (just as in Sumeria) the idea of *protection* is conceived more spiritually. It was considered to be the result of the help of the stars and the divine beings whose dwelling-places are the planets and other parts of the astral kingdom. Destiny, karma, was still experienced in those remote times as decisive factors in human life. The *cross* is the symbol of protection in Egypt, Sumeria and Babylonia, and the cross itself is a symbol of the stars, of the Divine.

(55) *The Cross is the Symbol of Protection*
in Egypt and Sumer.

To *advance* is pictured in Egypt by two legs moving forward, to *retreat,* by the same figure moving in reverse. A *pyramid* is expressed by a triangle with a large base, the profile of a pyramid. Some of the hieroglyphs or holy signs are already decadent; for example *heaven* is represented in a more or less unimaginative way as a simple roof geometrically drawn, not by three beautifully drawn lines hinting at the different spheres of the celestial vault as the Old Chinese pictured it.

(56) *Heaven Represented in Chinese and Egyptian Pictures.*

In Egyptian hieroglyphs rain, flood, tempest, hail are depicted by the same stylized roof from which water is pouring down in different directions. Oblique streams of rain show the effect of the wind and express the more dramatic aspects of a hurricane or of a thunderstorm.

(57) *Egyptian Hieroglyphs Representing Rain, Hail.*

With this brief glimpse of Chinese and Egyptian picture-writing and its development we have considered two of three Oriental centres where the art of writing first evolved. The third centre was in Mesopotamia, considered by many students to be the oldest homeland of Asiatic civilisation, its records dating back as far as 6000 to 7000 B.C. The Sumerian is the oldest nation to settle in that region. According to the prevalent opinion *Sumerians* developed the so-called wedge-writing or cuneiform writing (Latin, *cuneus,* wedge). These Sumerians had a somewhat Mongolian physiognomy as can be learned from the statues of their priest-kings or leaders. They were short, stocky, had rather round skulls and high cheek-bones, and wore a sort of turban or helmet. About 1910 Friedrich Delitzsch stated that those mysterious first inhabitants of the country located between the Tigris and Euphrates Rivers had spoken the Sumerian language and have left us specimens of it in the oldest records of mankind.

The Sumerian idiom is much closer to the original common tongue of mankind than Sanskrit, Greek or Latin. If we study a Sumerian vocabulary it appears as though certain words of that oldest recorded language were related to idioms

(58) *Sumerian Dingir (God) in Northern Asiatic Tongues.*

Sumerian Dingir	Turkish Tangr-i	Bashkir Tengr-i
Yakut Tangar-a	Buryat Tynger	Mongolian Tyngr-i

of the north of Asia, of Turan and the Far East, while other words seem to be connected with Western languages. The Sumerian word for *God* is *Dingir,* and its echo appears in all the Turanian idioms of Northern Asia.

(59) *Sumerian Pictures Preserved in Wedge-Writing.*

MEANING   PICTURE   MEANING   PICTURE

1. MOUNTAIN   6. STAR

2. FISH   7. HEART

3. BIRD   8. OX

4. HAND   9. WAVES

5. SUN   10. DOOR

The great antiquity of Sumerian records is proved by the wedge-writing itself. When it appears in history, it already possesses a decadent form, but its original character as a kind of picture-writing can still be recognized, for a number of images are preserved, such as mountain, fish, bird, hand, sun, heart, star, net, ox, protection (guard), waves, door and so on. As in Egyptian the hieroglyph *cross* meant *to protect, to help,* so the image of a cross in Sumerian meant *to guard,* and in Babylonian wedge-writing the cross developed out of a picture of a star designated *God.*

(60) *Transition from Picture to Ideograph in Mesopotamia.*

The older form of the signs still consisted of *lines*, not of wedges, and these ancient linear signs are much closer to

(61) *Same Pictures in Different Writing-Systems.*

MEANING	MESOPOTAMIA	EGYPT	CHINA
1. WATER			
2. FISH			
3. BIRD			
4. MOUNTAIN			
5. ENCLOSURE			

the original pictures than the later cuneiform writings. In the evolution of Mesopotamian script there are four periods:

(1) The *Sumerian* Epoch, when many pictures and linear signs still appear.

(2) An *early Babylonian* Epoch, when the transition from pictures, from linear to wedge-writing, begins.

(3) A *late Babylonian* Epoch, when more and more cuneiforms appear and pictures are replaced almost completely by ideographs.

(4) The *Assyrian* Epoch, when cuneiform writing became entirely abstract and no one could understand or read a wedge-sign without having first studied it.

The Sumerian Epoch came to an end about 3000 B.C., at the time when Semitic Tribes, speaking a Semitic tongue, conquered Mesopotamia and subdued the Sumerians but adapted their civilisation and particularly their writing, to their own mother-tongue. The Assyrian period comprises the first half of the first millennium before Christ.

In Mesopotamia we found certain pictures which exactly correspond with those of the writing systems of Egypt, China, or even of the Maya. In all these questions we are only at the beginning, and by no means at the end of knowledge, and further excavations may suddenly change the aspect of the present situation.

There are students who believe that Chinese writing derived from Mesopotamian. There are cases where such a relationship seems probable.

(62) *Chinese and Sumerian Pictures Almost Identical*

CHINA   MESOPOTAMIA

(CONSTELLATION)

Yet there are other cases where Chinese pictures show almost the same form as the Egyptian hieroglyphs, for instance the image for *heaven*.

(63) *Chinese and Egyptian Pictures Similar to Each Other.*

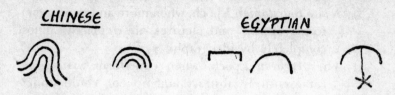

If the idea of a derivation of Chinese writing from Sumero-Babylonian is correct at all, this development must have occurred in a very remote epoch, since even the Sumerian pictures did not preserve the slightest trace of that originality and imaginative power which characterizes the older Chinese pictures. It can hardly be suggested that out of a dried out and almost faded writing system of a rather abstract character as the Mesopotamian, such a picturesque and artistic script could originate as that of the ancient Chinese images. A glimpse at such a figure as the Sumerian sign for *destiny* will confirm this fact. This empty geometrical drawing does not

(64) *The Sumerian Sign for Destiny.*

suggest any idea of Karma, reincarnation, destiny and fate, spiritual thoughts and facts which were common possession of men of old. On the other hand it cannot be denied that certain common principles concerning the basic form of the signs are manifest in Chinese, Hebrew and partly in Mesopotamian writing, such as the principle of the *square*. Each Chinese character is conceived and written in such a way that it fits into a square, and the same applies to Hebrew letters, and — to an extent — to Sumero-Babylonian linear signs and cuneiforms.

Until now we have dealt with pictures and ideographs, and not as yet with *phonetic* characters. There is a great break in human evolution, a change of human consciousness, when peoples passed from pictures and ideographs to sounds, to syllables and finally to written letters. More and more writing began to abandon the visualized thought, turning to the spoken word and language. With the transition to a phonetic system of writing, not only the eye, but the *ear* began to play a decisive role in the field of the written word.

The formation of our alphabet is one of the most important events connected with the story of language.

CHAPTER SEVEN

THE STORY OF OUR ALPHABET

In the beginning writing consisted of pictures only, and was a sort of visual reproduction of the things of this world. It appealed to the *eye* and presented things as a totality. Reading was easy in those times, for every person who saw the sign for a mountain simply pronounced the word *mountain* in his mother-tongue or dialect. This changed in all the three centres of picture-writing in the Orient, Mesopotamia, Egypt and China, when this system fell into decay and degenerated into mere ideographs whose significance did not immediately appear to the reader. However, even in this later, decadent stage the totality of every word was preserved in writing.

The great change took place when those nations who had invented picture-writing began to record the physical sounds of a word in combinations of consonants and vowels. This required a different attitude and method. It was an arduous and very long process of evolution which nowhere was achieved completely by any nation which had invented and for thousands of years used picture-writing. Other, younger peoples, with a different consciousness and a different thinking talent of a more analytical nature had to take up the task, to dissect whole words into their single phonetic elements. Man of old experienced great difficulty, when he had to drop the visual method of writing and adopt the acoustic and phonetic system, relying chiefly or exclusively upon his *ear* instead of his eye.

This difficulty is expressed in the Asiatic centres, Mesopotamia, China, in the fact that the whole change had to pass first through a stage of *syllable-writing* before it could attain to a true *alphabet*. Syllables — especially in olden times — were often complete words — and monosyllabic words are still very frequent in English.

(65) *Monosyllables very frequent in English.*

EYE	EAR	MOUTH	LIP	SKULL	HAIR	ARM	HAND
LEG	LUNG	BLOOD	TREE	LEAF	STEM	BUD	SUN
STAR	MOON	LIGHT	DAY	NIGHT	YEAR	SEA	WAY

Many, many others could still be mentioned. But though syllables in ancient vernaculars were very often identical with words, *phonetic* writing and reading was a very hard task for man of antiquity. This is why the Asiatic inventors of picture-writing did not go beyond the first stage of syllable-writing. To create and use an *alphabet* required a more abstract nature.

Now let us leave the writing of Antiquity and of the Orient for a while and turn to our own alphabets, English, Latin, Greek, German, Russian. Whence did they all come? When do they appear on the stage of history? Who brought them to Europe? *All European alphabets are derived from a common source.* They all are children of the East. We possess a traditional basis for this fact in an old Hellenic legend which describes the origin of the so-called *Cadmean Letters* of the Greek Alphabet. This is the tale of *Cadmus and Europe,* the legend of the spiritual birth of the European continent.

Europe and Cadmus were sister and brother, children of King Agenor of Phoenicia. Surrounded by a group of friendly girls, and well guarded by nurses and servants, the virgin Europe grew up in one of the king's castles located in the hills above the Mediterranean Sea. One night, about the time "when dreams are haunting mortals" Europe had a strange vision. Two women stood before her; one of these was her mother, Asia, the other a stranger. The strange woman used all her strength to drag the virgin along with her. "Come with me, darling, Zeus the Almighty has fallen in love with you and wants you to marry. A great destiny lies ahead of you. You will obtain immortality. Come, come, dearest, follow me."

While both women struggled for her, both dragging her this way and that way, Europe awakened, deeply troubled. What did this dream mean? Who was the strange woman?

Her play-mates came, inviting her to go down to the sea with them, and she followed most unwillingly. Down the slopes they jumped, picking flowers and branches, and twisting them into wreaths. The sky was bright, and the waves of the sea were calm. Suddenly a beautiful white bull swam to the shore, jumped out of the water, mounted the coastal hills and bent his knees before the royal virgin inviting her to sit upon his back. Europe caressed his soft neck, and yielded to his inviting gesture. However no sooner had she sat down, when the young fiery animal leaped up, ran as fast as he could toward the coast, plunged into the waves and swam away. Europe's play-mates badly frightened, screamed loudly, but the bull did not stop swimming until they landed at the island of Crete. There by magic art the animal turned into a young prince, and later married in Europe who, as a reward, was placed among the stars. In her honor the continent adjoining Asia received her name.

When King Agenor received the news of Europe's abduction, he ordered her brother Cadmus to search for his sister and not to come back without rescuing her. Cadmus wandered until he came to the oracle of Apollo at Delphi, and there he asked the God what he should do. Pythia told him he would meet a white cow marked by a yellow crescent on her forehead, and that he should follow her. Where that cow would lie down, there should he found a city and name it Thebes. Cadmus obeyed the oracle and founded the city of Thebes in Boeotia. Yet he did not find his sister. The cow rested beside a spring which was guarded by a dragon. Cadmus killed the monster, and sowed his teeth in the soil. After a short time the point of a spear emerged from the earth. This was followed by shafts, helmets, heads, arms and legs, and finally armed warriors arose from the earth, fighting and killing one another until only five survived. These five warriors became the ancestors of the Theban families. Later Cadmus was remembered by the Thebans as a great hero, as the inventor of many useful arts and as the great teacher who had introduced the *Phoenician alphabet* into Greece.

Thus far the legend. Is it true? Who are these mythical personalities, Cadmus and Europe? Their names are neither purely Hellenic nor Indo-European. They are both typical Semitic words. In Hebrew, as in Babylonian, *Kadam* means the *origin,* the *Orient,* the *primeval epoch,* while *Ereb* means

(66) *The Semitic Words Cadmus and Europe Mean Orient and Occident.*

Hebrew Kadam (Orient)   Ereb (Occident)

evening, darkness, sunset, west. Ereb in Hebrew is the same word as *Europe* in Greek, and the English pronunciation of the name Europe is the echo of the African name *Yorub-a* which means *west* too.

(67) *Phoenician and Greek Alphabets.*

	HEBREW NAME	OLD SEMITIC	GREEK	GREEK NAME	NUMERIC VALUE
1.	ALEPH		A	ALPHA	1
2.	BETH		B	BETA	2
3.	GIMEL		∧	GAMMA	3
4.	DALET	△	△	DELTA	4
5.	HE			E-PSILON	5
6.	WAW	Y	Y	VAU, DIGAMMA	6
7.	ZAIN	I	I, Z	ZETA	7
8.	HETH	⊟	⊟, H	ETA	8
9.	THET	⊗	⊕, ⊙	THETA	9
10.	IOD			IOTA	10
11.	KAPH		K	KAPPA	20

HEBREW NAME	OLD SEMITIC	GREEK	GREEK NAME	NUMERIC VALUE
12. LAMED	レ	レ, Λ	LAMBDA	30
13. MEM	ᙢ	M	MY	40
14. NUN	5	N	NY	50
15 SAMEK	军	军	XI	60
16. AYIN	O	O	O-MIKRON	70
17 PE	7	Γ	PI	80
18. SADEK	ᙁ		(SAMPI	90)
19. KOPH	φ	φ	(KOPPA	100)
20. RESH	ᖆ	P	RHO	200
21. SIN, SHIN	W	∑	SIGMA	300
22. TAW	✝	T	TAU	400

Thus, the myth of Cadmus and Europe shows the transition of human civilisation from Asia to Europe, from the Orient to the Occident. The spiritual birth of the Western Continent, the Occident of the Old World, is foreshadowed in it. Europe, which had remained quiet while Mother Asia played her important part in history and human evolution, awoke and began to prepare herself for her future task of the spiritual guidance of mankind.

Yet how can we prove that such a legend really contains historic truth, and does not consist merely of fancy? By the alphabet! Is it true that the Greek alphabet to which all other European alphabets are closely related is derived from the

Phoenician, Asiatic characters? On the other hand, were those systems of writing created in Europe? The correct answer is the key to this problem, for there are many more secrets involved in our alphabet than we generally realize.

There can be no doubt whatever that the Phoenician (Old Semitic) and Greek alphabet are absolutely identical. Both agree:

(1) in the form of the letters,
(2) in the name of the letters,
(3) **in their sequence,**
(4) in their numeric value
(5) in their direction.

From the time of Socrates, Plato and Aristotle on, the Greek alphabet appears to run from the left to the right, while the Phoenician, Hebrew, Arabic alphabets were written (and still today are written) from the right to the left. This however is a result of the evolution of the Greek alphabet after its reception, after its introduction by Cadmus. Originally most European alphabets Greek, Latin, even the Teutonic Runic alphabet were running just as their source, Phoenician or Hebrew writings, from the right to the left. The fact that the Greek letters stem from the Orient, from a Semitic source, is proved by another coincidence: the names of the Hellenic letters are not only identical with the Hebrew letter-names, but the words used are of Semitic origin and agree in their meaning with the Semitic names.

(68) *Names of the Hebrew and Greek Letters and Their Meaning.*

Hebrew names	Their meaning	Greek names
Aleph	ox	Alpha
Beth	house	Beta
Dalet	door	Delta
Iod	hand	Iota
Kaph	palm	Kappa
Lamed	illumine, teach	Lambda
Mem	water	My
Nun	fish	Ny
Ayin	eye	O-mikron
Pe	mouth	Pi
Koph	hind-head	Koppa
Resh	head	Rho

There is still another fact which corroborates the Semitic origin of the Greek alphabet. Some letters originally borrowed from the Old Semitic, but not needed in Hellas, were dropped later as for instance the *Koppa,* our *Q,* or the Sampi. They disappeared from the alphabet, but were preserved as numeric values in counting, in mathematics and geometry, and this numeric value was the same as in Semitic. Besides, the Greeks added to the Oriental alphabet which they had borrowed some particular Greek letters such as *Phi, Chi, Psi,* and these too were merely adaptations of forms found in the Old Semitic alphabet.

Let us now cast a glance at such an Old Semitic inscription as the stone of Mesha dating back to about 950 B.C.

(69) *The Stone of Mesha, an Old Phoenician Inscription.*

As it is usual in Western Semitic scripts only the consonants and half-consonants are written, while the vocalisation is to be combined by the reader. Thus the reader is presupposed to know the language in which a Semitic text is written. Many of the Old Semitic letters are today still the same as they were some 3000 or more years ago. We recognize our letter *K* in the Phoenician ⅄ when we turn its direction around. The word G-D (7, 8), identical with the English word *God,* is written in the same manner as in Greek except that it runs in Greek from the left to the right instead from the right to the left. Besides, in Greek we would have to add the vowel *A* or *O* in writing this name. The Moabitic word *Gad,* Hebrew, *Gad, God,* (the god of fortune, of destiny) is identical with the Teutonic name *God,* German, *Gott,* and is here first recorded in a Semitic inscription almost 1500 to 2000 years before it appears in Europe in any Germanic document.

This is a most important fact! Anglo-Saxon, Gothic, Old Norse, German words such as

> *God,*   *Earth,*   *Plough,*   *Shield,*

were used in Asia thousands of years before their recorded appearance in Europe! Not only were they spoken by nations dwelling at a great distance from one another, but we note that even the letters with which they were written stem from a common source. Hence their striking similarity ! Let us cast a glance at one example: the Anglo-Saxon Runic letter S. It was written as in (70) in its earliest appearance in the Eighth Century A.D., and called *Sigel* (sun) . In the Ninth Century A.D. it appeared in the Scandinavian Runic Alphabet, drawn as in chart 70, and called *Sol* (sun) in Sweden. This form of an S, phonetically corresponding to *S* in *Rose* (Hebrew *Zayin*) leads us back to the East, to Asia.

(70) *The Ancient Form of the Runic Letter S.*

We could even add here the *Phoenician* (Old Semitic) I=Z, the letter S I of the *Sinai* alphabet.

Who was the actual creator of our alphabet? From which writing system were the letters of the Phoenician or Cadmean alphabet derived? the Egyptian, the Mesopotamian, Hieroglyphs or Cuneiforms? Were the Sumerians the inventors of our letters, or the Phoenicians, Babylonian astrologers or Egyptian priests? Both hypotheses are possible: the Egyptian and the Sumero-Babylonian. However, there is no bridge leading from the Mesopotamian syllabary to a cuneiform alphabet. As to the Hieroglyphs as a source of our alphabet, not only does the difference between the Egyptian and the Phoenician alphabets present an obstacle, but many other facts too: the most decisive among them is the existence of an Egyptian alphabet in itself!

(71) *The Egyptian Alphabet.*

LETTER	PHONETIC VALUE	LETTER	PHONETIC VALUE
1.	A, ALEPH	8.	M
2.	I as in IS, Y „ „ YES	9.	N
3.	c, H, AYIN	10.	R
4.	U, W	11.	H, soft
5.	B	12.	H, sharp.
6.	P	13.	H (as German ACH)
7.	F	14.	H (very sharp)

LETTER	PHONETIC VALUE	LETTER	PHONETIC VALUE
15.	S, Ś	20.	T
16.	SH	21.	TH
17.	Q	22.	D
18.	K	23.	Z
19.	G		

From the viewpoint of recorded history the Egyptian alphabet is as old as the whole Egyptian writing system. Egyptian letters appear in the oldest inscriptions together with the pictures. The tragedy or the secret of the Egyptian script consists in the fact, that the people of the Nile River had at their disposal a complete alphabet, but never were able to make real use of it, until the downfall of their empire and civilisation.

Had the Semites in forming the first true alphabet intended to use the Egyptian letters as a model, then of course it would have been the simplest procedure to adopt the Egyptian alphabet as a whole, with a few changes, dropping the superfluous signs and adding for instance an L to the R. Such an adoption however never occurred. The Semites selected for their alphabet letters different from the Egyptian, as we can conclude from the difference of their names, and pictures.

(72) *The Old Semitic and Egyptian Letters Have Different Names.*

Egyptian Letter Names or Pictures	Semitic Letter Names
eagle	ox
reed	house
arm	door
quail	hook
cord	weapon
snail	wall
owl	hand
water	palm
mouth	illumine, teach
bolt	water
basket	fish
hill	tooth
basin	mouth
hand	hind-head
cobra	cross

Both alphabets use the acrostic for naming their letters: the Egyptians a drawing representing a *boot* (leg) for the *B,* the Semites the picture of a house, a *booth,* (Beth) for the same letter. But in almost all cases the pictures used are different, and even if the letters appear to be the same they are used in both systems for different sounds.

(73) *Same Egyptian and Semitic Letters Used for Different Sounds.*   *Egyptian*   *Semitic*

Form of the letter

Its sound value   S   P

Thus the derivation of the Old Semitic alphabet from the Egyptian alphabet appears utterly improbable. The more we proceed in our investigation, the more we are induced to believe that the creation of the Old Semitic alphabet, the mother of all alphabets, was not achieved in Egypt or in Mesopotamia, but in some ancient Semitic centre between Egypt and Babylonia. We used the term Old Semitic for this alphabet, because the Phoenician and Hebrew (as well as other Western

Semitic) letters are the same. Now we are confronted with another question: who were the true inventors of the Cadmean letters, Phoenicians or Hebrews?

There is an old Jewish tradition according to which Moses received the Old Hebrew letters from God on Mount Sinai. The creation of the Cadmean letters by Phoenicians had been put in question already in antiquity by Roman writers such

(74) *The Phoenician and Mount Sinai Alphabets.*

HEBREW NAME	SOUND VALUE	OLD SEMITIC	MOUNT SINAI
1. ALEPH	A	⪦	⌀ , ⌀
2. BETH	B	⅂	□ , ⊏
3. GIMEL	G	⅂	L , ∠
4. DALET	D	△	⅁ , ⅁
5. HE	H	⧣	⅄ , ⅄
6. WAW	W	Υ	⌒
7. ZAYIN	Z	I	= , ⌣
8. ḤETH	Ḥ , KH	⊟	⅀ , ⅀
9. ṬHET	Ṭ , TH	⊗	⊢�
10. IOD	I , Y	⟨	⟨ , ⟨

HEBREW NAME	SOUND VALUE	OLD SEMITIC	MOUNT SINAI
11. KAPH	K	⇗, ↓	Y, K
12. LAMED	L	𝖼, ʟ	𝟫, 𝟫
13. MEM	M	⌇, ⌇	ᴧᴧᴧ, ᴎ
14. NUN	N	𝟧	⸲, ⸲
15. SAMEK	S	≢	✕✕, 👉
16. AYIN	c, H	O	👁, ⟋
17. PE	P	⌐	▭
18. SADEK	Ṣ, TS	⤳	8, ∞
19. KOPH	Q	φ	⟜
20. RESH	R	⟨	⟨, 𝖰
21. SIN, SHIN	S, SH	w	ᨓ
22. TAW	T	+	+

as Tacitus and Pliny. About 1894 the British scholar, Sir Flinders Petrie indeed discovered inscriptions on Mount Sinai written in the Hebrew language in an alphabet much older than the Phoenician, for it dates from about 1800 B.C., and consists of the same type and number of letters as are contained in most Semitic alphabets.

How can we know whether the letters of Mount Sinai are older than those of Phoenicia? The Sinai alphabet is not as abstract as the Phoenician; its signs correspond with the meaning of their names, and 19 out of its 22 letters are drawings as they were used in picture-writing, in the hieroglyphic system, or in the Sumerian linear script. *Aleph* means an *ox*, *bull* in Semitic; as a matter of fact the Sinaitic *Aleph* still represents a bull's head, in the same manner as a bull is drawn in Egyptian hieroglyphs.

(75) *Sinaitic Letters Compared With Symbols and Pictures.*

LETTER	SEMITIC NAME	SEMITIC	MOUNT SINAI	EGYPT
1. H	HEY (JOY)			
2. TH	THET (CROSS)			
3. M	MEM (WATER)			
4. N	NAHAS (SNAKE)			
5. S	SAMEK (FISH)			
6. O	AYIN (EYE)			
7. R	RESH (HEAD)			
8. T	TAW (CROSS)			

B is called *Beth, house,* Greek, *Beta.* The Sinaitic B has the form of a house. The meaning of Gimmel, G, is obscure in Semitic; the Sinaitic G, representing a *corner*, explains it beyond any doubt. Hebrew *Dalet,* Greek, *Delta,* means a door; the *D* of the Sinai alphabet actually looks like a door, and it is also similar to the Anglo-Saxon Runic letter *Th* or *D*. The *H* is particularly interesting, for it is called Hey, and is literally the same pictured illustration of joy as the English word *Hey*! It represents a child jumping and leaping with joy just as in the hieroglyphs, while the abstract Semitic letter Hey (75) appears somewhat mysterious. *Thet* or Greek Theta, *Th,* is expressed by a mystic sign symbolizing eternal life which is the same as the Egyptian *Ankh.* M corresponds with the Egypto-Semitic *May, water,* Latin, *M-are, sea* our *M*oor, *wet ground,* or *M-oist.* N is the same as South Semitic *Nahas, snake,* and is represented by a serpent, while *S* (Semitic *Samek, fish*) has the form of an actual fish. The rude spirit, similar to *H,* Semitic, *Ayin, eye,* is drawn as a hieroglyphic eye. *T* finally, the Semitic and Greek *T,* is the symbol of the *Cross* and in the Sinaitic inscriptions is the same as our present day cross. Thus, the sign of the cross was by no means alien to the Hebrew people.

Here we see a connection with the Egyptian hieroglyphs on the one hand, and on the other such Sinaitic letters as *S* (*Samek, fish*) appear to be copies of the Sumero-Babylonian pictures.

Before we decide whether the hieroglyphs or cuneiforms influenced the Oriental alphabets, we must keep two facts in mind. *First*: In every sort of picture-writing the images as copies of things must show a certain inner relationship which is the natural result of *imitation.* Thus, independent similarities may appear in different writing systems without pointing to any immediate affinity at all.

Second — and this is more important — the Semitic alphabets, though created by spiritual leaders who doubtless were familiar with both hieroglyphic and cuneiform writings, are not simple transformations either of the Mesopotamian syllabaries or of the Egyptian alphabet. The Hebrews and Phoenicians, even though they knew both of them, did not pick these syllables or letters, but chose other characters for the different sounds of their own mother-tongue out of the wealth of pictures contained in both these systems of writing.

Finally, there were still many more channels through which connections between different kinds of writing were established in bygone epochs than we know of today. For some of these signs as Semitic *Thet,* Greek *Theta,* the Egyptian *Ankh,* symbol of our immortal part, the soul and the Ego, extend as far as to pre-Columbian America, to the writing symbols of the Maya.

Until the year 1929 no one — in spite of hints contained in Pliny and Tacitus concerning the existence of a Syrian ("Assyrian") *alphabet* — had the slightest idea that there was actually such a thing as a *cuneiform alphabet.* In 1929 however a French expedition sent to Ras Shamra in Syria, unearthed an ancient Phoenician Mystery Centre, Ugarit, which had flourished between the Twentieth and the Fourteenth Centuries B. C., having been destroyed about 1400 B. C. Numerous cuneiform tablets were dug up containing myths, legends, religious texts. Among the latter was an Adonis song, "Baal mat!", Baal-Adonis is dead! Other gods such as *El, Anat,* and the sun-god *Shapash* were mentioned also in these records.

Within about one year the Old Phoenician writing could be deciphered. The ability to read the old cuneiform and hieroglyphic writings had ceased in the last centuries before Christ, and in the first eighteen hundred years of the Christian Era not one human being upon earth was able to decipher such ancient texts as the Egyptian *Book of the Dead.* It was Champollion who solved the riddle of the hieroglyphs, and as we look back upon his great achievement we realize how ingenious this young man was in his approach to the solution of his very difficult task. He first deciphered not the ideographs, but the Egyptian Alphabet, the *cartouches,* containing names of outstanding personalities written phonetically, by consonants alone.

Were the Chinese ideography to fall into oblivion, it would take many centuries to decipher its forty to fifty thousand characters. Had Champollion tried to start with unveiling the mystery of the Egyptian pictures, instead of the hieroglyphic alphabet (some twenty three letters), a similar time would have been required. Champollion started with the letters and deciphered such first names as Cleopatra, Ptolemy, Caesar, Alexander, Berenice, and besides Arsinoë and Autocrator. When he told his elder brother "Je tiens l'affaire!" (I got it!), he was still very far from the complete solution, but the first great step had been made, and he had not only unveiled the mystery of the Egyptian alphabet, but discovered the right method of deciphering secret codes as used in modern warfare.

(76) *The Old Phoenician Cuneiform Alphabet of Ugarit.*

LETTER		HEBREW NAME	SOUND	LETTER		HEBREW NAME	SOUND
1	▷▷—	ALEPH	A	8.	▷—	WAW	W
2		ALEPH²	E	9.		ZAYIN	Z
3.		ALEPH³	E'	10.		HETH	H, KH
4.		BETH	B	11.		HET²	KH(CH)
5.		GIMEL	G	12.		THET	T, TH
6.		DALET	D, DH	13.		YOD	I, Y
7.		HEY	H	14.	▷—	KAPH	K

LETTER	HEBREW NAME	SOUND	LETTER	HEBREW NAME	SOUND
15. 𝕐	LAMED	L	22. 𝕐𝕐	SADEK	S̱, TS
16. ◁𝕐	MEM	M	23. ⋈	SADEK²	S̱²
17. ▷▷▷—	NUN	N	24. ▷—◁	KOPH	Q
18. Y, ▲▲	SAMEK	S	25. ▷▷▷—	RESH	R
19. △	AYIN	', H	26. ⋎, ◁	SIN	S'
20. ◁←	GHAIN	GH	27. ◁	SHIN	SH
21. ▷▷—	PE	P	28. ▷—	TAW	T

Thus the French scholars who faced the task of deciphering the cuneiform inscriptions of Ugarit in 1930 could profit from Champollion's experience. In all the different Phoenician tablets were only about twenty eight letters. Thus students immediately realized that this must be an alphabet; they discovered the old cuneiform alphabet of Ugarit.

To the best of our knowledge no scholar has compared these letters, perhaps the oldest true alphabet, with others. If we study the most important phonetic systems of writing from the viewpoint of their similarity, we discover that most of them — except those few created later, such as the Picto-Irish Ogham Alphabet of England — are so closely related that they must have derived from a common source. The ap-

parent different form and style of the hieroglyphs and cuneiforms by no means contradicts this fact. A thorough investigation will disclose that the cuneiform letters often show the
same pictures as the hieroglyphs or Semitic and early Greek
letters. In many cases we find that a letter is the same in most
of the writing systems of Asia and Europe, despite difference
of tongues, races and civilisations.

Let us examine a few identical letters in the Ugarit, Old
Semitic and Greek Alphabets.

(77) *Ugarit Cuneiform Letters Compared With Semitic and
Greek Forms.*

SOUND	HEBREW NAME	UGARIT	OLD SEMITIC	GREEK
1. T̤,TH	THET		+, ⊗	T, ⊕
2. E } H }	{ ALEPH² { HEY			, E
3. S	SAMEK			
4. S¹	S'IN			
5. K	KAPH		,	K

It is striking how similar the Ugarit letters E (Aleph 2) and
H are to Old Semitic He and Greek E-psilon. We observe here

a very important fact. The Ugarit letters, though adapted and used for a Western Semitic dialect, Old Phoenician, do not run as does the Cadmean alphabet exclusively from the right to the left, but as the Babylonian wedges and to an extent even the Sinaitic letters from the left to the right. Thus we are able to recognize immediately in Ugarit E (Hey) our own letter E.

(78) *The Letter "E" 3500 Years Ago and Today.*

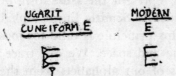

UGARIT CUNEIFORM E   MODERN E

There is no difficulty in realizing the relationship between Ugarit S (Samek), the Old Semitic S, and Greek Xi (Hsi). The same is true for Ugarit Shin, S, and strangely enough this Old Phoenician letter derived from wedge-writing directly is completely identical with modern Hebrew Shin, Sh.

(79) *Ugarit "SH" (Shin) and the Hebrew Shin Idientical.*

UGARIT SIN   MODERN HEBREW SIN

S' (S'IN)

More difficult is the explanation of Ugarit Thet and its connection with corresponding letters of other alphabets. However if we keep in mind that Th is related with T and a variety of it, and that it consists of two symbolic elements, the cross or Tau and the circle symbolizing the sun as still today in Astronomy, we easily find its links almost everywhere, in the most remote epochs. The Sinaitic Th (list 74) is similar to the Egyptian Ankh (immortality). Here the cross is outside the sun-circle, while in the Cadmean (Old Semitic) and Greek forms of Thet and Theta the cross is inside the circle. The same is true for the Maya symbol of the sun, called in the Maya tongue: IC! We turn the Ugarit letter Thet, Th to the left (by 90°) and we obtain a sign similar to the Ankh-cross.

(80) *The Theta in Hellas and Ankh in Egypt—Old Symbols.*

UGARIT	SINAI	OLD EGYPT	OLD SEMITIC	OLD GREEK	MAYA

By such comparisons it is clear that the Ugarit cuneiform
letters often represent the same form of the original picture
as that of the Old Semitic linear alphabet. Only the style is
different. This principle is valid for most alphabets independent of time and space. We can trace the development of
many letters of our alphabets from their appearance about
six to seven thousand years ago in Mesopotamia and Egypt,
in Phoenicia and Palestine, in Greece and in Rome, and
finally in England, Scandinavia, Germany, the Slavic countries and many other parts of the world. One example may
suffice to illustrate this fact.

(81) *The Letter D (Th) in Several Alphabets.*

SINAI	OLD SEMITIC	OLD GREEK	SOUTH ARABIC	ANGLO-SAXON	GERMANIC

Almost the same sign is used for D, Dh, Th. Of particular
importance is the fact that the Teutonic Runic letters, usually considered as derived from Greek or Latin, show in this
and in several other cases older forms than the classical European alphabets, signs which appear similar to corresponding Semitic letters. Generally speaking, the Semitic and European alphabets all appear to be somewhat clumsy in early
times, and are similar to the Runic writing. Whoever looks
at an Old Semitic, Phoenician, Greek or Latin inscription
of the last five centuries before Christ comparing them with
any Anglo-Saxon, Nordic or Germanic Runic texts, will see
that they are all written in the same primitive style.

Let us compare two Phoenician and Teutonic inscriptions,

that on the stone of Mesha, and that on Helmet B of Negau:

(82) *Semitic and Germanic Runic Inscriptions.*

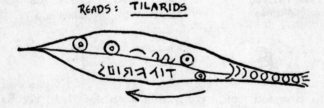

The Semitic text stems from the Tenth Century before Christ, the Germanic inscription allegedly from the Second Century before Christ. Both run from right to left, a common occurrence in the earlier age of Germanic Runic writing. The well-known spear of Kovel (Volhynia, Russia) contains the inscription TILARIDS (hitting the goal) again running from right to left. It dates from about the Third Century A.D.

(83) *The Spear of Kovel Bearing a Gothic Inscription.*

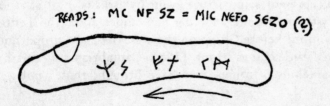

Thus it is apparent that writing from right to left is not especially characteristic of the Semitic races alone, but occurred in almost every nation in an early epoch of writing. Finally

(84) *Inscription of Maria Saalerberg, Carinthia.*

there is an enigmatic inscription of the First Century A.D. written on a knife found in Maria Saalerberg in Carinthia. The translation of this text is not as yet entirely agreed upon by all scholars, despite the fact that we know and can read the letters: M-C N-F S-Z (MIC NEFO SEZO?). This inscription is written in consonants only, the same as the Egyptian names in cartouches and in Western Semitic (Phoenician, Hebrew, Arabic) texts. Consonantic writing therefore was by no means confined to the Semites, but was practiced in early epochs even among the Germanic or Teutonic tribes.

At the end of this chapter on the development of the alphabet we may come back to the question from which we started: What are those mysterious signs (List 33) written in red and black on pebbles found in the grotto of Mas d'Azil in southern France? Are they pictures or alphabetic letters? It would be wrong to consider them as letters and to compare them with forms of historic characters, such as our E.

(85) Age of Our Letter E.

MAS D'AZIL PEBBLES	UGARIT CUNEIFORMS	GREECE
ABOUT 12.000 YEARS AGO	ABOUT 3600 YEARS AGO	ABOUT 2400 YEARS AGO

Such an assertion would contradict scientific truth. We have reasons for doubting whether the signs of Mas d'Azil were letters. Some 12,000 years ago human consciousness had not yet developed to a level which would have enabled any part of mankind to create an actual alphabet. Those signs were symbols, images as used millennia later in mythology and art to represent some actual event by a visual hint at it. Those mysterious immigrants who had landed about the Tenth Millennium before Christ on the west coast of Europe, and covered the ceilings of the Franco-Cantabrian caves with their marvelous paintings, may have brought those symbols with them, but certainly no alphabet, and later, out of these symbols generally used all over the earth in remote epochs, our writing systems developed.

Today we use the word alphabet thoughtlessly, in an abstract manner, as ABC. There was, however, a time, when people were conscious of the relations between the names and forms of our letters and the world of stars. They believed that our art of writing is but a residue of the art of reading the writing of the stars, of a celestial script. The symbols used in modern Astronomy are connected with the symbols of writing. We learned that Greek *alpha* is Hebrew *aleph* (ox, bull). The picture used for the *ox* in Egypt, on Mt. Sinai, in Sumer and Palestine is identical with the Astronomical symbol of the sign of the zodiac *Taurus, Bull,* and with our modern letter A, if we turn it upside down.

(86) *Alpha-Aleph Preserved in the Sign of Taurus, Bull.*

EGYPT	MOUNT SINAI	ASTRO- NOMY	SUMER	SEMITIC	MODERN A

The second part of the name *alphabet,* Beth-Beta (house) is connected with the zodiac again, for "house" in old Astrology meant the place of a sign of the zodiac. Further, the picture used for *house* in Egyptian, Sumerian, modern Chinese (enclosure), and Hebrew is identical with that of the sign of the zodiac *Gemini, Twins.*

(87) *The old picture for a house and the Sign of Twins.*

EGYPT	SUMER	CHINA	HEBREW	ASTRONOMY

Then there is the sign of the zodiac, *Aries, Ram,* whose exact likeness is found nowhere else but in China. There it is

(88) *The Sign of the Zodiac Aries, Ram.*

MODERN ASTRONOMY	CHINESE PICTURE FOR RAM	CHINESE IDEOGRAPH
♈	♈	羋

used as a designation for *sheep, ram.* How did this ancient Chinese symbol dating back to pre-Christian times arrive in Europe and penetrate into modern Astronomy as a symbol used for Aries? We find many more such connections between the ancient symbols of writing and signs of modern Astronomy, probably a heritage of ancient Astrology. The channels by which they were carried from continent to continent are one of the secrets of history with which we are faced in language again and again. We mention here but two more examples. One is the modern Astronomical sign for *Aquarius, the Water Bearer* which entirely corresponds with the Egyptian picture for *water* and its letter N, with Mount Sinai, Semitic and Modern M.

(89) *The Sign for the Zodiac Aquarius and Our M.*

EGYPTIAN PICTURE	LETTER N	SINAI	SEMITIC	ASTRONOMY	LETTER M
〰〰〰	〰〰	〰〰	⁊	〰〰	⋀⋀

Finally, we may mention the sign of the zodiac *Pisces, Fishes,* whose resemblance to the Old Semitic letter Samek, *S* and Old Greek *X* is striking, and which looks similar to our modern *X.*

A similar connection exists between the zodiac sign *Pisces, Fishes,* which is none other than Ugarit and Old Semitic *Samek, fish, S,* Greek X, and our modern X.

(90) *The sign of the zodiac Pisces, Fishes.*

ASTRONOMY	OLD SEMITIC	UGARIT	OLD GREEK	MODERN X
♓	羊	⯗	王	X

We already mentioned the astronomical symbols of the planets Sun and Moon, identical with the pictures used for them in four continents. Is not the symbol of *Venus* (Frey, Friday) the same sign as the *Thet* of Ugarit and on Mount Sinai, as well as the Egyptian Ankh?

(91) *The symbol of the planet Venus.*

There are numberless other links between ancient writing and the star symbols, so that we can realize that the wisdom of the stars was behind the creation of our letters and of their arrangement. The Runic alphabet is divided into 3 sections or 'staffs', German *Stab*. The western Semitic alphabets also fall under two 'staffs', one starting with aleph-bet, hence *alpha-bet*, the other with L,M,N. From the latter, Roman wisdom created the word *element, EL-EM-EN-tum*. Some Semitic alphabets such as the Abyssinian even start with the letters *L-M-N!*

There is 'hidden wisdom' even behind the arrangement of the Egyptian and Old Semitic alphabets. The hieroglyphic 'staffs' start with the letter A represented by an *eagle,* and end with a *Th* or *Z*, represented by a *serpent*, a cobra. The Semitic alphabets start with *Aleph, bull,* the *A,* and end with the *Tau, T,* a *cross.* What is the symbolic meaning of all these old images? The *eagle* and *bull* are apocalyptic animals. Their apocalyptic companion is the *lion,* often replaced in northern countries by the *dragon.* Besides all the four pictures, eagle, serpent, bull, cross, are well-known symbols of the age of picture consciousness, often used in ancient mystery centres.

The eagle is the symbol of initiation wisdom, while the snake ('uplifted' by Moses according to the Gospel of St. John 3, 14), the dragon, is the symbol of earthly knowledge. The *bull, the cow* — as Jacob Grimm and other linguists have pointed out — is the symbol of the *earth,* while the *cross* symbolizes spiritual spheres and divine forces.

There is a deep sense hidden in the sequence of our letters. In the Egyptian epoch the development of mankind was to lead people from higher wisdom acquired only through initiation, down to a more physical knowledge, to forces of nature, to the depth of mortal existence. The Hebrew people were to pave the way for Christianity by taking up the earthly knowledge of the 'snakes', transforming it and lifting it up to the heights of the cross.

CHAPTER EIGHT

VOWELS AND CONSONANTS
AND THEIR ROLE IN LANGUAGE

"IN THE BEGINNING WAS THE WORD, and the Word was with God, and the Word was God. The same was in the beginning with God. All things were made by him; and without him was not anything made that was made."

When St. John wrote these words, he expressed an attitude toward the Mystery of the Word which the whole of ancient humanity shared. All the nations of Antiquity regarded the profound mystery of speech and its written symbols with the greatest veneration.

In his Revelation, St. John the Divine depicts Christ as the Lord of Destiny, the Beginning and the Ending, which is, and which was and which is to come, the Almighty. The Christ says, "I am the Alpha and the Omega": the beginning and the ending *of the alphabet!*

"And I was in the spirit: and behold a throne was set in heaven, and one sat on the throne. And he that sat was to look upon like a jasper and a sardine stone: and there was a rainbow round about the throne, in sight like unto an emerald. And round about the throne were four and twenty seats; and upon the seats I saw four and twenty elders sitting; and they had on their heads crowns of gold. And out of the throne proceded lightnings and thunderings and voices; and there were seven lamps of fire burning before the throne which are the seven spirits of God." (Revelation 4)

A few centuries after the writing of this great description by St. John in his Revelation, a Christian painter depicted this grand imagination in the Simeon Monastery of Assuan in Egypt. In that wall-painting the Christ sits upon a throne in the middle; on both sides of him are four winged personalities, the evangelists, and at his feet sit twenty-four beings.

101

Above their heads are the Coptic inscriptions from A-ael,
B-ael, G-ael, D-ael to O-ael. The twenty-four letters of the
Greek alphabet are represented as divine beings; for Ael, El
means *god* in Hebrew as in the Greek Hel-ios, Ael-ios (*sun-
god.*)

Among the Hindus the sounds of our language were represented as seeds of *Brahma,* of the Universe. Brahma was the
Word, as *Brihas*-pati was its protector, the lord of blessing
and of speech. These names are intimately related to the
name *Bragi,* Odin's son, the lord of speech and poetry among
the Teutonic tribes. It contains the same word-stem as *Pray,*
Latin, *Prec*-or (I pray) and Hebrew *B'rach*-a (blessing,
prayer, mantram). German *S-prach-e* (language) is related
to these words.

(92) *The names of Brah-ma and Brag-i Mean the Word.*

India	India	Germanic
BRAH-ma (prayer)	BRIH-a (word)	BRAG-i (god of poets)

English	Latin	Hebrew
PRAY	PREC-or (I pray)	B'RACH-a (prayer)

The word in antiquity signified something important. The
words which we use today for 'talk' or 'speech' in remote
epochs meant *solemn announcement* or the *prophecy of an
oracle* as Anglo-Saxon Nef-na, the mother of 'to name'. The
wisdom of ancient India differentiated between the function
of the vowels and consonants in language. The vowels, according to the Chandogya-Upanishad, are incarnations of Indra. Different groups of consonants belong to different Godheads. The hissing and aspirate consonants are connected with
the creator, Prajapati, the builder of the Universe. The voiceless consonants (K,P,T) belong to the Mrityus or Spirits of
Death. The vowels ought to be pronounced with full tone
and power, with the idea "To Indra I entrust my force!"
According to Hindu tradition, the aspirate and hissing sounds
never should be swallowed or jolted, but formed out of the
consciousness "To Prajapati I devote my breath, my Self, my
Atma!" The voiceless sounds (K,P,T) should be shaped with

the will: "I shall protect my Self, my Atma, against the death-spirits, the Mrityus"!

In Ancient Mysteries, particularly in Egypt, priests sang hymns consisting but of certain vowels in honor of the Gods. The Greek language also possessed seven vowels. Ancient traditions connected these sounds with the seven planets, the seven colors of the rainbow and with the seven tones of the musical scale.

(93) *The Seven Vowels Connected With the Seven Planets.*

AO	I	A	E	O	A	OO
(as NOW)	(as MY)	(as SAY)	(BE)	(FOR)	(FAR)	(SOON)
⊙	☽	♂	☿	♃	♀	♄
SUN	MOON	MARS	MERCURY	JUPITER	VENUS	SATURN

These seven vowels were used instead of flutes and citharas as an accompaniment for prayers and hymns. The ancient Greek philosophers, Pythagoras, Heraclitus and others, considered the words to be *sounding pictures of things* (agalmata phonêenta) created by the Gods themselves. Socrates, in Plato's *Cratylus,* calls them the 'primeval names' (prôta onomata). In the teachings of antiquity the seven vowels were the hidden Word (the Lost Word), while the connection between the vowels and consonants was compared with the union of soul and body.

Plato, Socrates, and most great thinkers in the classical epoch knew that each sound, each consonant particularly, had its own meaning. As recently as the beginning of the Nineteenth Century, the French scholar, Fabre d'Olivet, in his book *The Hebrew Tongue Restored* published a complete alphabetical list explaining the meaning of every vowel and consonant. He as well as the great Court de Gebelin in his *Primeval World (Le monde primitif)* knew the varying functions of vowels and consonants in speech.

The *consonants* were considered the body of the words, while the vowels were regarded as their soul. The consonants imitate and repeat everything that appears in the Universe, all the objects which we grasp with our sense-organs. They depict and describe the earth, heaven, sun, stars, mountains, rivers, trees, animals and so on. Consonants are sound pictures of the outer world, of outer experiences. The *vowels* however express the effect which outer things exert *upon our soul life,* the impression brought about by outer objects and occurrences upon our inner nature, the feelings, sympathies, antipathies, astonishment, veneration, and fear.

(94) *What We Express by Our Basic Vowels (according to Rudolf Steiner)*

A (as in guard) (admiration)	E (as in net) (self-support)	I (as in fish) (joy, self-reliance)
O (as in for) (sympathy)		U (as in too) (fear)

We can illustrate *A* this way in almost every language by the exclamation of astonishment: Ah! *E* manifests its very nature in *Ego* and *Egotism, in Neg*-ation, in *sever, separate* and many other instances. *I* expresses joy in *Gee,* or in *cheer,* and self-reliance in *creed, free, believe, pier, pillar,* and so on. *O* appears as a symbol of *sympathy* in *love, home, boy, toy, joy, rose, comfort, common, compose* and others. Finally, U is the expression of something which *frightens* us in *ugly, umbrage, urus, shoo, moose, moo* and so on.

We often find in language the same consonants preserved in various words, while their vowels change. This is not only because the vowels are more subtle and 'frail' than the consonants, but because our inner reaction toward anything in the outer world may differ at different times. This is why in ancient times in most languages the change of present, past and future tense of a verb was affected by a variation of the vowels and a complete preservation of the consonants, a procedure which today survives in English, German and other Germanic tongues.

What gives the beauty to languages such as Italian or Spanish and many others is their vocalisation or the wealth of vowel elements in their words. According to Rudolf Steiner (lectures on Language delivered to teachers in Switzerland and Germany in the years 1919 to 1924) language developed its vocalisation step by step in different epochs. This evolution was manifested in *three stages* which followed closely the unfolding of human consciousness.

During the *first* stage of language, in remote epochs, speech was characterized by its strong *consonantic* nature rather than by the wealth of its vowels. There were many consonants in the words, and these consonants were generally *voiced* (B,G,D) and were spelled with great emphasis and force. Man imitated the outer world in the sounds of his speech which sculpted, painted and presented the whole brightness of the Universe to those who listened. In those remote times Man was still endowed with a certain visionary talent; he could penetrate into the inner nature of things, while his own soul-life and thinking-force remained on a lower level, as in children today. Man's inner reaction to things was comparatively unimportant in those distant epochs of antiquity. Hence the weakness of the vocalic element, the prevalence of the consonants in words. Heraclitus rightly called those primeval words *agalmata phonêenta,* sounding pictures; for behind the primeval sounds Man visualized the picture of the thing, not its idea. Picture-consciousness prevailed before thinking-consciousness developed.

Then came a great step forward, from the perception of the outer world to a stronger expression of the effect brought about by the appearance of things of the outer world before Man's soul and mind. The inner answer of humanity to the objects and events was expressed by a much *richer vocalisation.* This *second* stage marks a step forward *from without to within,* from an outer to an inner experience of the Universe. At the same time the *quality* of vowels begins to change, words are characterized by a greater flexibility in the transition from one vowel to another within the same word-stem, in the formation of different tenses and in the passage from a verb to a noun. Thus Man became not merely a spectator of the Universe, but an active participant in the life of the world.

The *third* stage in the evolution of speech is not a state of youth and of growth, but of age and decline. The vocalisation becomes less beautiful; not only the quantity but also the quality of vowels declines, and their flexibility comes to an end. Man does not change the vocalisation and the quality of vowels once he starts to separate himself from life, expressing no longer his inner feelings but rather his more abstract viewpoints.

Let us illustrate this by a few instances, first showing the flexibility of the vocalic element in the *second* stage, in English and in German.

(95) *Flexibility of Vowels in English Conjugation.*

Vowels:	Present	Past	Past Participle	Consonants
i-a-u	shrink	shrank	shrunk	sh-r-nk
i-a-u	sing	sang	sung	s-ng
i-a-u	begin	began	begun	b-gn
i-a-u	drink	drank	drunk	d-r-nk
i-u-u	dig	dug	dug	d-g
i-o-i	write	wrote	written	wr-t
u-a-u	run	ran	run	r-n

The flexibility of the vocalic element is characteristic of an ancient state of languages. The more ancient the language, the more changes of vowels we encounter, particularly in conjugation. The flexibility is still much better preserved or more intense and frequent in German than in English, and it is particularly characteristic of the Semitic tongues. There it was and is so evident, that it was consciously used in writing as a kind of shorthand. What do we notice at the first glance when we examine Table 95? We discover that while the vowels of the words change in the present, past and perfect tenses, the consonants do not change at all. They express the stable element of the words, while the vowels are more flexible.

(96) *Flexibility of Vowels in German Conjugation.*

Vowels Consonants	A	E	I	O	U	Meaning
w-r-d	Ward	Werd-e	Wird	Word-en	Wurd-e	become
b-r-g	Barg	Berg-e	Birg	ge-Borg-en	Burg	hide
w-r-f	Warf	Werf-e	Wirf	ge-Worf-en	Wurf	throw
b-r-ch	Brach	Brech-e	Brich	ge-Broch-en	Bruch	break
sp-r-ch	Sprach	Sprech-e	Sprich	ge-Sproch-en	Spruch	speak

Thus in modern German (strong) conjugation the vowels pass sometimes through the whole scale while the consonants remain unchanged. Such words in every tongue, ancient or modern, are called irregular verbs. Today we can observe the tendency to regularize such forms, to transform language, a fount of eternal creation, into a sort of stable, immobile, easy, artificial and regular tongue. This is because the poet is more and more dying out and the writer appears in his stead.

We no longer stand amidst the sphere of speech, deeply involved in its destiny and unfolding; we are no longer partakers in the divine creation, co-workers of God as St. Paul has called us, but only cool, disinterested observers and skeptics. We use our speech so cleverly and superficially that we slur over the strings of this marvelous instrument without becoming aware of the whole power and beauty of their tunes. Thus the laws of language are mysteries to us.

In Hebrew — unlike other Semitic tongues — a vowel must be put between two consonants, even between two double-consonants such as NN, LL, SS and so on.

(97) *In Hebrew a Vowel is Put Between Two Double-Consonants.*

English	English	German	Hebrew
RUN	RUNN-ing	RENN-en	RANAN
		(to run)	(to leap for joy)

The abundant vocalisation of ancient tongues compared with the meagre quantity of vowels in modern idioms prevents many scholars from realizing the relationship between such words as RANAN and RUN or German RENN-en. If we look backward a few centuries in English, we shall find a great difference in the vocalisation of words. Thus, Anglo-Saxon was richer in vowels than is modern English.

(98) *Richer Vocalisation in Anglo-Saxon than in English.*

Anglo-Saxon	Modern English
MONTH	MONETH
CHURCH, KIRK	CIRIC-e, KIRIHH-a
MILK	MEOLUC
THROUGH	THURUH, THORUH
THUNDER	THUNOR
BENT (-reed)	BEONOT

In modern English we find *THROUGH and THO-ROUGH* side by side, two differently vocalised forms of the same word. When we go back only a few centuries, to the age of Chaucer, English appears still as a far more beautifully sounding language on account of its richer vocalisation.

(99) *Vocalisation of English Words in Chaucer's Time and Now.*

Chaucer	Modern English
FITHELE	FIDDLE
HEVED	HEAD
LODE-STERRE	LODESTAR
JOLILY	JOLLY
NORICE	NURSE

Once we understand this development as it occurred in all languages, it becomes easy to recognize the relationship of words as well as the age of a language from its vocalisation. Sanskrit is much younger than Hebrew, for the holy idiom of India appears in history in a strongly consonantic form. Among the modern Indo-European vernaculars Czechoslovak and Yugoslav actually contain vowelless words. These Indo-European words are not only written but also spelled (pronounced) without any vocalic sound: something quite extraordinary

(100) *Indo-European Words Containing no True Vowels.*

Sanskrit	Czechoslovak	Yugoslav
HRD (heart)	KRK (neck)	PRST (finger)
	VRCH (top)	GRK (Greek)

in language. This is impossible in the Egyptian and Semitic groups: their vocalisation is as rich as is usual in the *second*

(101) *Same words in Hebrew and English.*

Hebrew	English	Consonantic Scheme
SALAP	SLAP	S-l-p
SARAP	SERP-ent	S-r-p
ERETZ	EARTH	E-r-tz/th
SHELET	SHIELD	Sh-l-t/d
SHEVET	SHAFT	Sh-v/f-t
DEREK	TRECK	D/T-r-k
CHALIF	CLIPP, CLIFF	C-l-p/f
KALAP	CLAP	C-l-p
PALAKH	PLOUGH	P-l-kh/gh
BARA	BEAR	B-r
THERASH (Aramaic)	THRASH	Th-r-sh
SHARAB (Arabic)	ab-SORB	S-r-b

stage of evolution while Sanskrit and most Indo-European tongues show all the characteristics of the *third* stage of evolution. If we compare English and Hebrew words we find that they do not disagree because of the difference in language, but because of the difference in their ages. Comparing Hebrew and English words is the same as if we compared the picture of an old man with his photo when he was a boy. This is the point. Once we know this, it is easy to overcome an artificial barrier called the *Triliterality* of the Semitic tongues.

We are told that all Semitic word-stems consist of *three* consonants, that the vowels do not belong to the root, and that on account of this particular characteristic Semitic words cannot be compared with or related to Indo-European words. This idea was first introduced into the field of linguistics by Jewish students and Orientalists, yet the theory is completely erroneous. *First* of all, it was the Egyptians and not the Phoenicians, Hebrews or Arabs who established purely consonantic writing.

Egyptian consonantic writing dates from about four thousand B.C., while Phoenician and Hebrew records go back only to about two thousand before Christ. *Second,* the Babylonians (Eastern Semites) were unable to use this sort of consonantic writing, because they never developed any formal alphabet, but only a syllabary. *Third,* consonantic writing is a question of *script* alone, not of spoken language. It would be possible to write the words of each language by recording consonants only and after becoming accustomed to this kind of script everyone could read it.

(102) *English Words Written Only by Consonants.*

SLAP	SEARCH	MARK	CLOTH	MONK	CREEP	DRAB	FILM
S-l-p	S-r-ch	M-r-k	C-l-th	M-n-k	C-r-p	D-r-b	F-l-m

We can use this same procedure in every language and this will help us to recognize their relationship and their common structure.

Why did the Egyptian and Semitic spiritual guides who established alphabets introduce consonantic writing and even develop a style where most words were written by only three consonants? What does this *triconsonance* mean? Of course the consonantic writing poses a lot of difficulties. D-s-c-v-r could hardly be read otherwise than 'discover', yet st-r-ng could be spelt either 'strong' or 'string' or connected with 'strangle'. F-r-m could be read 'farm' or 'form' or 'firm', or even 'frame' or 'from'! And f-l-d could possibly be 'flood' or 'field' or a 'fold' or finally be read as he 'fled'! It is when we solve such puzzles as these that we can learn very useful facts about the secrets of the origin of words.

Some scholars believe that the Egypto-Semitic method of writing was a first attempt at writing shorthand. Without doubt, this is partly correct. All scribes of Antiquity and in the Middle Ages, copying the same texts many times year after year, sought for devices to shorten their labors. However this does not explain the whole riddle.

The Egyptians and Semites, out of their imaginative power, looked at the words and realized that in spite of the flexibility and transmutation of the vowels *the words with the same consonants form a unity, are identical*. The vowels change, they almost fly away from the words, like winged beings, while down here upon earth what remains is but the body which continues its life-functions. There is still life around the consonantic skeletons of words. They are not dead corpses, they are organs of a living body. *Stick, stock,* and *stake* are the same word, in spite of the change of their vocalisation. The ancients, upon looking at such words as *string* and *strangle* could realize their relationship through the scheme *ST-R-NG*, for a string has something to do with strangling. It may happen that an abbreviation such as *F-L-D* embraces both 'field' and 'flood'. Already Jacob Grimm had pointed out that the poets of Hellas compared a plough with a floating boat and the tilled field with the 'water-field' of the ocean. Groups like *F-R-M* which connect such various words as 'form', 'from', 'frame', 'farm', and even 'firm', are the problem-children of language. Are these words really

related to one another or do they look similar as a result of
some accident during their development?

The great teachers of Antiquity knew that there were
words in the various languages which consisted of one or two
consonants or vowels only such as the exclamation *Ah!* or *Oh!*
But they also knew that the great majority of words were
characterized by *three radical consonants.* This was not a
peculiar feature of the Egypto-Semitic tongues but a characteristic common to every language in every epoch and in every
corner of the world. Whether we go to the languages of the
Far East, to Africa, to Europe, or to the American Indians,
we can note the following organic principle: most words consisted or still consist of *three consonants,* and never of more.
It is true that we find words in many languages which contain
more than three consonants, yet these surplus-consonants actually do not belong to the original root or are merely pho-
netical extensions of simple basic sounds, as *ST* instead of *T*
in *STEER* and *TAUR-us* or *STUMBLE* and *TUMBLE,* or
in Polynesian *TOK-i* (*staff*, emblem of the chieftain) and
STICK, STOCK

(103) *The Word CROWN K-R-N* (*wreath, king*) *in Different Continents.*

America, Aymara
KARAN K-r-n (vice-king)

Europe, Latin
CORON-a C-r-n (crown)

Europe, Greek
KARAN-os K-r-n (prince)

Asia, Manchu
KURUN K-r-n (royal family)

We can also note many other examples such as the Peruvian (Quichua) *MARK-a* (territory), Arabic, *MARG'*
(field), Gothic *MARK-a* (territory): their common symbol is
M-R-K. Such consonantic symbols facilitate the recognition
of the relationship of languages, and the fact that they are
at the foundations of the structure of words found all over
the world is further evidence that all tongues derive from the
same source.

CHAPTER NINE

THE SPIRIT OF WORDS

Germanic mythology tells of the beautiful legend of Ymir, the primeval giant from whose body the Gods shaped the Earth. Who was this mysterious Ymir or Ymer? To answer this question, we must start from the language, and from a state of consciousness reflecting the spirit of those early epochs of mankind which we may call mythological.

Why does the myth tell us that the earth was made of the flesh of Ymir and the sea, the water, of his blood? *Blood* and *Flood* do not only rhyme, they are the same word, with a change of the initial *B* into *F*. The *Blood* is the *Flood* of life. And *Flesh* was the word used in antiquity and in the Gospels to express our modern term *matter*. 'The *Spirit* is willing, but the *Flesh* is weak'! The earth is the material, the physical part of the Universe, and that the mountains and rocks are called the 'bones' and 'ribs' of this earth is a common symbolic use of words.

What a strange name is this Ymir or Ymer! It is contained in the Scandinavian *Edda* and it is not found in any other Teutonic vernacular except in a shortened form in the German words *MAER*-e (report, message) and *MAER*-chen (fairy tale). When we turn from the mythology of Northern Europe to the Hebrew record of the creation of the world, in *Genesis* we discover the name Ymer once again: "Va-Yomer Elohim, yehi Or, va-yehi Or!" . . . "And the Elohim spoke: Let there be Light! And there was Light". The Hebrew word *Yomer,* from *Amar,* to *speak,* is the same stem as *Ymir, Ymer.* It means the *Word.* Thus we discover a bridge between the strange Germanic myth of Ymir, the Old Testament and the Gospel of St. John. Here again, "In the beginning was the Word, and the Word was with God", the world has been created out of and by the Word. Here again, the Word has become *Flesh* — Matter.

It was not without just cause that the philosopher Schelling called language "faded mythology", for the pale shadows of the Gods still dwell in our words. The words of our modern languages still contain in faint outline the silhouette of a divine world. We recommend the study of myths and legends in an objective, scientific way, because they can reveal much of the background of the spirit of the words, of language. For example, if we consider the names which we give to the different parts of the earth, we shall find that we give them the names of Ymir's limbs as the legend has it, for we describe our earth as a living being, almost as a human being. Do we not speak of the *foot* of a hill, of the *mouth* of a river, of an *arm* of the sea? The coast of the ocean is its *rib* (Latin, *costa*, rib). A *beach* is a *mouth* (French *bouche*, Italian *bocca*, mouth), a gulf is a *bosom* (Greek kolp-os, bosom). Do we not speak of the *ridge* of a mountain as if it were its *back*, and of the *peak* or *crest*, as if we were describing a cock or some other bird? A promontory, a slope, is called a *naze*, simply because it is similar to a *nose*. We speak of the *tip* or *top* of a hill or mountain and hardly realize that actually we are calling it a *head*. In Old Egypt T-P (*TAP*) means *head* and is shown in hieroglyphic writing as a head. The universality of this representation of a head for the upper or the highest part is proved by its vast expansion, for the word is found in four continents of the Old and New World.

(104) *The word TIP, TOP (peak, head) in various continents.*

Europe, English	Africa, Egypt	Asia, Turkish	America, Mexico
TIP, TOP	T-P, TAP (head)	TEP-e (hill)	TEP-etl (hill)

Their consonantic scheme *T-P* is completely identical. Thus we can understand and trust mythology as a source of information and knowledge for the light it sheds upon words.

The English word *ACRE* means simply a measured area of ground, and in German, Latin and Greek, we find that it means a field or tilled soil. When we go back to Asia, to Babylonia and Palestine, the word passes from the soil to the man who tills the ground, to *the peasant*. Finally if we turn still farther to the Old Egyptian divinities, we encounter A-K-R (Aker), the earth-god or spirit of agriculture.

(105) *The Word ACRE in Different Meanings.*

English	German	Latin	Greek
ACR-e	Acker	AGER	AGR-os
	(soil)	(soil)	

Hebrew	Babylonian	Egyptian
IKKER (peasant)	IKKER-u (peasant)	A-K-R (earth-god)

Thus, on its way from the Egyptian epoch to our present age, the word *Acre* changed its meaning, passing from the designation of a God to a name for an area of the earth.

Such changes of the spirit of words are very frequent. When we speak today of Astronomy or Astrology, the word *Astro-*, from Latin or Greek, means a *star*. In almost every continent we encounter the word *STAR*, in German, *STERN*, in Persian *SITAR-eh*, even in Tierra del Fuego, *SETER-e*, according to Magalhaens.

(106) *The Word STAR in Different Continents.*

America, Patagonia	Europe, Latin
SETER-e (star)	SIDER-a (stars)

Africa, Berber	Asia, Persia
ITER-i (star)	SITAR-eh (star)

In Russian the word for star is quite different, *Zvezda* (white, luminous), and in the Semitic tongues the word ASTR- is not used to represent the celestial body, a planet, but the spiritual, the divine being himself was called *STAR*. Thus we find *ISHTAR*, the goddess of love and spring, the

(107) *The Star-Name ASTAR-te (Venus) Used For the Love-Goddess.*

Europe, Basque	Hellas	Africa, Egypt
OSTIR-ala	ASTAR-te	HATHOR (SATHOR)
(Venus-day)	(Venus)	(Venus)

Asia, Phoenicia	Babylon
ASHTOR-et (Venus)	ISHTAR (Venus)

Venus of Babylonia, *ESTHER* in the Old Testament, *ASH-TOR*-et in Phoenicia, *ASTAR*-te in Hellas. Even the name of the Egyptian love-goddess *HATHOR (SATHOR)* is part of this group.

As to the name *Esther* of the Biblical 'Book of Esther' for a Jewish virgin whose father is *Mordecai,* while the Persian leader *Haman* is their enemy, this whole book is a symbolic presentation of a struggle between three divinities, Haman (Hebrew, *Hamon, Ammon,* the sun god), Mordec-ai (Babylonian, Mard-uk, *Mars*) and Esther *(Astar*-te, *Venus).* We can also link with the *Astarte*-group our *EASTER,* German, *OSTER* (spring-time), for according to the Venerable Bede the Anglo-Saxons worshipped a spring-goddess, *EOSTRE,* quoted by Jacob Grimm as *OSTAR-a,* and she was none other than the love-goddess *ASTAR*-te or *ISHTAR.*

We see that language descended from its former heights and gradually became a means of conversation. In its early childhood speech was still the utterance of music. A song (Latin, *CARM*-en) was then a *charm.* The *Edda* and the early literature of the Germanic and Celtic tribes is a witness of this fact for Anglo-Saxon and German literature start with such songs of charm. In one of the Anglo-Saxon poems the goddess Herke is mentioned in the Tenth Century A.D. Jacob Grimm refers to this goddess *Harke,* as a deity of the earth, and in Palestine, Hebrew mysticism mentioned the name of the Earth-Spirit, *Harki-el.*

(108) *An Old Name of the Earth-Goddess: HERKE.*

Anglo-Saxon	German	Hebrew
HERK-e	HARK-e	HARK-iel
(earth-goddess)	(earth-goddess)	(earth-spirit)

In Latin times this goddess had been forgotten, and the name was used merely for *clay*: ARG-illa, as in *argillaceous.* A cosmic transformation had occurred, a deep change in human consciousness. In the chapters on writing and the alphabet we showed that the human mind moved from a picture-consciousness growing out of a strong imaginative power to a more abstract thinking consciousness where pale ideas replaced the vivid colorful images which had emerged as a kind of light-accompaniment of the sounds produced by speech. A shadow of that state still appears in such a word as re*mark*: for this word unites the idea of speech activity with that of a visual activity. In the time of Chaucer *MERK* meant *image*, and this word-stem contains the old root *MIR* as in *MIRR-or*, *MIR-ador* closely related to the Egyptian word *M-R* (*MER*), *eye*.

Ralph Waldo Emerson in his essay on *Language* pointed to these pictures lying behind the sounds of our words. We speak of good and of *Right* because we face the image of a *straight path,* as we call something *Wrong* because it is *twisted.* That which is wrong goes a round-about-way and has something in common with *wring* and *wriggle*. The same is true with *Tort*: it is *tortuous, tortile,* similar to the move-ment of a reptile, a *Tort-oise* or a *Turt-le*. The same picture appears behind words such as *Crime* corresponding to the German word *Krumm* (curved), and *Crooked* which means both *fraudulent* and *twisted*. The same idea applies to *trick, treach-ery, be-tray, treason,* German, *Trug,* betrayal.

In the *Zend Avesta,* the holy book of Persia, the struggle between *Ahura Mazdao,* the spirit of good and of light, and *Angra Mainyu* (*Ahriman*), the spirit of evil and darkness, is described. There Ahriman is called *DRAOGA,* the 'be-trayer'. Is this not the same word and symbolic picture as that of the treacherous serpent of the Bible, the *DRAG*-on who seduced Eve in paradise? Language is still a symbolist that loves to illustrate the meaning of sounds by images, yet *these images are realities* and not mere comparisons. Language can be called a symbolist, because every word contains some deeper symbolic sense in addition to its usual, every-day meaning. And each word has many more different meanings than we imagine.

Of course, *Avestan, Draoga* is related to the *Drag-on,* Greek *Drak-on,* and the Egypto-Semitic writing of this word, *D-R-K,* reminds us of another word which is related to the dragon, namely *DARK*. The Greek word *DRAK-on* (dragon) and the English word *DARK-ness* would be written in Egypt and Palestine with the same letters, *D-R-K*, thus revealing to the reader that there is a relationship between both of them. We only find the bridge leading from one to the other if we touch their symbolic, hidden picture-values.

In Hebrew, the snake, the dragon, is called *NAKHASH*, in Arabic, *NAKHAS*, in Sanskrit, *NAGAS*, as in English S-*NAKE*. Take the Latin word *NOX* (night, darkness), and the Greek word *NYX* (night) and compare them with the Arabic *NAKHAS*: is there not a similarity between them? Can we not notice a similar symbolic relationship between *NAUGHT-y*, *NAUGHT* and *NIGHT?* *Evil* and *Darkness*, *Evil* and *Dragon* are symbolic twins in speech; their images are related.

Light and darkness and the beings who manifested in them or stood behind them played a far greater part in antiquity than they play today. The sun, the moon and the stars affect us much more intensely and frequently than we may think. We say that we will take something into consideration, and yet do we have the slightest inkling of a connection with the starry sky, with the stars themselves, when we make such a promise? In List 106 we note that the Latin word *SIDERA* means *stars*. To be *con-SIDERA-te* is literally to be *in close contact with the stars,* to read the writing of the celestial lights, to try to act in favor of a balance between our past, present and future, our destiny. Thus, to take something into *con-SIDERA-tion* signifies much more than an abstract, superficial thought, since it refers to our inner connection with the stars and the whole astral world. Behind each consideration of ours we can recognize a faint necessity of asking the stars, the heavenly beings, about what we should do.

In Latin there is still another word for *Star, STELL-a.* If we replace one star-name by the other instead of con-SIDERA-tion we discover the related word *con-STELLA-tion!*

If we choose a word such as *desire,* we think of it as a word meaning merely a wish or a whim. However, *Desire* stems from the Latin word *de-SIDER-ium* which has survived in our words *desiderate* and *desideratum*. De-SIDERA-tum really means something which we wish to bring down from heaven, from the stars! It is not a mere whim, but a serious and sincere connection of our souls with the world of stars, of celestial forces and beings.

A similar link between our earthly life and the stars appears in the word *Dis-ASTER*. *Aster* in Greek means *star,* and a *dis-ASTER* is not merely an accident but a most tragic event in our life, a severance from our life-star, our guardian-angel. The people of Antiquity felt they were doomed because the link connecting them with higher worlds had been cut. This is the very meaning of the word disaster. Thus we see that our words are indeed 'faded mythology', that they still preserve something of the spiritual atmosphere which once pervaded all human speech.

(109)   *Consideration, Desire, Disaster Are Words Linked With the Stars.*

Latin	Greek	English
SIDERA	ASTER	Con-SIDERA-tion
(stars)	(star)	(linked with stars)

English	English
de-SIDERA-tum	dis-ASTER
(implored from the stars)	(severed from the stars)

In India the sun was called 'The Eye of Indra', and in Egypt it was the right eye of Osiris, while the moon was his left eye. The Germanic Odin is described as a pilgrim with a black plaster over his left eye. He is a sun-god, hence the moon-side of his sight is covered. A remnant of the deeper meaning of *EYE* survived in Hellas. While the current Greek word for eye is *Ophthalmos*, there is an old poetic synonym *AUG-ê*, identical with the German word *AUG-e* (eye), yet meaning both *splendor* and *eye*.

(110)   *The Word EYE in Indo-European and in Hebrew.*

Greek	Old German	Armenian	Hebrew
AUG-e	AUG-on	AG-n	AY-in
(eye, splendor)	(eye)	(eye)	(eye)

Some forms of this stem are extended by a final -*n* (Old

German, *AUG-on,* Armenian, *AG-n,* Hebrew, *AY-in*), hence we can include in this group the name of the Hindu fire-god *AGN-i,* and the Middle English form of Eye, *IGH-e.*

(111) *The word-stem EYE Used for Eye and Light.*

America, Maya	Europe, Basque
IC (light, day, sun)	IG-i (eye, sun)
Africa, Soudan	Asia, Sumer
EK-e (day)	IG-i (eye)

On the reverse side of the United States dollar bill is printed the symbol of the Great State Seal. It represents a pyramid whose upper point is severed and lifted. In this triangle an eye floats in a sea of light. What does this eye in the middle of the triangle represent? The triangle is an old symbol of the Trinity which we encounter in Egypt. In its center is the sun, in Maya, *IC,* and this same word IC meant in Anglo-Saxon *I,* the *Self,* the *Ego* or spiritual light of a higher consciousness.

(112) *The Maya Symbol of the Sun and the Egyptian Ankh.*

MAYA	ITS	EGYPTIAN
SUN SYMBOL	ELEMENTS	ANKH CROSS

 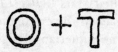

The Maya picture of IC shows the *Tau-symbol,* a cross or a star surrounded by two ovals similar to an Egyptian cartouche. If we remove the ovals toward the top of the Tau, then the Maya hieroglyph of the sun, a symbol of light, turns into the Egyptian *Ankh,* the *Crux ansata,* a symbol of immortality carried by gods and the souls of the dead.

The Latin sun-name *SOL* is related to the Gothic *SAUIL,* in Munda vernaculars, *SOL* (shining), to Samoan, *SUL-u*

(113) *Latin SOL (sun-god, sun) and Irish SUIL (eye).*

Europe, Irish	Gothic	Asia, Munda	Australia, Samoa
SUIL (eye)	SAUIL (sun)	SOL (shining)	SUL-u (torch)

If we take the Samoan word *SUL-u,* torch, we can compare with the word *TORCH* the Irish term *DORC* (eye). *TORK-a* was the word for star in Old Peru; in Yugoslav, *ZORK-a,* means sunrise, the goddess of Dawn, Eos, as Hebrew ZER-AKH means morning, orient, east. One group of words after another shows the same parallelism of meaning: the symbolic use of an eye to express a higher idea of light, of consciousness.

(114) *The Word Torch Used for Eye and for Light.*

Irish	Greek	Russian
DORC (eye)	DERK-omai (I look)	ZORK-i (eagle-eyed)

Yugoslav	Hebrew	Aymara, Peru
ZORK-a (sunrise)	ZERAKH (sunrise)	TORK-a (star)

The parallelism between "light" and "eye" is confirmed once again by the word *LIGHT* itself whose semantical counterpart we find in the Breton word *LAGAD* (eye).

(115) *The Word Light Meaning Both Light and Eye.*

Aymara, Peru	German	Gothic
LIKHUT-a (light)	LICHT (light)	LIUHATH (light)

Breton	Hebrew	Babylonian
LAGAD (eye)	LAHAT (light)	LA'AT-u (light)

This is a very old name used in ancient mythologies. In Latin the god Mars was called *LEUCET-ios*, the shining one, and the Hindu called Mars *LOCHIT-a*. We have mentioned the sun as being named the eye of Indra or Siva, of Osiris or Horus. The ancient Sumerians designated the planet Saturn as the eye of *Anu*, and the American Indians called the sun the eye of the Great Spirit, of Manitu.

What does Manitu's eye literally mean? Is it not the *Mind's eye* mentioned by Shakespeare through Horatio in *Hamlet?* The old Hebrew mystics also depicted the seven planets as the seven eyes of God, and in the Revelation of John the Divine we encounter the same kind of symbolism, the same pictures: the cosmic lights are described as eyes. "And out of the throne proceed lightnings and voices and thunders. And there were *seven lamps of fire* burning before the throne, which are the *seven Spirits of God*. . . . And I saw in the midst of the throne and of the four living creatures, and in the midst of the elders, a lamb standing, as though it had been slain, having seven horns, and *seven eyes,* which are the *seven Spirits of God,* sent forth into all the earth."

A grand cosmic conception is set forth here. For *eye* to the man of Antiquity, capable of visions and imaginations, meant a fount of light, and seeing still expressed the power of spreading light. This was a conception shared by the deepest thinkers of ancient and classical times, and Goethe himself described it in one of his most ingenious sayings.

GOETHE AND THE MIND'S EYE
Wär' nicht das Auge sonnenhaft,
Die Sonne könnt' es nie erblicken.
Läg' nicht in uns des Gottes eigne Kraft,
Wie könnt' uns Göttliches entzücken?"

"Were not the eye alike the sunny shine,
How would it ever catch its beaming light?
Were our heart not full of force divine,
How could it God-like take of such delight?"

In conclusion let us note the English word *WEIRD* which is derived from the Anglo-Saxon word *WYRD* (destiny, fate, fortune) which in turn comes from *WEORDH-an* (to become, to be), the same as the German word *WERD-en* (to become). This word-stem is usually connected with the Latin word *VERT-o* (to turn), and this is correct, as we can realize from expressions such as "to turn sour" where "to turn" really means "to be transformed". In addition, Sanskrit preserved in the word VRT all these meanings: *to turn, to roll, to become.* But the deeper sense of this stem is contained in the Old Norse word *URDH-r* (fate) which reminds us of the Three Norns of the Nordic mythology: *Urdh, Verdandi,* and *Skuld,* Past, Present and Future. They fulfilled a function of life similar to that of the three Parcae in Italy, and the Three Fates in Ancient Greece: *Klotho* who spins the thread of life and represents the Past, *Lachesis,* the Disposer of Lots, who determines the length of life, the Present, and finally *Atropos,* the Inflexible, who will cut the thread in the Future.

This is a conception of Fate and Destiny which is confined only to the length of earthly life. The original dramatic representation of Destiny by Three Parcae, Three Norns, is intimately connected with the idea of reincarnation. In Hindu mysticism, Destiny is Karma, self-made fate. The Romans expressed this idea in their proverb, "Suae quisque fortunae faber est" — Everyone is the fashioner of his own fortune. Thus fate turned more and more into destiny, but destiny embraces all three acts of the trilogy of time, past, present and future. It works from one age into the next, from one life into the following lives. The personality is the unity of our earthly existence between birth and death; it links together day with day, night with night. Our individuality, however, is our eternal essence, whatever changes we may undergo in the course of our existence in the Universe. It is our individuality which embraces all our lives, all our incarnations, whenever, wherever they took place or will take place. It is in this sense that Jehovah called himself *Ehye Asher Ehye,* "I am he who was, who is and who shall be," and this is why the Christ is called "The Lord of Destiny".

The Christ in the conception of the "hidden wisdom" of which St. Paul spoke in his letters to the Corinthians, is the Spirit of the Sun, and at the same time the power of our higher Ego. Hence the words of St. Paul: "Not I, but the Christ within me" which can be paraphrased, "Not my lower human Self, but my higher Ego pervaded with Christ's spirit."

The deeper meaning of *WEIRD* is symbolized by that image of the cross which is surmounted by a circle of seven deep-red roses expressing the overcoming of death and a new beginning in life. We do not discover the words *WEIRD* (destiny) or German *WERD-en* in Semitic idioms or in Egyptian, because these Oriental tongues did not follow the road of decay and abstraction which our western vernaculars took many centuries ago. However we find this word-stem in the Near East when we think of the symbol of the rose cross, for in Egyptian, *UARD-a,* and in Hebrew, *UERED* or *WE-RED* mean *bud, blossom, rose.*

(116) *English WEIRD and Anglo-Saxon WEORDH-an in Different Tongues.*

Anglo-Saxon	English	German
WEORDH-an	WEIRD	WERD-en
(to become)	(destiny)	(to become)

Hebrew	Egyptian
WERED (rose)	UARD-a (rose)

Thus the idea of transformation and destiny can be approached more easily when we understand what is contained in the pictures behind all these words. Life, death and reincarnation are but different acts in the same drama of existence. One life is the germ of a new life, and our deeds in one incarnation are the seeds for the following revival. Our experiences in life which we call destiny are the budding branches of a tree, a kind of Tree of Life which we ourselves planted once upon a time in a remote epoch of a former earth-existence.

CHAPTER TEN

THE WORLD-UNITY OF SPEECH

Why is it so difficult to rediscover the original words of the common tongue of mankind in the languages of the various nations?

The Roman poets noticed that many words have disappeared from languages, and they compared this with the falling of leaves in autumn and the appearance of new foliage in spring. These changes are periodic; our languages relentlessly renew their vocabularies, and words become archaic, obsolete, or regional. Thus we find Americanisms such as *shack* (hut, shanty), and a wealth of very old, most interesting words in Scotland: words which are still in popular daily use, while they are entirely forgotten in other parts of the English-speaking world. It is very difficult, sometimes even impossible, to link such words with relatives in other Indo-European languages. On the other hand, it is often easy to find missing links outside this family: for instance Scottish *SKEAN* (dagger).

(117) *Scottish SKEAN (dagger) in Semitic languages.*

Scottish	Hebrew	Arabic
SKEAN (dagger)	SAKIN (knife)	SIKIN (knife)

These Scottish survivors of remote ages are interesting, and it is regrettable that the editors of *Webster's Collegiate Dictionary* stopped the publication of Scottish words from the fifth edition onward.

This list includes only a few out of many available examples. Most of these words are known to be old, probably outdating the Anglo-Saxon conquest of the British Isles. Can we conclude from this close relationship between Scottish and German that Germans settled in Scotland before the Fifth Century A.D.? This would be a mistake. It is possible

(118) Scottish Words Still in Daily Use in German.

SCOTTISH WORDS		GERMAN RELATIVES	
CREAGH	(plundering incursion)	KRIEG	(war)
CRAG	(neck, throat)	KRAG-en	collar, neck)
HALS	(neck, throat)	HALS	(neck, throat)
KEN	(to know)	KENN-en	(to know)
KITTLE	(to tickle)	KITZEL	(tickling)
KNAVE	(lad)	KNABE	(lad, boy)
WALE	(choice)	WAHL	(choice)
WISSLE	(money change)	WECHSEL-n	(change money)
WON	(to dwell, abide)	WOHN-en	(to dwell, abide)
WISE	(to guide)	WEIS-en	(to guide)
WOOD	(furious)	WUT	(fury, rage)
YAMMER	(to lament)	JAMMER	(lament)
YAWL	(howl, scream)	JOHL-en	(howl, scream)
YEWK	(to itch)	JUCK-en	(to itch)
FRIST	(to postpone)	FRIST	(delay)
FREMD	(foreign)	FREMD	(foreign)
CANGLE	(to quarrel)	QUENGEL-n	(to quarrel)
COFF	(to buy)	KAUF-en	(to buy)
DOUF	(stupid)	DOF	(stupid), **Berlin dialect**
EARN, ERN	(eagle)	ARN-	(eagle in **Arn**-old)
KEMP	(champion)	KEMP-e	(champion)
GANG	(walk)	GANG	(walk)
HANDFAST	(agreement)	HANDFESTE	(agreement)
HOAST	(to cough)	HUST-en	(to cough)
LAIR	(learning, lore)	LEHRE	(learning, teaching)
LICH	(corpse)	LEICHE	(corpse)
MICKLE	(great, much)	MICHEL	(great, much), **MHG**
MUTCH	(a cap)	MUETZE	(a cap)
STERN	(star)	STERN	(star)
SNELL	(quick)	SCHNELL	(quick)
SPEER	(to follow the track)	SPUER-en	(follow the track)
SHEEN	(beautiful)	SCHOEN	(beautiful)

that some of these words were originally German, e.g. *HAND-FAST* corresponding with *Handfeste* (agreement) in German, used by the Nineteenth Century Austrian poet, Grillparzer. Yet a thorough investigation of some of these words proves that their use and relationship must go back to a very remote antiquity, to an epoch long before the arrival of Celtic tribes in the British Isles.

(119) Scottish and German Words Linked with Oriental Idioms.

Scottish	German	Oriental
CREAGH (invasion)	KRIEG (war)	Hebr. HARAG (kill)
KNAVE (lad)	KNABE (boy)	Egypt. (H)ANAB (boy)
ERN (eagle)	ARN (eagle)	Assyr. ERN-u (eagle)

The comparison of English (Scottish) words with the oldest vernaculars of the Orient: Sumerian, Babylonian, Egyptian and so on, is of a great help in obtaining information about British and other European names, their form and their meaning in prehistoric times. Let us consider the word *DEER*. What does *DEER* mean? In answering this question correctly, we discover a principle of speech. The word *DIR* meaning *horned animal* is found in Sumerian at least four thousand years before it is recorded in English. A deer is a horned animal, and if we wish to discover its relatives we must not only look for *"deer"* but for *"horn"* or *"horned"* and for other connected pictures and ideas. Thus, if a connection is correct, it can be verified by the reappearance of such parallelisms as "deer" and "horn".

(120) *DEER in English Related to DIR (horned) in Sumerian.*

English	DEER (stag)	Sumer.	DIR (horned)
French	CERF (deer)	Finnish	SARV-a (horn)
English	ELK	Brazil.	ALC (horn)
Hebrew	TSON (sheep)	Japan.	TSUN-o (horn)
Tungus.	HUKUR (ox)	Hebrew	HUACR-a (horn)
Assyr.	SHAPAR-u (goat)	Peru	SHOPHAR (horn)
Bulgar.	RUG-ach (deer)	Arabic	RUK (horn)
English	BUCK	"	BUK (horn)
Peru	GUANAC-o (goat)	Mexican	QUANAC (horn)
Mexican	KWAKWA-way (bull)	"	KWAKWA-witl (horn)
Polish	SARN-a (roedeer)	Caucas.	SURN-a (horn)

It is as if the primeval common speech had broken into national idioms and word-forms which are but parts of a whole, mosaic stones of a common picture, stones which we must put together to obtain an actual understanding of the true character of a word.

Today the old words are scattered about the earth. Even within the same linguistic family many important words are different. Consider the word "frog" within the Indo-European circle.

(121) *The Names of the Frog in Indo-European Idioms.*

Sanskrit	Greek	Albanian
BHEK-a	BATRACH-os	BRET-ek
Latin	French	German
RAN-a	GREN-ouille	FROSCH

All these names are more or less different, they are *synonyms,* but they are not relatives. Did the Indo-European speaking nations, the so-called Aryans, not know frogs or toads? The Sanskrit name, *BHEK-a,* frog, is related to the Old Persian word *BAK* (toad), to the Yakut dialect *BAG-a* frog, and to *POGG-e* (frog) in certain German dialects. Further, in the Fiji Islands the crocodile is called *BOK-ai,* and the same word is used in several islands in the vicinity. There the name survived the animal, for "big frogs" (crocodiles) have been extinct in Fiji for a long time and yet the tribes in the inner parts of that island still use for them the same name as other clans on neighboring isles.

(122) *The name PUKA (toad) in Basque Used in Five Continents.*

America, Chile	Europe, Basque	Africa, Egypt
POK-o (toad)	PUK-u (toad)	PAK-it (tortoise shell)

Asia, Kirghiz	Fiji
BUK-a (frog)	BOK-ai (crocodile)

Thus we learn a very important rule. Words which we use today are either used in place of expressions long ago dropped or they are sometimes survivors of a remote epoch which lost their connection because their relatives have been moved or omitted in other dialects or tongues. A dialect word such as German *POGG-e* (frog) which appears in fairy tales or in folklore may be the term in use in the country now inhabited by German speaking people some five to ten thousand years ago. They may be the missing links which we are to look for when establishing a complete word-chain. There was a time when a fish was not yet called a fish, a frog not yet a frog, a dog not yet a dog, and a stork not yet a stork. Other *synonyms* were applied or were predominant. Hence, when we wish to re-establish the unity of speech by any act of science, we must try to find the precise synonym which thousands of years ago was the common name used by the majority of mankind for certain objects.

WHELP, rather than dog was the name of a canine in early

ages. We find this word first within the Indo-European group where it means a young animal, a dog, a fox, a wolf.

(123) *WHELP used for a young animal, a dog, a fox, a wolf.*

English	German	Old German
WHELP	WELP, WELF	HVELP
	(young dog)	(young dog)
Latin	**Greeek**	**Gothic**
VULP-es (fox)	ALOP-ex (fox)	ULF (wolf)

We obtain an insight into the workshop of Nature as well as into that of Speech when we learn that dog, wolf, fox, jackal and hyena formed a unity in olden times before they fell asunder into different sub-species.

(124) *Different Names for Dog in the Indo-European Family.*

Sanskrit	Greek	Latin	English
SHU	KYON, KYN-	CAN-is	DOG
German	**Polish**		**Russian**
HUND	PIES		SOBAK-a

These names contained within a family are almost all different, and there are even more variants in this name group. Only a few of them however can be connected with relatives in other linguistic families, for example the Greek *KYON* and Chinese *KYAN* (dog). In the Semitic circle the predominant dog-name is the Hebrew word *KELEB*, related with *WHELP, HVELP* and its variant *GUELPH.*

(125) *The Dog-Name WHELP in Old Idioms of the Old and New World.*

America, Chile	Europe, Anglo-Saxon
CULP-eu (dog)	HVELP (young dog)
Asia, Hebrew	**Assyrian**	**China**
KELEB (dog)	KALB-u	CLOW

The Chinese name *CLOW* is contained in the Dan Yao dialect. Many other links such as Arabic *KELB* (dog) could be added. What does a dog do? It *yelps*, and to *YELP* is the English echo of *KELB* (dog). The German word *KLAEFF-er* (dog, literally the 'yelp-er') resembles the Chinese *CLOW*, and the French word *GLAP*-ir (to yelp) sounds similar to

GUELPH. Further, since *WHELP* originally meant any young animal, we may connect the Babylonian *KALB-u* (dog) with the German *KALB*, our *CALF* (young animal). The same principle applies to *Fish*.

(126) *Different Names for Fish in the Indo-European Family.*

Sanskrit	Greek	Latin	English
MATS-ya	ICHTH-ys	PISC-is	FISH

Slavic	Armenian	O. Pruss
RYB-a	TZUKN	ZUKAN-s

Fish seems to be a more modern term, and it is impossible to find the ancient name of this animal, so long as we confine our investigation to the single field of Indo-European tongues. Speech as a world-chronicle does not permit any restriction: we must search for connecting words in every corner of the earth, in every epoch. If we wish to find relatives of the Old Prussian word *ZUKAN-s* or the Armenian *TZUKN* (fish) we must look to the Far East.

(127) *Relatives of Old Prussian ZUKAN-s, Fish, in Japan.*

Old Prussian	Armenian	Japanese
ZUKAN-s (fish)	TZUKN (fish)	SAKAN-a (fish)

In this instance it is the *sounds* which lead us to the right connection; in another it is the *meaning*, the *picture*. Where are we to look for links with the Slavic fish-name, *RYB-a*? We discover them in America, Africa and Australia, yet they seem to be lacking in Asiatic idioms. However, if we ponder the meaning of *RYB-a*, we can find a missing link in the Germanic tongues spoken on the shores of the North Sea, the German *ROBB-e*, Dutch *ROB*, Frisian and Danish *ROBB-e* (seal, *Phoca vitulina*). *RYB-a* was originally a general ap-

(128) *Slavic RYB-a (fish) Related With German ROBB-e (seal).*

America, Cariban	Europe, Danish
RAPA-RAPA (fish)	ROBB-e (seal)

Africa, Egypt	Australia
RAM-i (fish)	KARAV-a (fish)

pellation for *Fish,* and only later on it has been restricted to one of its species, the *Seal.*

Thus we see that animals originally were named from their form without regard to their size. In German, a little worm is called *WURM* and a giant dragon, a saurian a Lind-*WURM* (a creeping worm or flying worm). As a matter of fact the word *WHAL-e* was used in the earliest epochs for *fish*: whale originally meant every kind of fish.

(129) *WHALE an Ancient General Name for Fish.*

America, Cariban	Europe, Iceland
WALA-WALA (fish)	HVAL-r (whale)
Africa, Somali	Asia, Samoyede
KUL-un (fish)	KUAL (fish)

We could add to this chain an Australian link: *KUAL*-ba (fish), and find in other languages the following phonetic variations of *WHALE* representing fish or whale: KUAL, KWAL, KAL, CHALL, HVAL, HAL, WAL, BAL, PHAL, and so on. Thus we encounter this word *WHALE* in all the five Continents, especially in the northern parts of Europe and Asia, of America and Australia, and in certain vernaculars of Africa. It is however a striking fact that the most classical tongues of the southern half of the earth, Sumerian, Babylonian, Egyptian, Sanskrit, Hebrew and others, do not possess this old fish-name but only its word-stem, while the Greeks and Romans used it only for the whale.

The fact that animals obtain their names from their form and not from their size can easily be extended. One of the most interesting instances is a stork-name found in Arabian fairy-tales, *Abu Lak-Lak,* Father Lak-Lak. If we go to the Euphrates Valley, we find in Old Babylon the same redoubled name, *LAKU-LAKU,* for "a big bird". This duplication

(130) *Father Lak-Lak, the Stork, in the Old and New World.*

Arabic	Assyrian	Chukchee
Abu LAK-LAK	LAKU-LAKU	LAKH-LAEKH
(stork)	(a big bird)	(goose)
Greenland		Peruvian
LLEKH-LLEKH (stork)		LLEKA-LLEKA (a heron)

characteristic of very ancient tongues can be traced throughout Northern Asia, to Greenland and to America.

We could add further links to this word-chain such as the Siberian Eskimo word, *LUK-LUK*, a brent-goose, Aino, *LAKH-LAKH*, a wild goose, and Californian (Yokuts) La'-LA', goose. The Peruvian name *LLEKA-LLEKA* designates the *Sherardius resplendens*, a kind of heron. Can we find this strange, old name in English? Yes, it has survived in *gray-LAG* (*Anser anser*), the name of the common wild goose of Europe! We can add also the Irish word *LAKH* (duck) and the Czech *LICH-e* (duckling).

What does the name *Abu Lak-Lak* mean? It is the same word as English *LEG* and the Old Norse *LEGG-r* (leg). In Zoology the stork belongs to the group of wading birds. Thus *Abu Lak-Lak* is Father Leg-Leg!

(131) *The Stork-Name Abu Lak-Lak Means Father Leg-Leg.*

English	Old Norse	Old Aramaic
LEG	LEGG-r (leg)	LEG-er (leg)

Mandaean	Babylonian
LIG-ra (leg)	ALAK-u (to go)

In Sanskrit too *LAKH* means *to go*. Even today German fairy tales call the stork "*Langbein*" or "Long-Leg".

Before passing to other examples we must note one reason why it is often difficult to find the thread connecting words in different idioms and in different historical epochs. Writing will be of a help in this case. It is the loss of an imaginative perception of the pictures behind the words which makes the sounds appear pale and insignificant to us today, particularly in a mixed language such as English which contains many Latin or Romance words. How can a person without a knowledge of the Latin word *TEC-tum* (roof) unveil the mystery of the meaning of the word *Protection*? Protection means to put somebody under a roof, to cover him with something which prevents him from being hurt or injured. *To shelter* has a similar meaning and can be represented by a similar picture. The Latin word *TEC-tum* (roof) should not be unfamiliar to us, because in Anglo-Saxon *THAEC* meant a roof, and *THATCH* is used today in a similar sense. This is the same word as Swedish *TAC* (roof, cover), German *DACH* (roof), Greek *TEG*-os (thatch). However, it is not easy to

(132) *Protection Originally Meant Thatch, a Covering.*

Anglo-Saxon	English	Swedish
THAEC (roof)	THATCH	TAC

Latin	Greek
TEC-tum	TEG-os (thatch)

pass from the concrete picture of a roof to the abstract idea of protection without a bit of imagination. Yet the Chinese who still use the ideographs in writing paint the meaning of words directly. No artificial, auxiliary bridge is needed to understand what they intend to convey to us.

(133) *The Abstract Idea Protection In Speech and in Writing.*

Old Chinese Picture

Latin Word

pro-TEC-tio
from
TEC-tum (roof)

We see here how much more difficult it has become to disclose the picture behind the words when we listen to their sounds only, instead of visualizing in an imaginative way what they intend to express. When we pass from *TEG-os* (roof), in Greek, to *TAG-os* (leader, general), to a modern abstract-minded human being the last clue of the former image is lost: the leader as the *pro-TEC-tor*, the *roof*. Hence the difficulty of understanding such a word as Arabic *SULT-an*. We translate it simply "ruler, sovereign", and can hardly imagine that such a name from the Arabian Nights could have anything to do with our Western tongues. Yet we can discover its word-stem in English as well as in German, once we disclose the true nature of what it depicts. In Hebrew the Sultan is called *SHALIT*, and in German *SCHALT-en* (schalten und walten) means *to rule*. These designations are not original, but are derived from a concrete picture, the *shield* and the *shelter*. SHIELD, German *SCHILD*, Go-

thic *SKILTH-us,* is an ancient word which the Germanic
tribes share with the Semites: Assyrian *SHALT-u,* Hebrew
SHELET, Aramaic *SHILT-a* (shield).

(134) *Sult-an, Shield and Shelter All Mean Protection.*

Anglo--Saxon	Gothic	Danish
SCYLD (shield)	SKILTH-us (shield)	SKJOELD (shield)

Hebrew	Aramaic	Assyrian
SHELET (shield)	SHILT-a (shield)	SHALT-u (shield)

There can be no doubt about all these relationships. Shelter is explained by Webster as *protection* or *place of protection;* to *shelter* means to *protect.* He derives it from *SCILD-
trum,* a troop of men with shields who shield the people or
the ruler. To shield is described as to cover *with a shield, to
protect. Sult-an* and the Hebrew word *SHALIT* (ruler) thus
are the shielders of the nation.

(135) *Orient and Occident Have the Stem Sultan in Common.*

O. Norse	SKJOELD-ung	(king)
English	SHELT-er	
Hebrew	SHALIT	(ruler)
Arabic	SULT-an	(ruler)
Egypt, Manetho	SALAT-is	(ruler)

Here we stand only at the threshold of the mysteries of the
past. According to Manetho, the first Hyksos king of Egypt
was called *SALAT-is* which in the Canaan idiom meant *sovereign,* just as Joseph (Genesis I, 42) who became vice-king of
Egypt in the same period was called *ha-SHALIT,* the vice-
king. The younger Edda contains the same word, SKJOELD-
ung (king). In the Beowulf-saga a young boy came floating
over the sea, slumbering in a sparkling shield, and landed on
Denmark's shores. This boy was Odin's son and they called
him *SKJOELD,* that is, *king.* Again we see here the clues of a
remote antiquity which we touch by such mysterious connections between Egypt and Palestine on the one hand, and
Scandinavia, Germany, and the British Isles on the other. Let
us keep in mind that the Vedas do not mention shields at all,

(136) *Different Names for Shield in the Indo-European Languages.*

English	SHIELD
Latin	CLIP-eus
Greek	ASPIS
O. Norse	TARG-a
Russian	SHCHIT
Persian	SIPAR
Aramaic	SHILT-a

and that the Indian and Persian names for this defense weapon are all recent. The different members of the Indo-European Linguistic group use entirely different names for it. The Germanic words however are related to the Egypto-Semitic tongues in this case. They appear in texts which can be directly or indirectly compared with records dating almost 2500 to 3000 years before these words emerge in Northern and Western Europe. Thus in the Orient as well as in the Occident, the word-stem *Shield* is connected with mythology and sagas, with the most ancient traditions.

Many other words could be compared in the same way, disclosing their secret, underground connections. We classify not only words of different and distant idioms, but the same words of any tongue when they appear with various meanings, as two different stems, e.g. *HID-e* (skin) and *HID-e* (to conceal, shelter). The *HID-e* is the picture behind both words: the skin which conceals our muscles against injuries, and the act of hiding something by putting covering over it. The same applies to the word *MASK,* since in earlier epochs *MASK* meant *hide, skin, leather.*

(137) *In Early Times MASK Meant Hide, Skin, Leather.*

English	MASK	
Egyptian	MASHK-a	(hide)
Babylonian	MASHK-u	(skin, hide)
Aramaic	MASHK-a	(hide)
Caucasus	MOSHK-u	(leather)
Greek	MOSKH-e	(hide)

Teutonic warriors, when they first appeared on European battle-fields, wore heads of animals instead of helmets, and Greek drawings and paintings represent Hercules after he killed the Nemaean lion, with his head covered with the lion's head and skin as a trophy. In Sumerian *MASHK-im* was the designation for a *demon*, as in Gaul, in the region of the Celtic Druids, *MASC* meant a *sorcerer* or *witch*, a picture which is still preserved in our word *Mascot*. We learn from reports on American Indians that the Mayas and Incas in their Carnival processions (Festival of Raymi in Peru) wore animal skins as did the Teutons.

These connections between, a *hide, hiding* and *sheltering* are by no means isolated. They are the result of a principle which helped to form and develop speech, and we observe their interplay even between quite different tongues.

(138) *The Hide, to Hide and a Hut All Arise from the Same Stem.*

English to HID-e	English the HID-e	English the HUT
English to MASK	Egypt MASHK-a (hide)	Egypt MASHK (tent)
German HUET-en (to hide)	German HAUT (skin)	German HUETT-e (hut)
German SCHUTZ (protection)	Greek SKYT-os (hide)	English a SHED
Latin PARC-o (to save)	English BARK (of tree)	English BARRACK
Latin CEL-o (conceal)	English SCAL-e (of fish)	English CELL
Latin CAV-eo (to hide)	Japan KAW-a (skin)	English CAV-e
Hebrew SHALIT (protector)	Latin CUT-is (skin)	English COTT-age
Greek KEUTH-o (conceal)	English SHIELD	English SHELT-er

What renders the connection of these different terms difficult, and sometimes puts almost insurmountable hindrances in the way of linguists, are the so-called *homonyms* and *synonyms*, words of the same phonetic structure and apparently quite different meanings as quoted in list 138, or, on the other hand, words which have entirely different sounds and the same meaning as *land, earth, country, territory* etc.

Democritus, a Greek thinker, could not accept the idea of a common origin of speech because of such irregularities as homonyms and synonyms. As a matter of fact, from a concrete scientific viewpoint, these irregularities can be conceived of as the cause of the "Confusion of Tongues." We search for the relationship of languages, and generally expect their vocabularies to be identical, to find for *HORSE* a corresponding word of an identical or similar structure in every other related tongue. This however is not the case in idioms which are close cousins such as German and Dutch, Russian and Bulgarian. Every tongue has its own individual character, possesses an identity, and this independence of languages is largely due to synonyms, to the freedom of choosing this or that name from a series of synonyms and making it predominant. Let us illustrate this fact with names of the *Earth* in the Indo-European Family of languages.

(139) *Various Words for Earth in the Indo-European Family.*

English	Latin	Greek	Polish	Sanskrit
EARTH	TERRA	GAIA	ZIEM-ia	BHUMI

The fact that these words differ is matched by the fact that the Germanic earth-names correspond with the Semitic.

(140) *Earth Compared with Earth-Names in Semitic Tongues.*

Anglo-Saxon	Gothic	Dutch
EORTH-e	AIRTH-a	AARD-e
Arabic	**O. Phoenician**	**Babylonian**
ARD	ARS	ERS-itu

In Hebrew the earth is called *ERETZ*, a word similar to the German *ERZ* (ore, metallic earth). Again we note this strange surprising link between the Teutons and the Semites! How about the other synonyms? Are they isolated, or can we link

them with distant languages? We can do this, for instance
with the Greek word *GAI-a, GE,* contained in *GE*-ography,
GE-ometry, *GE*-ology.

(141) *The Greek Earth-Name Gaia, Ge in Various Continents.*

Europe, Greek	Irish	Africa, Galla
GAI-a, GE	GE'	GE
Asia, Sumer	Annam	Australia
GU, GI	GIA	GAW-e, GO-

According to Pherekydes or Syros, the Earth was first called
CHTHON, and Zeus turned it into *GAIA* by giving it the
gift of grain, thus covering it as it were with a garment. We
could add many more examples to these two earth-names
which are very, very old. Both are mythological names:
Erda was the goddess of earth, Odin's consort, as Hera was
that of Zeus. *GAIA* likewise was the spouse of the father of
the gods and the mortals, and even in German mythology
Jacob Grimm mentions a "Frau Gouwe" (Lady Gouwe=
Lady Earth), a Teuton goddess. Again we encounter the
name *GAI* in Hebrew, meaning *a valley:* GE-henna = Gay
Hinnom, the valley of Hinnom near Jerusalem.

Thus we see that two Indo-European synonyms have their
relatives in Hebrew and in many other distant tongues of
the Old World, and in Australia. The different synonyms
are scattered, but are not lost entirely.

Let us close this chapter with a very significant example:
the synonyms for the *Hand,* one of our most important bodily
organs. Again the same impression appears in the Indo-European
language-group: almost as many words for *hand* as
there are vernaculars. Whence that variety? What does it
mean?

(142) *Different Words for Hand in the Indo-European Group.*

English	Latin	Greek	Russian	Sanskrit
HAND	MAN-us	CHEIR,	RUK-a	PAN-I

When we pass to the Egypto-Semitic group we have a similar impression, though we do not have such a variety of words as in the Indo-European languages. We find Sumero-Babylonian *KAT-u* (hand), Hebrew *YAD* (hand), *KAPH* (palm), Egyptian *KAP* (hand). The Sumerian name, *KAT-u*, extends over Siberia and Northern Europe, particularly embracing the Ural-Altaic family, a Turanian branch.

(143) *Sumerian KAT-u (hand) in the Ural-Altaic Family.*

Sumerian	Vogul	Ostyak, Cheremiss
KAT-u	KAT	KET

Hungarian	Finnish	Lappish
KEZ	KAET-e	KAET, KIET

We could add here Danish KAIT-e (the left hand), and the Alaskan KAT-in (hands). We could speak in greater detail of these words in a chapter on the human body. In conclusion we shall note a few names for *hand* in the Western Hemisphere.

(144) *Names for Hand in American Indian Vernaculars.*

Kolyush, Alaska	Peruvian	Maya
KAT-in (hands)	MAK-i	CAB

Quichua, Peru	Kuril	Aino
PAN-a	TEK	TEG-i

At the first glance even a small selection of specimens as this appears as a numberless variety of names for the same organ. How can we find our way out of this labyrinth of diversity to the idea of unity, to the common origin of tongues? It is not so difficult as it first appears, for there are many parallelisms in these words. The Quichua word *PAN-a* (hand) can be linked with the Sanskrit *PAN-i* (hand), and with the Latin *PON-o* (to put down, deposit), and the Alaskan word *KAT-in* (hands) — with a pure plural ending as it is used in Christ's language, Aramaic, — with the Sumerian *KAT*, or the Mayan *CAB* with the Egyptian *KAP* and the Hebrew *KAPH* (open hand). However, with which word for hand in our own vernaculars can we link the Kuril word *TEK* or the Peruvian *MAK-i* (hand)?

This is not possible it we confine ourselves to a synonym

for hand. However, spoken language itself tells us how and where to find the links. In Peruvian *MAK-i* means *hand,* while in Mexican *MAC-a* is *to take, to give;* in Egypt, *MAKH* is *to seize, grasp, create,* in Annam *MAK* to take, seize, grasp, and in Semang (Munda-Polynesian) *MAK-i* plainly means — *to make!* From the name of an organ the meaning passed to *the function* of the organ: from hand to *handle,* from Peruvian *MAK-i* (hand) to our *MAK-e,* German *MACH-en* (to make). Now the door has been opened, and many other missing links can pour in from many sides.

(145) *Hand Meaning the Organ is Used also for its Function.*

Peruvian	Mexican	Egyptian
MAK-i	MAC-a	MAKH
(hand)	(to take)	(create)
Annam	Semang	English
MAK	MAK-i	MAK-e
(seize)	(make)	

We can now ask the question: What does the Peruvian do with his *MAK-i* (hand)? *He makes . . .* ! And the Mayan, Egyptian, Hebrew with his *CAB* or *CAP*? *He keeps . . .* or *CAP-*tures . . . ! And the Kuril with his *TEK* (hand)? *He takes . . .* ! And the Russian with his *RUK-a* (hand)? *He reaches. . . .* ! We can represent such relations by a chart:

(146) *Words for Hand in Different Tongues Contained in English.*

English	Latin	Russian	Hebrew	Sumerian	Peruvian	Kuril
MAN-age	MAN-us					
REACH		RUK-a				
KEEP			KAP			
GET				KAT		
MAK-e					MAK-i	
TAK-e						TEK

Thus we learn that words may be different in various tongues, and yet this does not in any way exclude their existence in our mother-tongue. Words did not vanish in the course of many, many ages: they were merely pushed aside and we can discover them at will. We call the organ of speech *MOUTH,* and the French call it *BOUCH-e,* but this does not matter! The French use *MOT* (word) for the product of the mouth, and we use *BEACH* for a gulf that looks like a *BOUCH-e*.

It is true on the other hand, that not every case is so easy to handle as are the names for bodily organs. Yet once we understand in a concrete manner what actually happened to the language of humanity, then we can rebuild the lost community of speech.

The way of evolution leads from a unity to a diversity, and from that half-conscious diversity we can return consciously to a higher degree of unity.

CHAPTER ELEVEN

THE CRADLE OF HUMANITY

WHEN THE ancient Biblical tradition concerning the common origin of all tongues and the unity of mankind fell into oblivion with peoples such as the Sumerians, Babylonians, Egyptians, Hellenes, the reminiscence of a common homeland of humanity also vanished. There was a time when historians and philosophers became convinced of the idea that every nation that was reported to have settled first in a certain part of the earth, had originated and developed there independently of the other nations. The Cretans were considered by Herodotus to be the aborigines of that island, the Pelasgians were the primitive people of Hellas, the Arabs and Semites originated in Asia, the Egyptians in Africa, and according to Tacitus, the Germanic tribes were the aborigines of Germany.

This acceptance of such doubtful and somewhat inconsistent conclusions was very simple for the Roman historian who lived in the First Christian Century. Germany was a country of swamps and fogs, with a cold and unfriendly climate and very little sunshine. Who then, concluded Tacitus, would leave his original homeland, risk crossing wide oceans at the hazard of his life and settle in such a poor corner of the earth? The Teutons must have been born in the swamps and virgin forests of Germany and Scandinavia, the "womb of nations."

When America was discovered, many people looked upon the American Indians as the aborigines of the Western Hemisphere, and a minority of students still do today. Likewise when the "Aryans" (Indo-Europeans) first appeared in history, in spite of their lack of an impressive pedigree, scholars immediately sought for a common habitat of that family where they must have originated. About the middle of the

141

Nineteenth Century, most students considered Mother Asia as the probable homeland of the "Aryan" group.

Thus Asia once again was the favored continent, but later, especially since the start of the present century, more and more scholars have given preference to Europe, considering that the "Aryans" came from Germany, Scandinavia, the British Isles, the swamps of Rokitno, the Baltic Sea, or the Black Sea. The old proverb "Ex Oriente Lux!" (*From the East, Light!*) lost all attractiveness and the struggle for the Western origin of the "Aryans" was begun, until finally — for reasons transparent in our day — Germany and the region around the Baltic were given the preference by German students.

Again this is not the right attitude toward a scientific problem. As a matter of fact the old theory of Asia as the cradle of mankind is one-sided and incorrect. In the course of human evolution mankind had to migrate several times into different, nay opposite directions. There were far older movements from the West to the East than the postdiluvian transplantations connected with nations such as Indians, Persians, Sumero-Babylonians, Egyptians, Hebrews, Greeks, Romans and those Northern and Western tribes that took part in the migrations of peoples in prehistoric and historic times. Language does not leave any doubt as to the validity of these facts.

There are words which can only be linked with the East, sometimes even English words can only be connected with names of the Far East, and on the other hand the vernaculars of the American Indians, Mexican, Peruvian (Quichua), Brazilian (Tupi), Chilean (Araucan), etc., contain numberless terms which we find recorded far earlier in the ancient idioms of the Old World. The possibility of a migration from the West to the East, from the direction of the Atlantic to the shores of Western Europe (Hybernia) must be seriously examined, for such a direction of early human pilgrimages will provide the solution to the great enigma of the Franco-Cantabrian caves and their amazing art.

In Table 1 we pointed out that words such as *DRUM*, *TRUMP*-et, *STAMP*, *SELF* do not appear in European languages before the migration of peoples, before the Teutonic tribes appeared in history. Such a word as *Self* is usually not borrowed from other vernaculars or nations. It is a term which most peoples shape for themselves. As a matter of fact each branch of the "Aryan" language group uses its own synonym

(147) *Different Words for Self in the Indo-European Idioms.*

Sanskrit	Greek	Latin
SVA-	AUT-os	IPS-e
Italian	English	Slavic
MEDESIM-o	SELF	SAM-y

for *self*, and there are at least five different terms in use. Words like the Anglo-Saxon *SYLF*, German *SELB*, Venetian (inscription of Canevoi) SSELB-oi SSELB-oi (self) appear late in Europe. Where do we find their relatives? First of all on the east coast of Italy, and then in the Far East, in the Manchurian, *SILB-a*, (same name). Thus far we have not been able to discover any link anywhere else, certainly not in the American Indian vernaculars. This clue undoubtedly points to an eastern origin, to an East-West migration in a post-diluvian epoch.

(148) *Relatives of the Germanic Word-Stem Self.*

English	Anglo-Saxon	Old German
SELF	SYLF, SEOLF	SELB-o
Venetian, Canevoi	Manchurian	
SSELBOI-SSELBOI	SILB-a	

The *ox* is an animal belonging to a late period of civilisation. It is not Man the *hunter* who tamed this animal but Man the *farmer*, who captured the aurochs, the bison, the buffalo and tamed him in a late period of evolution, in post-diluvian times. Agriculture did not start in the earliest ages of man's life on earth, and thus we do not find a common name for the ox in the Western and Eastern Hemispheres, and no indigenous name for this animal in most of the Amer-

ican Indian dialects. Even the Indo-European tongues use
different terms for the ox.

(149) *Different Names for the Ox in Indo-European Idioms.*

Sanskrit	Greek	Latin
GO, GOV	BOU-s	BOS, BOV-

French	Anglo-Saxon	Slavic
BOEUF	OX-a	WOLL

GO is the predominant name of the ox and cow in Old India; yet the name ox also existed there as a synonym: *UKSH-
an,* as it existed in Egypt and in many other countries except
America. This we must keep in mind, for it is a key to many
secrets of the past, a clue which follows the path of migration
of the Indo-European speaking tribes.

(150) *The Word Ox in Northern Europe and Asia.*

English	German	Gothic
OX	OCHS	AUHS-a

Sanskrit	Turkish	Ostyak
UKSH-an	OKUS	UKYS

	Yakut	
	OGUS	

All these word-forms are pronounced nearly the same as
in English. There are however in several tongues variances
of spelling the final consonant, some of them within the same
family, as the Dutch *OS* instead of English *OX*.

(151) *OS Instead of OX in Various European and Asiatic
Idioms.*

Dutch	Kymric	Irish	Caucasus
OS	YCH	ES	OS, IS

Votyak	Zyrian	Manchu	Japan
OSH	YSH	ISH-an	USH-i

A strange fact faces us here, for we discover a wide *gap*
between the zone containing the name OX in Europe and the
corresponding zone in Asia. This gap extends from the Baltic
to the Mediterranean, with an interruption in the Caucasus
Mountains, for neither the Slavo-Baltic, nor the Greek languages possess the stem *OX*. The Slavic idioms use *WOLL*

which corresponds to our *BULL,* and the same applies to the word *COW.*

(152) *The Name COW in Europe and Asia.*

English	German	Albanian	Armenian
COW	KUH	KAU (ox)	COV (cow)

Sanskrit	Sumer	China	Japan
GAU	GU	KU	GO
		(wild ox)	

This word extends from England and the Germanic zone in North-Western Europe, Holland, Germany, Scandinavia, to China and Japan. Yet within the Indo-European group we encounter quite different names for this domesticated animal, and again in the East of Europe, from the Baltic Sea to the Bosporus and Mediterranean we find the same gap as in the

(153) *Various Names for the Cow in the Indo-European Group.*

Sanskrit	Greek	Latin	Anglo-Saxon	Slavic
GO, GAU	BOU-s	VACC-a	CU	KOROV-a

extension of the word *OX.* The name *COW* is lacking in Europe all around the Germanic region in the South-Western part and in the Eastern zones, yet is found in the North of Asia, throughout Siberia to the Far East, and in many other regions of the Old World including Egypt. We notice a kind of Slavo-Baltic and Hellenic wall between Northern and North-Western Europe on the one hand, and Asia and Africa on the other. As a matter of fact, we find a link of this greatly extended word-chain even in America. In Table 120 we already mentioned the Mexican word *KWA-KWA-way* (bull) and *KWA-KWA-witl* (horn). Yet we shall see later that this is not a genuine genealogical link in the word-group *COW,* but a later term used for horn and horned animals probably after America had been discovered.

To these two words, the *ox* and the *cow,* which are characteristic of the Germanic idioms and alien to their eastern neighbors, the Slavs, we can add a third important animal-name, the *horse.* However it is not *HORS-e* which the different European and Asiatic vernaculars have in common, but the word *MAR-e*. Again we find quite different names for this animal in the Indo-European idioms.

(154) *Various Names for Horse in the Indo-European Dialects.*

English	German	French	Latin
HORS-e	PFERD	CHEVAL	EQU-us

Greek	Polish	Russian
HIPP-os	KON-y	LOSHAD-y

We could add Sanskrit *ASV-a* (horse). This is quite a nice variety of synonyms including six different names (*Equus, Hippos* and *Asva* can be derived from the same stem). On the other hand we find the name *MAR-e*, common to most vernaculars of the Old World, particularly wide-spread in Asia, while in Europe it is confined only to the Germano-Celtic group, but is lacking in the other Occidental zones and in the Slavo-Balkanic regions.

(155) *The Word Mare in the Germano-Celtic Idioms.*

English	O. German	Anglo-Saxon
MAR-e	MAR-ah	MEARH

Breton	Irish	O. Norse, Swedish
MARCH	MARC	MARR

This name also appears in European recorded texts not earlier than the Migration of Peoples. It spread over all Europe in the term *MARSHAL* from the Old German *MA-RAH-scalc* (horse-servant, groom). However before we encounter it in Europe it appears in the old hieroglyphic and cuneiform records of Egypt and Babylonia. In Egyptian *MAR-i* was a groom, a "marshal", and *MAR-iannu*, the same as the Babylonian *MAR-iannu*, was the name of warriors in Palestine, probably Egyptian and Babylonian cavalry, or a term designating the Khurri (Hittite) warriors in Syria and in Asia Minor. In Arabic *MUHR* means a *colt.*

This is very important in view of the fact that many students suggest that the horse is characteristic of the Aryans, that it appears in history with the Aryan group of peoples.

Now we can see that Germano-Celtic horse-names are found in Egypto-Semitic records far earlier than in Indo-European texts, and this applies not only to the word *Mare*, but to other horse-names as well. Further, *Mare* is the principal horse-name in the Far-East: Indo-Chinese (Sokpa) *Mar-i* (horse), *MOR-in* (horse) in the Buryat, Tungus, Kalmuck, Mongol and Manchu vernaculars, and in the latter tongue *MOR-itsi* again means a horse-groom, *a marshal*. Yet no trace of this name is found in the Western Hemisphere.

(156) *The word MAR-e in African and Asiatic Tongues.*

English MAR-e	Africa, Egyptian MAR-i (horse-groom)	Asia, Assyria MUR-u (colt)
	Mongol, Manchu, Buryat MOR-in (horse)	

No doubt the name MAR-e points to the East as the place of its origin, while there is no connection at all to be found in America. We encounter traces of this stem in the Japanese *UMA* (horse), Chinese *MA* and Korean *MAL* (from *MAR*, horse) but no clue whatsoever in the Western Hemisphere, either in Alaska, in Mexico or in Peru. The names of the *ox* and the *cow* show a similar extension, and there are still other words with the same characteristics.

STAMP is a word which emerges within the European languages in the post-Christian epoch, after the Migration of Peoples, and from that time onward plays a great part in the vocabulary of modern tongues. The first fact we observe is the difference of terms for *seal* (stamp) in the Indo-European idioms.

(157) *Different Terms for Seal, Stamp in Indo-European Idioms.*

English STAMP, SEAL	German STEMP-el	Latin SIGILL-um	Greek SPHRAG-is	Russian PECH-aty

Again we have quite different synonyms in the Indo-European family. The Teutonic word *STAMP* is a post-classical word, characteristic of the Germanic vernaculars with the same Balto-Balkanic wall existing between this Northwestern Ger-

manic territory and that part of Asia where we find the links
of the word-chain STAMP in the Semitic idioms.

(158) *Links with the Root STAMP in Egypto-Semitic
Tongues.*

English	Babylonian	Hebrew	Egyptian
STAMP	HUTUM-u	HOTEM	HATAM

Coptic	Aramaic	Schemes	
SHETAM	SETAM	H-T-M	S-T-M

In remote epochs the highly civilised peoples of the Near
East used the word HATAM-SETAM for a seal. The classical tongues of Greece and Rome did not contain this term,
nor did the Celtic and Slavic idioms. The Teutons introduced
the word STAMP for *seal,* the same term which had been
used in Egypt, Babylonia and Palestine thousands of years
before. This late-comer among European words designates
an object unknown in primitive ages. Since barbarians such
as the Teutonic tribes did not know writing, how could they
use seals? As a matter of fact, STAMP does not appear as a
noun in *Anglo-Saxon* or in *Middle English,* but only as a verb.

(159) *STAMP Used As a Verb Before the 15th Century.*

Anglo-Saxon	Middle English	Modern English	Polish
STEMP-an	STAMP-en	STAMP	STAMP-ich
(to trample)	(to tread)		(to tread)

The eastern gap has vanished because the Slavic tongues
possess this word-stem in common with the Germanic vernaculars, but only in our modern sense of *to tread,* not as a
noun designating *a seal.* However the word is not found outside the Germanic, Slavic and Egypto-Semitic zones, in the
Far East or in America. It must go back to a very distant epoch
when the Teutonic tribes and the Egypto-Semites were neighbors. This is a hidden fact, because it belongs to prehistory,
but the archives of language have preserved it for us.

Another word which again points to an origin in the East
is *Massacre.* What a strange term this is! Webster and others
mention its provenience from the Old French MAÇACR-e,
MACECL-e (shambles, slaughter), and leave its true origin

unsolved. It appears first in the "Chanson de Roland" (*The Roland Song*) in the Twelfth Century, and from France was carried to Britain. Strangely enough this word at first glance seems to be isolated in Europe, but in the Far East, in the old idiom of the ancient inhabitants of Yedo, Japan — the Aino — we encounter *MASSAKAR-e* (axe). The French and Aino words are antipodes, yet in German there is a link between them in the word *METZGER* (butcher), Middle German *METZYER*, and the still older word *METZJAER-e*.

(160) *Relatives of the Word MASSACRE in the Far East.*

English	French	Old French	German	Aino, Japan
MASSACR-e	MASSACR-e	MACECR-e	METZGER	MASSAKAR-e
(slaughter)			(butcher)	(axe)

At first glance we see again an example of an enigmatic Eastern connection. The French *MASSACR-e* (slaughter) and the Yedo, Aino *MASSAKAR-i* (axe) are evidently the same stem. Many more links are to be found, if we pass from that prolonged root *M-SS-C-R* to a shorter stem, *M-S-K*, without the final R which in this case is merely an addition. In French there is the word *MASSOQU-e* (club), and in English *MATTOCK* and *MAC-e*, or French *MASS-ue* (club) and we can discover many more related words in all parts of the earth.

This shows how careful we must be before drawing too far-reaching conclusions from certain facts. In many cases the material from which we conclude is entirely insufficient. Most theories about the cradle of mankind and human civilisation were established between th middle and the end of the Nineteenth Century, before the Sumerian, Babylonian and Egyptian records were fully translated, even before the first vocabularies of Sumerian were published and scholars agreed that Sumerian was an actual language. What can we expect of such vague theories? The word examples published in this chapter are by far insufficient to establish any theory, whether Eastern or Western. They are but illustrations. The following is an example of migrations from the West.

(161) *A Possible Western Origin of the word Mind (spirit).*

English	Anglo-Saxon	Latin
MIND	**ge-MYND**	**MENS, MENT-is**
	(memory, spirit)	(intelligence)

		Algonquin
	Sanskrit	**MANIT-oo**
	MANAS	(great Spirit)

MANIT, MANAT (spirit) are names of several Semitic divinities, one of them mentioned in the Koran. The possibility of the Western origin of this important word-stem *M-N-T* cannot be denied, but must be examined carefully. The same applies to many other examples.

When America was discovered, and Spanish monks came in contact with the Indians of Central and South America, most of the former had such a one-sided conception of their faith that they could not gain a correct approach to the religious ideas of the primitive savages as they considered the Indians to be. When they learned about human sacrifices in Mexico and other parts of the Western Hemisphere, they more and more abhorred Indian rites and ceremonies and denied that the American Indians had any notion of a divine being. A correct interpretation of the god-name *Manitoo* (Great Spirit) not only shows that the American Indians knew about the existence of God and worshipped Him but that in their religion and cultural life they used names of God which are identical with those of Europe, Asia and Africa. *Manitoo* is not the only example of this kind. Mexicans, Mayans and others used even the same classical god-name as the Greeks and Romans: Greek *THE-os,* Latin *DE-us, DIV-inus* (divine)!

This is so much the more amazing when we realize that the Indo-Europeans even today do not possess a common name for the divinity.

(162) *Various Synonyms for God Used by Indo-Europeans.*

Anglo-Saxon	German	Latin	Greek
GOD	**GOTT**	**DE-us**	**THE-os**

	Sanskrit	Slavic	Persian
	DEV-a	**BOG**	**KHAUD-a**

There are at least three different synonyms for God, *THE-os, BOG* and *GOD,* scattered over the earth, with wide gaps between their various zones of use. Two of these Indo-European God-names are found in American Indian vernaculars and in languages of the Far East.

(163) *The Greek God-Name THE-os* (in *THEO-logy*) *in America etc.*

Mexico	Nicaragua	Anglo-Saxon	Greek
TEO-tl	TEO-t	TIW (TUE-sday)	THEO-s

China	Annam	Japan
TI	DE	TEI, TAI

J. G. Müller in his *Geschichte der Amerikanischen Urreligionen,* Basel, 1867, (History of the American Primeval Religions) reports that the first Spanish missionaries did not dare use the Mexican name *TEO-tl* for the Christian God. The Jesuit *Acosta* stated that Indians had no name for God, much to the disappointment of another Jesuit, *Clavigero,* who considered the Mexican word *TEO-tl* as significant as the Spanish word *DIO-s.*

TEO-tl in Mexican is the same word-stem as *THEO-s* in Greek; -tl is an Axtec ending, and *TEO* is the root. We can discover this root in such names and compounds as the Mexican *TEO-calli* (Greek *KAL-ia,* hut, *KAL-ias* chapel) which actually means *God's house* and is a temple atop a step-pyramid. *TEO-amoxtli* means *the holy book, TEO-teuktli,* a priest, or literally, a *leader in God,* while *TEO-nenemi* meant the *march of the Gods.* There were towns and cities bearing the name *TEO-,* which were cultual or mystery centres, such as *TEO-ti-huacan* (divine sanctuary) ; from Peruvian *HUAC-a,* in Greek *HAG-ios* (holy), Hebrew *HAG* (festival.) In Nicaragua, *TEO* (God) was used as the stem of *TEO-t,* in *TEO-bat* (temple), where *BAT* is the same word as the Hebrew *BETH* (*TEO-bat* could be in Hebrew *BETH-EL,* God's House), and English *BOOTH* (hut). Since we find this name of God in the Far East (Ti, De, Tei) as well as in America, we might think here of the possibility that it was carried to Europe from the East (Asia) as well as from the West beyond the Atlantic Ocean.

We can say the same of the God-name God which seems typically Teutonic. This too extends in both directions, East and West.

(164) *The Name GOD in the East and West.*

English GOD	German GOTT	Arabic HAUDH	Persian KHUD-a

Turkish KHUD-ai	Manchu HUT-u	Kamchatka KUT

The Chukchee call God, *AGHAT,* quite similar to Greek *AGATH-os* (good); *GOOD* and *GOD* are related with one another as well as the *DEVIL* with the *EVIL.* In a Semitic legend we find the name *JEUD,* the son of the God *Baal* whom he sacrificed for the salvation of mankind. *GAD* in Hebrew was the God of Destiny, as Christian mystics consider the Christ the Lord of Destiny. The Cuban word COT-i

(165) *GOD a God-Name in pre-Columbian America.*

Cuba COT-i (god)	Haiti GOEIZ (spirit)	Vilela, S. America GHOT-o (heaven)

Vilela GOZ (ghost, demon)	Hebrew, Moab GAD (God of Destiny)

(God) and some Arawac and Cariban forms of this word-stem may be borrowed from the Dutch language, but even this is doubtful, since both names as well as other American God-names may well be indigenous. The possibility of certain words having been brought to the Old World from the West must be admitted, as well as the carrying of certain words from Asia to Europe in the course of the successive Migrations of Peoples which took place in several ages.

But what does an indigenous language mean? Can it be that mankind and our language originated in America? Is the Western Hemisphere the cradle of humanity, or did the ancestors of the American Indians, as their own legends and holy books relate, come from the East, from *Aztlan* or *Atlan?*

On the other hand, are the American "aborigines" the descendants of the Turanians, Siberian tribes who crossed the Behring Strait into Alaska, later to migrate to the South? The few word examples which we have noted do not suffice to answer this question precisely. We must first compare tongues spoken on both shores of the Atlantic and the Pacific Oceans to find out whether language can help us to clear up these problems. Language is more informing and reliable than most archaeological evidences such as skulls and skeletons, stone-tools and weapons. The latter only can tell us indirectly about the remote Past, while speech can inform us directly.

For thousands of years, before 1492, America had been separated from the Old World and even knowledge of its existence had been forgotten. It had to be rediscovered by Columbus. Its story must contain certain vestiges of the Past, and the American Indian languages are the key which we shall use in our study of man's history upon earth.

CHAPTER TWELVE

IDENTICAL WORDS ON BOTH SHORES
OF THE ATLANTIC

THOMAS PAINE wrote in his book, *Common Sense,* that America was to play a particular part in world history. He felt that even the distance which the Almighty has placed between England and America is a strong and natural proof that the authority of the one over the other was never the design of Heaven. The time likewise at which the continent was discovered adds weight to the argument, and the manner in which it was peopled increases the force of it.

The Reformation, Paine continued, was preceded by the discovery of America, as if the Almighty graciously meant to open a sanctuary to the persecuted in the future years, when home should afford neither friendship nor safety. Thus such a strange man as Thomas Paine saw the hand of destiny acting in the discovery of the Western Hemisphere.

In a similar way one could look at Christopher Columbus and the way he was inspired to start his voyage to a new, unknown continent. Very often, while waiting for some important decision to further his undertaking and his plans, the great explorer used to sit on a rock by the Spanish shore of the Atlantic gazing at the wide surface of the ocean and listening attentively to the breaking of the waves. For many years he had studied Plato's account of the Lost Continent of Atlantis and was convinced of its seriousness and truth. He stared at the vast sea, fixing his mind's eye as it were upon a dim blue line on the horizon, seemingly the shore of a distant land.

The waves approached the coast with a rhythmic regularity, throwing upon the rocks all kinds of objects. One day, while Columbus was watching the strange play of the waves, the ocean cast up a wooden log with carvings. The explorer ran to the spot, picked up the log and stared amazed at the carvings. What a strange style of art! Never before had he seen anything like these odd, distorted figures and forms! What kind of people could have carved them? Certainly no artists of the European world he knew. Columbus stared at that strange piece of wood as if enchanted. Again he gazed at the blue line on the horizon. The log must have come from that direction, from some land in the Atlantic, some island, or perhaps even from the other shore of the sea. And since the wood was covered with carvings there must be human beings living on the other side of the Atlantic! This was as clear to Columbus as the light of the sun. Many other people, fishermen, peasants, artisans, perhaps even learned men, may have encountered similarly carved logs without paying any attention to them, but to Columbus the finding of that log bearing those strange carvings became a key leading to the re-discovery of America.

Another explorer, this time in the field of languages and unrecorded history, was Thomas Jefferson. In the newly discovered Continent he was the first to realize that the vernaculars of the American Indians could become most important in disclosing their origin and the source of their civilisations. In his *Notes on the State of Virginia* written about 1780 Jefferson said, "A knowledge of their (i.e. the Indians') several languages would be the most certain evidence of their derivation which could be produced. In fact it is the best proof of the affinity of nations which ever can be referred to ... Were vocabularies formed of all the languages spoken in North and South America, preserving their appellations of the most common objects in nature, of those which must be present to every nation barbarous or civilized, with the inflections of their nouns and verbs, and their principles of regimen and concord, and these deposited in all the public libraries, it would furnish opportunities to those skilled in the languages of the old world to compare them with these, now or at any future time, and hence to construct the best evidence of the derivation of this part of the human race."

According to Jefferson's biographer, John Dewey, the author of the Declaration of Independence collected vocabularies of fifty American idioms and deposited them in libraries. Yet this was just a beginning, for there was as yet no method for the discovery of the relationship between languages of the Old and New Worlds. The whole idea of encountering in America, among the Indian "primitives" and their "savage" vernaculars words identical with the noble appellations used in the Old World seemed so unfamiliar and strange to many scholars that they did not even dare identify or connect American and European words.

The best illustration of this state of mind is the example of two German students of American Indian languages who, in the sixties of the last Century, went to Peru and other parts of the Western Hemisphere, intent upon collecting American Indian words related to words of the Old World. They were Julius Platzman and Fr. W. Middendorf. After having spent many years of study, Middendorf could not discover a single root of Chinese, Malayan or Indo-European provenance either in the Quichua or Aymara tongues of Peru, in Mexican, in the Guarani idiom of Brazil, in the Chibcha of Colombia, or in the Chimu dialect of Northern Peru. Not one equation was to be found, as he related in the preface to his book, *Die einheimischen Sprachen Perus,* Leipzig 1890 (The Indigenous Idioms of Peru).

On the other hand, Platzmann, in a far shorter time, succeeded in collecting about 700 word-stems common to American Indian and Old World idioms. He published them in 1870 in a book titled *Amerikanisch-Asiatische Etymologien via Behring-Strasse (American-Asiatic Etymologies via Behring-Strait),* and most of them are irreversible and highly important. Thus it appears that a student may know a few languages fairly well, so as to publish vocabularies of them, and yet be almost deaf and blind in the field of comparison. There are people who only note the diversity of things, while others have an innate ability in discovering similarities and relationship.

In one of his reports to the king of Spain in 1498, Columbus, then governor and vice-king of the Spanish possessions in America, mentioned the Arawakan and Cariban boat-name *CAN-aoa*. From this report the Indian boat-name penetrated into Spanish as *CAN-oa,* and into French, English and most modern Western tongues, as a "loan-word": *CAN-oe.*

(166) *Cariban CAN-aoa a Loan-Word of Most Modern Idioms.*

Cariban	Spanish	French	English
CAN-aoa	CAN-oa	CAN-ot	CAN-oe
	German	Dutch	
	KAN-u	KAN-oe	

This word entered into the European idioms after 1498 in a form quite similar to its Indian original. That is one point. The other point however, by far more important, is the fact that the same word-stem (though not the same word-form) appears in the Eastern Hemisphere in different tongues, at a time long before the discovery of America. *KHAN-u* was the name of the death-barge of the sun-god Sokharis mentioned four to five thousand years ago in the

(167) *The American Root CAN-oe Appears Long Before in the Old World.*

American, Cariban	Old French	O. Danish
CAN-aoa (boat)	CAN-art (boat)	KAN-e
German		Egyptian
KAHN		KHAN-u (barge)

Book of the Dead. In Old French *CAN-art* (boat) appears about the 12th Century, and in Old Danish *KAN-e* (boat) probably earlier, since the French word likely is borrowed from the Vikings, the Normans, who occupied Northern France about the Ninth Century. In modern Danish, *KAN-e* does not mean a boat, but *a sledge,* a "boat" that slides on ice or snow. As a matter of fact, the death-bark of the Egyptian sun-god, Sokharis, who carries the souls of the dead to the

Netherworld, was represented as mounted on a sledge.

(168) *Words Common to Tongues Spoken on Both Shores of the Atlantic.*

EUROPEAN and AFRICAN SHORE		AMERICAN SHORE	
Basque	IG (day, light)	Maya	IC (day, sun)
"	HURM-a (cold)	Quiche	HOROM (cold)
"	TUT-a (play on bagpipe)	Chile	TUT-uca (bagpipe)
"	PUK-a (toad)	"	POK-o (toad)
"	IZOK-in (fish)	Peru	SUKI (fish)
Breton	TUS (to dance)	Peru	TUS-uni (to dance)
"	PRAG (flower)	Chile	PRAG-yn (flower)
"	KUMM (wave)	Maya	CUM (wave)
"	KER (house, town)	Chile	KAR-a (town)
"	AR (on, upon)	Brazil	AR-a (over, upon)
"	BELEC (priest)	Peru	VILLC-a (priest)
"	PAOTR (youth)	Comanche	PAOTR-a (daughter)
Irish	HUA (son)	Omagua Br.	HUA-HUA (son)
"	MACC (son)	Cape Horn	MAK-u (son)
"	CILL (house)	Mexico	CALL-i (house)
"	BOCC (buck)	Kiriri Br.	BUK-e (deer)
"	LAN (land, earth)	Mexico	LAN (country)
"	SEARP-an (swan)	Maya	SARP-on (eagle)
M. Irish	NIMB- (a drop)	"	NIMB-u (water)
Gaelic	ALP (highland)	Peru	ALLP-a (earth)
Kymric	GUAR (to defend)	Brazil	GUAR-ini (warrior)
Celtic	BEAL, BEL (sun-god)	Maya	BAAL (lord)
"	KELT, CELT (knife)	Kolyush	KYLT-ai (knife)
O. French	HELLEQ-uin (wild hunter)	Kinai, Al.	UELEK-en (wizard)

French	GON-e (Lyon) (child)	Mexico	CON-otl (son)
"	RIV-e (bank)	Arawak	RIF-u (sea-side)
Anglo-Saxon	THAEC (thatch, roof)	Maya	TAK-e (shelter)
"	TIU (god, TUE-sday)	Mexico	TEO-tl (god)
"	CYN-e (king)	Maya	KIN (priest)
"	MON-a (moon)	Carib	MON-a (moon)
"	ATTOR (perfume)	Peru	HUATAR-a (perfume)
"	HYP-e (hip)	Brazil	UP (hip)
"	TADIG-e (toad)	Br. Guarani	TATAG (toad)
"	TUN (fence)	Peru	TAUN-a (rod, branch)
English	STAR	Patagonia	SETER-e (star)
"	GHOST	Maya	GOZ (demon)
"	to TIN-e (to hedge)	Cariban	TIN-i (to twist)
	to PICK	Peru	PIC-a (to pick)
"	TERN (gull)	Quiche	TEREN (cock)
"	CRAG (rock)	Botocudo	CRACK (mountain)
"	AL-e	Yunka, Peru	YAL-a (beer)
"	HOL-e	Maya	HOL (hole, door)
"	KEN (to know)	"	CAN (to learn)
"	YOK-e	Peru	YUK (to tie)
"	CARAB-in (soldier)	Cariban	CARIB (a valiant man'
"	BIND	Peru	PINT-uni (to bind)
"	MIND	Algonquin	MANIT-oo (great Spirit)
Breton	TITIRIK (cock)	Maya	SITIRAC-a (cock)
O. Norse	YNG-vi (king, prince)	Peru	INC-a (king)
"	DIOG (rain)	Quiche	TIOKH (rain)
Old German	PINUZ (bent-grass)	Peru	PINT-ok (bent-grass)
"	PACH (BECK, brook)	Maya	PAC (river)
Nuba, Afr.	OROM (cold)	Quiche	HOROM (cold)

This idea of considering languages in terms of their age as a sort of chronological device, is still novel in the science of language, but we can recognize the importance of certain tongues just from this viewpoint. Sumerian is an idiom spoken in Mesopotamia for many thousands of years which died out as a spoken (living) tongue in the Third Millennium B.C. Egyptian became a dead tongue at the end of the pre-Christian Era. If we find a Sumerian word in the New World, it is clear that it hardly could have been carried to America as a loan-word later than about 3000 B.C., or almost 5000 years ago. Further, migrations from Sumer to Mexico or Peru let us say in the year 3800 B.C. are unknown. Thus in such a case there is usually but one conclusion left: that similarities or identities of Sumerian and American words can be explained only by a common origin of both vernaculars, or by a contact of both nations or groups of nations, in remote epochs long before the year 3000 B.C. A few such examples however would never suffice as a basis for such far-reaching conclusions. This is why we must proceed here step by step, methodically investigating the different idioms in order to obtain fundamental answers to our questions. The first step is to discover whether there are common words in the idioms spoken on both shores of the Atlantic Ocean.

Only one example of African-American relations has been quoted in this Table, but dozens of such word-chains could be mentioned. On the other hand we note a great number of relatives in the tongues of Hybernia extending from Scotland to the Basque country and to the New World. Thus we are certain that there must have been some old contact between all these nations. Words such as *Inca, Manitoo, Huracan* which were considered to be typical of the American Indians, suddenly lose their exotic nimbus and appear in Old European tongues. In this list we quoted several Peruvian and Chilean words, although Peru and Chile are on the shore of the Pacific. This is for the purpose of checking whether words could not have been brought to the New World from the East and later on have been transmitted to the shore of the

Pacific across the American continent. We shall deal with this possibility still more extensively, but must compare many more tongues for this purpose.

As an example let us take the Basque word TUT-a (to play on the bagpipe) and the Araucan TUT-uca (bagpipe, shawm). In German we find DUD-eln (to play on the bagpipe) which we can connect with the Yankee DOOD-le. There is doubt whether TUT-uca (bagpipe) is a genuine Chilean word at all, because in Russian the shawm or bagpipe is called DUD-ka — assonant to Araucan TUT-uca — from Turkish DUD-uk (flute). Since Alaska formerly belonged to the Russians, there is a possibility that the use of this Russian word DUD-ka may have extended down the Pacific coast to California, Peru, and Chile as a loan-word of the Indian tribes.

(169) *Araucan TUT-uca (bagpipe) Could Be a Russian Loan-Word*

Araucan, Chile	Russian
TUT-uca (bagpipe)	DUD-ka (shawm)
Turkish	**German**
DUD-uk (flute)	DUD-eln (play on the bagpipe)

We can link with this word-chain the English word TOOT and the Hebrew word TOOT (to blow a horn).

Thus we could eliminate the Canadian French word OR-IGN-al (deer) which probably stems from the Basque Oreñ-a (stag), and replace it by the Bororo Brazilian word OROG-o (fallow deer) which is related to Basque ORK-atz, goat, and to the Greek ORYX, ORYCH-os (antelope). For OROG-o is without doubt an indigenous word not imported from Europe or other continents. We must keep in mind that in

(170) *Bororo, Brazil OROG-o (Fallow Deer) Related to ORYX.*

Canadian, French	Basque	Basque
ORIGN-al (deer)	OREGN-a (stag)	ORK-atz (goat)
Bororo		**Greek**
OROG-o (fallow deer)		ORYX (antelope)

such lists as Table 168 and some of the following, words are merely given as examples as yet not actually compared. Each line can be extended and linked with terms of many other vernaculars. Then only would we be able to draw definite conclusions from such comparisons.

We pick an example such as the Breton word *KOK* (red) which is related to the Mexican word *QUAK* (red) or Mayan *KIAK* (red). At first such a name for red seems very strange and unfamiliar, yet do we not use it daily in our own tongue? Is not *COCH-ineal* (scarlet) based upon the same stem?

(171) *Mayan KIAK (red) related to COCH-ineal (scarlet).*

Breton	English	Mexican	Mayan
KOK (red)	COCH-ineal	QUAC (red)	KIAK (red)

We shall encounter another name for *red* in Peruvian which is related to Hebrew, Greek, and Latin cousins. The color red played a great part in painting the bodies and mummies of the Indians, and thus its name has been preserved for thousands of years in New and Old World languages.

It is amazing to discover such a familiar word as *MAC* (son) as used in *MAC*-millan, *MAC*-pherson, *MAC*-beth, *MAC*-duff etc. in the Jagan dialect of Cape Horn in the word *MAK-u* (son). This is identical with the Old Irish word *MACC* (son). However it would be premature to draw any conclusions from this coincidence until we have searched for further relationship. In Egypt also *MAY* meant *son*, while in the Dravido-Australian vernacular *MAG-u* is a *child*, and *MAG-an a son*. The word-stem *MAC* (son) is found in all

(172) *MAC (son) Found in America and elsewhere.*

Jagan, Cape Horn	Old Irish
MAK-u (son)	MACC (son)
Egyptian	**Dravido-Australian**
MAY (son)	MAG-u (child)

the five Continents. Two further examples of the use of the same words on both the European and American Continents are the Irish word *CAOR-a* (lamb) and the Peruvian *KAU-*

R-a (lamb), and the Peruvian word *MISG-i* (sweet) identical with the Breton word *MISK-i* (sweet, honey).

(173) *Irish CAOR-a (lamb) and Breton MISK-i (sweet)*
Found in Peru.

Irish CAOR-a (lamb)   **Peruvian** KAUR-a (lamb)
Breton MISK-i (sweet)   **Peruvian** MISG-i (sweet)

We can extend this word-chain by linking with it the Hebrew words *KAR* (lamb) and *METEK or METHEK* (*MESEK*) "sweet, honey". The fact that these words extend much farther than this shows us how careful we must be in establishing theories upon insufficient basis. In the following list we note that related words are not only encountered on both shores of the Atlantic but in languages spoken in distant countries as well.

(174) *Common Words in Tongues Spoken in Various Continents.*

Peru
1 POKPUK (bottle)   Malta, BAKBYK-a (bottle)
2 MIT-a (goal)   Latin, MET-a (goal)
3 ANT-uy (flower)   Greek, ANTH-os (flower)
4 SIS-a (flower)   Egypt, SIS (flower)
5 HUANAC-o (sheep)   "   HANAK (sheep)
6 HAMP-atu (frog)   Caucas., GAMB-io (toad)
7 TARUK-a (deer)   Tuareg, TURIK (antelope)
8 CHARAP-a (turtle)   French, CRAP-aud (toad)
9 SIR-a (snake)   Assyrian, SIR (snake)
10 KUM-u (hump)   English, HUMP

Maya
11 SARP-on (eagle)   Irish, SEARP-an (swan)
12 PAPAL-otl (butterfly) Latin, PAPIL-io (butterfly)
13 CARB-at (fruit)   "   CARP-o (to harvest)
14 CUM (wave)   English, HUMP

Quiche
15 TIOKH (rain)   O. Norse, DIOGH (rain)

Mexico
16 MOY-otl (a fly)   Greek, MYI-a (a fly)
17 MASH-atl (deer)   Sumer, MASH (deer)

Brazil
18 UP (hip)   Gothic, HUP-a (hip)
19 ACAR-a (heron)   Cyprus, AGOR (hawk)
20 CARAP-aoa (fly)   Finnish, KAERP- (a fly)
21 TAPIR (deer)   Egypt, TSAPUR-uma (antelopes)
22 GUR-a (chicken)   Wendic, KUR-a (chicken)

Cariban
23 BALAN-a (sea)   Latin, BALN-eum (bath)
24 AKIR (mother-in-law) Cornic, HVIGER-en (mo.-in-law)

Galibi
25 MAK-o (midge)   Cymric, MAK-ai (worm)
Arawac
26 DOP-u (lizard)   Egypt, DAP-i (crocodile)
Chile
27 MEN-u (hair)   Syriac, MEN-o (hair)
Paraguay
28 MOUT-eu (speak)   English, MOUTH
Peru
29 PILC-o (bird)   Latin, BILC-o (falcon)
Algonquin
30 CARIB-ou (deer)   Celtic, CARB (deer)
Shoshone
31 TERM (summer)   Greek, THERM-os (warm)

The Same Words Found in Other Tongues.

1. **Hebrew**
   BAKBUK (bottle)
2. **Lithuan.**
   MIT-as (goal)
3. **Sanskrit**
   ANDH-a (flower)
4. **Hebrew**
   ZIZ (flower)
5. **O. Phoen.**
   ANAK (sheep)
6. **Sanskrit**
   AJAMB-a (frog)
7. **Babylon**
   TURAK-u (deer)
8. **Malayan**
   KRAB-ö (crocodile)
9. **Sanskrit**
   SIR-a (snake)
10. **Sanskrit**
    KUMBH-a (hump)
11. **Latin**
    SARP-a (heron)
12. **Letton**
    PEPEL-is (butterfly)
13. **Greek**
    KARP-os (fruit)
14. **Sanskrit**
    KUMBH-a (hump)
15. **Hebrew**
    DAG-anim (rain)
16. **Chinese**
    MIEH (flies)

17. **Sanskrit**
    MESH-a (sheep)
18. **O. German**
    HUP-a (hip)
19. **Hebrew**
    AGUR (heron)
20. **Greek**
    KARAB-os (beetle)
21. **Hebrew**
    TSAPIR (deer)
22. **Hebrew**
    KOR-e (partridge)
23. **Russian**
    VOLN-a (wave)
24. **Greek**
    HEKYR-a (mother-in-law)
25. **Korea**
    MOK-ui (mosquito)
26. **Hebrew**
    TSAB (lizard)
27. **China**
    MAN (hair)
28. **French**
    MOT (word)
29. **Hawaii**
    PELEH-u (turkey)
30. **Arabic**
    KHARUF (goat)
31. **Hebrew**
    DEROM (south)

In this list there are examples of different American Indian dialects among them Peruvian (Quichua), Mexican, Mayan, Brazilian (Tupi) and Chilean (Araucan) which from a certain viewpoint we could consider to be the classical tongues of the Western Hemisphere; for the more we shall proceed in our investigation, the more we shall realize that these tongues not only contain the highest percentage of the Old World's classical words (Greek, Latin, Hebrew, Egyptian, Sanskrit, Babylonian etc.) but have preserved them in a very pure form so that is is possible to recognize them almost at first glance. A language such as the Peruvian (Quichua) or Aymara contains nearly fifty percent of words which seem to be copies of Greek, or Sanskrit, Gothic or Latin terms. Whenever the sound and sense of a word, regardless of its nationality, have been preserved, it is not too difficult to rea-

(175) *American Words Perfectly Resembling European Terms.*

Peruvian	MARC-a (territory)	Gothic	MARK-a (territory)
Aymara	KARAN (vice-king)	Greek	KARAN-os (king)

lize its kinship. The next step consists in discovering its likeness in modern tongues which we know. If we are able to do this then and only then do we live up to a full understanding of the nature and spirit of words.

In Table 174 we noted the Chilean word *MEN-u* (*hair*) compared with Syriac *MEN-ô* (*hair*) and Chinese *MAN* (*hair*). Thus we might be inclined to believe that we are faced with a word-chain uniting both shores of the Pacific: Chile with China. However the same word appears in Europe too, in the German word *MAEHN-e,* and the English word *MAN-e.*

(176) *The Word MAN-e on the Shores of Both the Atlantic and Pacific.*

America, Chile	Europe, England
MEN-u (hair)	MAN-e
Asia, Syriac	China
MEN-o (hair)	MAN (hair)

By means of another example we shall note that all those exotic names, however distant from European centres, are frequently found in European and Asiatic classical vernaculars. How typically American does the name *CARIB-ou* (deer) sound! Does it not have a Canadian, an Algonquian smell? And yet we have linked it already with the Celtic word *CARB, CARV* (deer) and can even add the Latin word *CERV-us* (stag) and the French word *CERF* (deer).

In Table 174 we find a French word *CRAP-aud* (toad). Its origin is unknown and it seems to be quite isolated in France. As a matter of fact quite different names for frog or toad are used in the Indo-European tongues. The French word *CRAP-aud* stands apparently quite alone, until we discover a relative

(177)   *Various Synonyms of Frog and Toad in Indo-European Idioms.*

English	French	Latin	German
TOAD	CRAP-aud	RAN-a	KROET-e

Greek	Slavic	Sanskrit
BATRACH-os	ZHAB-a	BHEK-a

of this strange word on the shores of the Pacific, in Peru: *CHARAP-a* (turtle). Did *CRAP-aud* migrate to the other shore of the Atlantic, then cross the South American Continent and settle in Peru? A toad is a *rep*tile, from Latin *REP-o*, Greek *HERP-ô* (to creep), related to our own word *CREEP*, *C-R-P*, and to the French word *CRAP-aud, C-R-P*. How would the Egyptians and the Phoenicians have written these words in their alphabets? *C-R-P!* In other words, with the same symbol. Thus there is no doubt concerning the relationship of the words *CRAP-aud* and *CHARAP-a*.

(178)   *Words Found on the American and Asiatic Shores of the Pacific.*

Peru	CHARAF ₁ (turtle)	Malay	KRAB-ö (crocodile)
Peru	PILC-o ₁ ird)	Hawaii	PELEH-u (turkey)
Chile	MEN-u (hair)	China	MAN (hair)

There are no general abstract formulas which we can use as schemes in stating whether nations migrated East or West in ancient times. It is not easy to answer such difficult questions in a reliable manner. If we wish to do this, we must first investigate numerous examples thoroughly, step by step. We shall continue this examination in the following chapter by comparing words found on both shores of the Pacific to discover whether the words which we find in Oregon, California, Mexico, Peru or Chile are related to words found in Western Asia, in Central Europe and in Hybernia. Relationship of a few tongues does not prove anything, so long as we do not determine whether it is restricted to that linguistic group or whether it can be extended to other vernaculars also. Much harm has been done to our human knowledge in the course of the Nineteenth Century by theories built upon a limited section of the available facts.

Now let us shift our study to Siberia, China, Japan and Australia on the one side of the Pacific, and to Canada, Washington, California, Mexico, Peru and Chile on the other. It is easy to imagine that words which were brought to Mexico together with the early conquerors might have been transmitted from the Atlantic to the Pacific shore of that vast country. Yet it is more difficult to explain how—by migrations alone — words of the European coast of the Atlantic could have landed in Peru or Alaska. One fallacy will have to be removed before we can reach reliable conclusions: the idea that those "primitive" people of early epochs were not able to cross such vast oceans as the Atlantic or Pacific. Language will prove to be the best way to solve this problem.

CHAPTER THIRTEEN

IDENTICAL WORDS ON BOTH SHORES OF THE PACIFIC

In his book *La Esfinge Indiana* (*The Indian Sphinx*) published in Buenos Aires in 1926, J. Imbelloni presents an interesting comparative list of Peruvian and Maori (New Zealand) words. In comparing these two vernaculars Imbelloni followed instinctively the geographical method which is consciously applied in this book: for Peruvian and Maori can be considered as idioms spoken on both shores of the Pacific.

(179) *Words Used on Both Shores of the Pacific* (*From Imbelloni*).

QUICHUA (Peru)		MAORI (New Zealand)	
AP-ay	(to lift)	HAP-ay	(to lift)
ARAP-a	(Venetian blind)	ARAP-aki	(Venetian blind)
AWK-i	(father, prince)	AUK-i	(old man)
CUR-aka	(tribal chieftain)	KUR-a	(chieftain)
HUAC-a	(holy object)	WAK-a	(holy object)
ING-a	(prince, king)	ING-a-nui	(the Lord)
KAR-a	(skin)	KIR-i	(skin)
KOKOT-uai	(pigeon)	KOK-o	(bird)
KUMAR-a	(potato)	KUMAR-a	(potato)
MUN-ay	(to love)	MUN-ay	(to love)
NYOC-a	(I)	NOC-u	(my, mine)
MUT-u	(mutilated)	MUT-u	(mutilated)
PAPAYA	(a fruit)	PAPAYA	(a fruit)
PAH-uai	(to run)	PAH-u	(to leap, run)
PAR-a	(rain)	PAR-aara	(thunderstorm)
PAR-ia	(bird)	PAR-irau	(bird)
PUR-a	(both)	PUR-ua	(between both)
UN-u	(water)	UN-u	(to drink water)
NAK-a	(near by)	NAK-a	(next to)
KOT-o	(small things)	KOT-o-KOT-o	(small)

In Imbelloni's list there are still other words mentioned, some of them from the Rapanui or Easter Island vernacular, others from Formosa, Rarotonga or Hawaii. As a matter of fact there is no difference in quoting a dialect of a single Pacific island or some spoken in its vicinity; for there is relationship between almost all these vernaculars, and we can draw the same conclusions from tongues of any of the Pacific tribes.

(180) *Words Common to Tongues Spoken on Both Shores of the Pacific.*

AMERICAN Tongues		ASIATIC Tongues	
California	CANAC-o (dog)	Samoyede	KANNAK (dog)
,,	GAT-uc (worm)	Samoa	GAT-a (snake)
,,	LA'-LA' (goose)	Chukchee	LACHLECH (goose)
,,	TAIK (see)	Munda	TAK-au (look)
Comanche	TAK-en (speak)	Mongol	DAGH-on (voice)
Greenland	IGN-ek (fire)	Chukchee	EGN-ek (fire)
,,	NEKK-e (meat)	Japan	NIK-u (meat)
Mexican	TE-TEK-a (weave)	Chinese	TEK (weave)
,,	NAK-a (flesh)	Chukchee	NAK-a (meat)
,,	TSAQ-a (to close)	Annam	TAK (to close)
,,	NAM-eya (to rob)	China	NIAM (to take)
,,	COTON-a (to cut)	Japan	KATAN-a (sword)
,,	COU-a (to buy)	Japan	KU (to buy)
,,	PAN-tli (flag)	China	FAN (flag)
,,	TELP-ochtli (stupid)	Manchu	TULB-a (thoughtless)
,,	SARP-on (eagle)	Aino, Jap.	SHIRAP (eagle)
,,	ALC-o (wild dog)	Korea	ILH-ei (wolf)
,,	TOC-atl (spider)	Munda	TAK-oe (to spin)
Mayan	AKH (owner)	Korea	EK (owner)
,,	SEG-u (word)	Yakut	SAG-a (voice)
,,	BALAM (magician)	Tibet	(B)LAM-a (magician)
Antilles	TON-a (sun)	China	T'UN (sun)
Cuba	COT-i (God)	Kamchatka	KUT (God)
Peruvian	TAMP-o (house)	Japan	TAM-oya (house)
,,	KAUR-a (sheep)	Siberian	KER-e (reindeer)

"	MUN-ay (love)	Maori	MUN-a (love)
"	PAQU-iy (to break)	China	P'EK (to burst)
"	MANK-uni (to cut)	Munda	MANG (to cut)
"	YUK (to tie)	Korea	YOK-ta (to tie)
"	SAT (to fill)	Mongol	ZAT-o (satiated)
"	SISS-i (ant)	Yurak, Sib.	SIS (ant)
"	VANAC (eagle)	China	PHENG (phoenix)
"	TAK-i (chant)	Maori	TAKI-TAKI (song)
"	HUANAC-o (sheep)	China	YANG (sheep)
"	SIM-i (speech)	Manchu	SEM-e (word)
"	TOK- i (axe of chief)	Maori	TOK-i (axe)
Chile	QUETAL (sun)	Vogul	KOTAL (sun)
"	DUG-u (speech)	Annam	DOC (to say)
"	POK-o (toad)	China	PO(K) (toad)
"	KAR-a (town)	Samoyede	KARR-a (village)
"	HVINC-a (chief)	China	HUANG (sovereign)
"	TU-e (earth)	China	THU (earth)
Brazil	AR (to be born)	Japan	AR-u (to be born)
"	NHEEM (to whisper)	China	NYM (to speak)
"	POROK-o (thunder)	Australia	POOROK (thunder)
"	MEN-a (man)	China	MIN (mankind)
Bororo	OROG-o (fallow deer)	Mongol	ARG-al (wild sheep)
Guarani	TAK-oa (bamboo)	Japan	TAK-e (bamboo)
Cayriri	DZU (water)	Samoa	SU-a (water)
Chaques	KAMUR-u (cloud)	Japan	KUMOR-i (cloud)

It is physically impossible to present here even one of these word-chains in a complete form by quoting every link which we can discover in any of the spoken or faded tongues, because one word-chain alone of sufficient importance would fill a whole book. This is why we use here a *representative* system, quoting but a few words out of numberless relatives, sometimes mentioning only one word as representative of a whole continent. There are a few instances where the links of a word-chain so far discovered are very restricted in number. As a rule however each of the quoted word-chains can easily be extended by adding to it many various forms of the same word-stem out of a great number of languages.

Let us pick from Imbelloni's list 179 the Peruvian word *CUR-aca* (chieftain) which he rightly compared with the Maori word *KUR-a* (chieftain).

(181) *Extension of the Maori Word KUR-a (chieftain)*.

America, Peru	Europe, Greek	Asia, Sumer
CUR-aca	KYR-ios	GUR-ush
(chieftain)	(Lord)	(Lord)

Sanskrit	New Zealand
GUR-u	KUR-a
(teacher)	(chieftain)

To this we could add the Hungarian word *UR* (Lord) and many other links. Why did we connect the Sumerian word *GUR-ush* (Lord, man) and the Sanskrit word *GUR-u* (teacher) with this group? Because in remote antiquity kings were still initiates or priest-kings, political and spiritual authorities at the same time. The chieftain was the wisest man of the tribe or clan, its ruler as well as its teacher.

In like manner we can extend the Quichua word *KAR-a* (skin) and Maori *KIR-i* (skin).

(182) *Extension of the Peruvian Word KAR-a* (skin).

American, Peru	Europe, Latin	Greek
CAR-a	COR-ium	CHOR-ion
(skin)	(skin)	(skin)

Asia, Hebrew	New Zealand
(H)OR	KIR-i
(skin)	(skin)

This word appears in such Slavic tongues as Polish *KORZ-a* (skin, leather), in Phoenician *(H)OR-t* (skin), and the chain can be extended still further when we connect with it the term *bark* as the "skin of a tree".

(183) *Further Extension of Peruvian CAR-a (hide, bark).*

America, Peru	Europe, Latin	Slavic
CAR-a (bark)	COR-tex (bark)	KOR-a (bark)
Perm	**Ostyak**	**Asia, Tataric**
KOR-a (bark)	CAR (bark)	CAR-y (bark)

Of greatest importance is the Peruvian word *NYOC-a* (I
Ego) mentioned by Imbelloni (list 179) and compared with
Maori NOC-u (my, mine). First of all it proves that the con-
cept of the individuality, the Ego, goes back to the earliest
epochs of mankind before its split into various nations. For
NOC- is an abridged form of the Semito-Egyptian word
ANOK-i (I) which we already know from the Moabitic in-
scriptions of the stone of Mesha (Table 69).

(184) *Extension of the Word-Stem NOC-a (I)*, Semitic
ANOK-i.

America, Peru	Europe, Albania	Africa, Coptic
NYOC (I)	UNEH (I)	ANOC (I)
Asia, Assyr.		**New Zealand**
ANAK-u (I)		NOC-u (my)

This is of course but a small section of the available material which could be linked with this important group.

(185) *Further Extension of Semitic ANOK-i (I).*

America, Chile	Mexican	African, Lybian
INCH-e (I)	NECH (me)	NEK (I)
Asia, Khmer		**Chukchee**
ANH (me)		WANG-a (I)

The latter form *WANG-a* can easily be connected with the
Chinese word WENG (soul). Actually, the deeper original
meaning of the Ego, the I, was *soul, spirit.* Hence the similarity of the Egyptian word *ANOK* (I) with the *ANKH* (cross,
the symbol of eternal life), with the Brazilian word *ENCG*
(soul), Chilean *ANC-a,* soul, with the Esthonian word *HENG*
(soul) so similar to the Chinese word *HUN* 5244, in Foochow
HUNG (soul).

(186) *Egyptian ANKH (soul, spirit) Related to ANOK (I).*

America, Chile	Europe, Esthon.	Africa, Egypt	Asia, China
ANC-a (soul)	HENG (soul)	ANKH (soul)	HUNG (soul)

However it must not be forgotten that there are certain words which only particular regions such as the American Pacific coast and Polynesia or Malaysia have in common, at least so far as we can judge from the present state of knowledge. *PAPAYA* (a fruit) and *KUMARA* (potato) quoted by Imbelloni are part of this group, but they are exceptions, while as a rule we find more links to almost all of the words mentioned in the Tables 179, 180. Let us now apply the representative method and replace the words in Table 179, American and Polynesian, by other words of European and Asiatic or African type thus extending these word-chains.

(187) *Words of Table* 179 *Replaced by Those of Other Continents.*

EUROPE		ASIA OR AFRICA	
German	HEB-en (to lift)	Sanskrit	UP-a (up)
Greek	RHAP-to (to sew)	Hebrew	ARUB-a (lattice window)
"	HAG-ios (holy)	"	HAG (festival)
Iceland	YNG-vi (king)	Phoenic.	ANAK (prince)
Latin	COR-ium (skin)	Hebrew	(H)OR (skin)
Polish	KOGUT (cock)	Malay	KAKAT-ua (cockatoo)
German	MINN-e (love)	China	MAN (to covet)
English	MUT-ilate	Annam	MOT (destroyed)
Greek	PHEUG-o (to run)	Hebrew	PAK-a (to run)
Latin	UND-a (wave)	Samoyede	OND-oi (barge)
English	NIGH (near)	Hebrew	ANAH (to meet)
Hungar.	KIS (small)	Egyptian	KIT (small)

We could link with the Greek word *PHYG-e* (flight) the Latin word *FUG-a* (flight) and the Slavic word *BYEG* (flight) and thus obtain six different links of the chain instead of four. Likewise the apparently typical Peruvian name *INC-a* would lose its whole American Indian nature, if we linked it with the Greek word *ANAX, ANAK-tos* (sovereign, king, prince, lord, first) and were to translate the words of Homer's Iliad, "ANAX ANDRON AGAMEMNON", literally: 'Agamemnon, the *Inca* of the tribe'! For the Hellenes too called their leaders *Incas!* Castor and Pollux were worshipped in certain places as 'Great Gods' and in Hellas as *ANAK-es*, the *Incas!* In Argolis the festivals in memory of the deluge were celebrated in honor of *INACH-os*, while the Phrygians called their postdiluvian ancestor *ANNAC* or *HANNAC*, a name identical with *NOAH* of the Bible, Hebrew *NOAKH*. In Rome *ANC-us* Martius was the name of the fourth of the *Seven Kings* who ruled from 641 to 616.

In Egyptian as in Hebrew and other Semitic tongues, *HANAK* meant *to initiate*, so that *INC-a* may well have been the designation of an initiate, particularly of someone who had been initiated into the Sun Mysteries; for *UNG, UNG-i* in Egyptian meant a son or a messenger of the solar deity. In the Younger Edda, *YNG-ling* or *YNG-vi* were designations of kings, unmistakably assonant to *Inca*. Not only the Phoenicians used the word *ANAK* for a prince, but the Arabs still use *(H)ANAK* in the same sense, and the Zulu tribe of Natal calls its chieftain *INC-osi*. The old families who lived in Palestine long before the Hebrew conquest, in the vicinity of Hebron, and whose last remnants were known in historic times as living in the Philistine cities of Gaza, Gath, and *ASDOD* (now *Asdud* or *Isdud*) were designated in Hebrew as *ENAK-im*, sometimes translated as *giants*. Strangely enough, this Inca-name is linked here with the name of *Asdod*, Arabic Isdud, so evidently assonant to one of the earliest names of America, *Estoti-Land*, contained in medieval maps.

(188) *The Name INCA Found in All Continents.*

America, Peru	Europe, Greek	Africa, Zulu
INC-a	ANAK-es	INCO-si
(king)	(kings)	(chieftain)

Asia, Phoenicia	Maori
ANAK	ING-a
(king)	(chief)

Even the classical Aryan tongues of Old India and Iran contained the same name: Sanskrit *JANAK-a* (king), Avestan *ANH-us* (king, lord), and in Chinese still we have the word *HUANG* (sovereign). Does not Avestan *ANH-us* sound similar to the Roman king-name *ANC-us* and to the Scottish king-name *ANG-us*?

If we now turn to Table 180 which contains fifty words found on both shores of the Pacific, we understand that we can extend them in the same way as was possible with Imbelloni's list of twenty names. A few of these words are identical in both lists (179, 180); in fact we may say that there are at least sixty five different names contained in both. This, of course, is a very great part of the dictionary of any tongue, for out of one word-stem many different words can be formed, at least a tenfold number. In addition in all our languages words are interwoven with one another, one word leading directly to various other words. Consider such example as (Table 180) Mayan *AKH* (owner) and Korean *EK* (owner).

(189) *Extension of Mayan AKH (owner) and Korean EK (owner)*.

America, Maya	Europe, Greek	Anglo-Saxon
AKH (owner)	EKH-o (I own)	AG-en (own)

	German	Asia, Korea
	EIG-en	EK (owner)

It is fascinating to observe how deeply interwoven this name is with the individuality of a person. Long before the genius of the Roman law passed from common property of the tribe to single property of the individual, primitive man established the same connection in his language. He considered his property to be what he owned or what his *Ego* owned: hence the Anglo-Saxon word *AG-en* (own) is connected with and even

(190) *Greek EKH-o (I own) Is Connected With EG-o, the Individual.*

Anglo-Saxon	German	Greek
IC (I)	ICH, IK (I)	EG-o (I)
AG-en (own)	EIG-en (own)	EKH-o (I own)

derived from *IC* (*I*) just as the German word *EIG-en* (own)
is linked with *ICH* (I) and the Greek word *EKH-o* (I own)
with *EG-o* (*I*).

Another link of this kind can be found between the Latin
word *MAR-e* (sea) and *AMAR-us* (bitter), so that *MAR-e*
actually means *bitter water*. *MOOR, MARSH,* and *MORASS*
are its relatives. The Indo-European family of tongues shows
quite a variety of synonyms for *ocean* or *sea*.

(191)   *Various Synonyms for Sea Used in Indo-European*
Idioms.

English	German	Latin	French
SEA	SEE	MAR-e	MER

Slavic	Greek	Sanskrit
MOR-e	THAL-atta	SAV-a (water)

We cannot suggest that the Indo-European tongues used entirely different names for the ocean, hence their original home
must have been at a great distance from the open sea. The
Germanic vernaculars do of course use the words *SEA* or *SEE*
for *ocean,* but the Germans also use *MEER* (ocean, sea)
which they have in common with the Romans and Slavic peoples. The Greek word *THAL-atta* is quite a particular stem,
but the word *SEA,* German *SEE,* seems one of the oldest designations for "water" in general, later applied to an ocean or
sea. It is related to *SAP* and to *SWAMP,* and survived in
Europe in such old river names as *SAV-a,* German *SAU,*
SAW-e, in Yugoslavia, while *SAV-a* (water) in Sanskrit,
Gothic *SAIW-e* (lake, swamp), Hebrew *ZUV* (to flow), and
Babylonian *ZAB-u* (to flow) are its relatives.

(192)   *SEA an Old Name for Water Used*
in Both Hemispheres.

Europe, English	Asia, Sumer	China
SEA	SU	SHU, SEI
	(sprinkle)	(water, river)

Korea	Japan	Samoa
SU	SUI	SUA
(water)	(water)	(water)

In Japanese, Malayan, Javanese and Sunda *SAW-a* means

swamp. A variation occurs where the initial *S* is replaced by *TH* or *T,* as in the Sanskrit word *TOY-a* (water), Annam *THUY* (water), and in America Chepewayan *TU* (water). We note that *SEA* is actually a very old name for the ocean. Perhaps it was originally a designation for *sweet water,* later used for water in general and finally applied to sea and ocean. Other nations replaced this original name by an adjective meaning *bitter,* little by little extending the use of it to include brackish or sea water.

(193) *Latin MAR-e (sea) Meant Originally "Bitter Water".*

Latin	French	Hebrew
MAR-e (sea)	MER (sea)	YAM (sea)
AMAR-us (bitter)	AMER (bitter)	MOR-r (bitter)

We learn a new principle from this example. The appearance of different synonyms in various languages or the lack of certain terms and the use of others does not weigh against the relationship of these tongues. The Hebrew idiom neither includes the Latin word *MAR-e* (sea) nor such English words as *MOOR, MARSH* and *MORASS,* yet the word-stem *MOR* exists in Hebrew in the sense of *bitter,* and once the form is found to have been preserved, it is a link in proving relationship of words.

If we wish to extend Table 180 we may replace the words from the Asiatic shore of the Pacific by European words (except in a few cases).

(194) *Extension of Table 180 Replacing Asiatic by European Words.*

	AMERICA		EUROPE
Californ.	CAN-aco (dog)	Latin	CAN-is (dog)
"	GAT-uc (worm)	Russian	GAD (worm)
"	LA' LA' (goose)	English	Grey-LAG (wild goose)
"	TAIK (to see)	"	TOK-en (sign)
Comanche	TAK-e (speak)	Latin	DIC-o (to say)
Greenland	NEKK-e (meat)	Greek	NAK-e (skin)

"	IGN-ek (fire)	Latin	IGN-is (fire)
Mexico	TE-TEK-a (weave)	Latin	TEX-o (weave)
"	NAK-a (flesh)	Swiss	ANK-e (fat)
"	TSAQ-a (to close)	Latin	TAC-eo (keep silent)
"	NAM-eya (to rob)	German	NEHM-en (to take)
"	COTON-a (to cut)	Caucasus	KOTAN (plow-share)
"	COU-a (to buy)	German	KAUF (buying)
"	PAN-tli (flag)	German	PAN-ier (banner)
"	TELPOCH-tli (fool)	"	TOLPATSCH (fool)
"	SARP-on (eagle)	Latin	SARP-a (heron)
"	ALC-o (wild dog)	Iceland	YLG-r (she-wolf)
"	TOC-atl (spider)	O. Slavic	TUK-ati (weave)
Maya	AKH (owner)	Greek	EKH-o (I own)
"	SEG-u (word)	Iceland	SAG-a (a saga)
"	BALAM (magician)	Latin	FLAM-en (priest)
Antilles	TON-a (sun)	English	SUN
Cuba	COT-i (God)	M. Germ.	COT (God)
Peru	TAMP-o (house)	Latin	TEMP-lum (God's house)
"	KAUR-a (sheep)	Irish	CAOR-a (sheep)
"	MUN-ay (love)	German	MINN-e (love)
"	PAQU-iy (break)	Italian	S-PACC-o (break)
"	MANK-uni (to cut)	Latin	MANC-us (mutilated)
"	YUK (to tie)	English	YOK-e
"	SAT' (to fill)	Latin	SAT-ur (satiated)
"	SISS-i (ant)	Greek	SOS (insect)
"	VANAK (eagle)	Irish	FANG (vulture)
"	TAK-i (chant)	English	TAC-t (rhythm)
"	HUANAC-o (sheep)	Russian	YAGN-ia (lamb)
"	SIM-i (speech)	German	STIMM-e (voice)
"	TOK-i (axe)	"	STOCK (stick)

Chile	QUETAL (sun)		ADIL-ia (God's Sun)
"	DUG-u (speech)	Latin	DIC-o (say)
"	POK-o (toad)	German	POGG-e (toad)
"	KAR-a (town)	Breton	KER (town)
"	HVINC-a (chief)	English	KING
"	TU-e (earth)	Egypt	TA (earth)
Brazil	AR (to be born)	Latin	OR-ior (to be born)
"	NHEEM (to whisper)	"	NOM-en (name)
"	POROK-o (thunder)	Lithuan.	PERK-unas (thunder-god)
"	MEN-a (man)	English	MAN
Bororo	OROG-o (fallow deer)	Greek	ORYX, ORYKH- (antelope)
Guarani	TAK-oa (bamboo)	French	TIG-e (shaft)
Cayriri	DZU (water)	English	SEA
Chaques	KAMUR-u (cloud)	Slavic	KHMUR-a (cloud)

Here again we can observe that behind many words which today are used in a rather prosaic way there were once names of Gods, that language indeed represents 'faded mythology'. Take the Chilean word *QUETAL* (sun) and connect it with a Mexican divine being, *Quetzal-coatl*. In Mexican, *Quetzall-i* means a *feather* and *Coa-tl — a snake*. Hence the usual explanation: *Quetzal-Coatl — a feathered snake*. Snakes (as the imperial Chinese dragon) were an occult symbol, used in the Bible and in the Gospels in the sense of the 'uplifting of snakes' (compare page 99). However we ought not to confuse the symbol with its reality. *Quetzal* (feather) is a curtain or veil for *Quetal* (sun), for the |sun-god. *Quetzal-Coatl* means, word by word, *Sun-God,* and this meaning is contained in related words found in vernaculars of Northern Siberia. According to an old tradition Saint *Odilia* who is linked by a Christian legend with Mount Odilia in the Vosges was called the *Sun of God,* and the old name *ETHEL* in English does not only mean *noble* as in German *EDEL,* but also *the sun.*

In Babylonian mythology *EDL-u,* the same word as German *EDEL* and English *ETHEL,* was most frequently used as a name for Shamash or Bel, the sun-gods. Further, in Mexico itself *Quetzalcoatl* was originally worshipped under the older name *Quetzal-Ton,* and *Ton or Tona* means *sun.*

Quetzalcoatl was considered to be a hero of culture, a king of the nation, a high priest and founder of a religion. He was depicted as a human being of white complexion, large eyes, black hair and a strong beard. *HUE-mac* or *HUE-matzin* was the name of his companion, and his symbols were three: the sparrow, the flint and the snake. Some traditions identify the Mexican Quetzalcoatl with the Peruvian *Huitzilopochtli,* where *HUITZIL* means a 'humming bird'. The Aztecs considered Quetzalcoatl as a son of Huitzilopochtli. Müller in his book *Ur-Religionen Amerikas (America's Primitive Religions, p.* 77) points to the fact that the priests of Quetzalcoatl bore the name of their god. In British Columbia the corresponding deity worshipped by the natives was called *YETL,* the same name as the Chilean *QUETAL* (sun).

(195) *Chilean QUETAL (Sun) and its extension.*

America, Chile	Arawak	Europe, German
QUETAL	HADAL-i	ODIL-ia
(sun)	(sun)	(Sun of God)
Asia, Vogul	Ostyak	Philippines
KOTOL	KHOTUL	ADL-o
(sun)	(sun)	(sun)

This name also appears in Anglo-Saxon where the word *WADHOL,* Middle German *WADDEL* means the *moon,* while in Gaelic *EADHAL* meant *a fire, a brand.* This curious change in meaning has something to do with another strange fact: in German today the *sun* is considered to be feminine (*die* Sonne) and the *moon* masculine (*der* Mond), thus their places in the Cosmos are reversed. However in all sun-religions the sun was worshipped as the brother and the moon as the sister, by the Greek, Roman, Hebrew nations etc. The Arabs, the Tuaregh tribes of North Africa, several American Indian tribes and others call the moon the brother and the sun his sister.

(196) *Sun and Moon Are Brother and Sister, or Vice-Versa.*

	Latin	**Greek**	**Hebrew**	**Egyptian**
m.	SOL	HEL-ios	SHEMESH	OSIRIS
f.	LUN-a	SEL-ene	LEVAN-a	ISIS

	Arabic	**German**
m.	HILAL (moon)	der MOND (moon)
f.	SHAMS (sun)	die SONN-e (sun)

There are still many questions which should be touched upon here. *HUE-mac* and *HUE-matzin,* the name of Quetzal-coatl's companion, reminds us of the same prefix in the name of the highest Celtic divinity, again a sun-god, *HU-Aeddon.*

Another instance where the name of an element brings us back to a deity, is the *fire-name,* Greenlandic *IGN-ek,* Chuk-chee *EGN-ek,* Latin *IGN-is* (our *IGN-ite*), Lithuanian *UGN-is,* Slavic *OGON-y,* African (Fernando Po) *UGON-i* (fire). In Sanskrit it was still used as the name of the fire-god *AGN-i.* Agni was the god of the altar fire and as such the mediator between Gods and men.

(197) *The Former Name of the Fire-God AGNI Used for the Fire.*

America, Greenland IGN-ek (fire)	**Europe, Latin** IGN-is (fire)
Africa, Bantu UGON-i (fire)	**Asia, Sanskrit** AGN-i (fire-god)

Another very archaic name is that of the Mayan *BALAM* (a magician) which we connected with Latin *FLAM-en* (a priest of the old Roman mysteries) and Tibetan *LAM-a,* *BLAM-a* (a priest). In Chile we encounter *PULM-en* (a noble man), in Hellas *PALM-ys,* an old name for a king, and the Biblical name *BILEAM,* written in medieval translations

(198) *Old Bileam of the Bible an Ancient Term for a Magician.*

America, Maya BALAM (a magician)	**Europe, Latin** FLAM-en (a priest)	**Greek** PALM-ys (king)
Asia, Tibet BLAM-a, LAM-a (a priest)	**Hebrew** BILEAM (magician)	

BALAAM (as in the German legend of Baalam and Josaphat) can be added to this word-chain since it is the name of a magician and priest.

The connection between the meaning *priest* and *king* is quite natural, since in the earliest epochs both functions were united in the person of a priest-king. In many languages, as in Slavic and Lithuanian, the names for a king and a priest are built from the same stem.

Another interesting word-chain is connected with the Brazilian word *POROK-o* (thunder), Australian, *POOROK* (thunder) which we can link with the Lithuanian name of the thunder-god, *PERK-unas.* However it is not so much the connection of the simple word *POROK-o* (thunder) with the old god-name *Perkunas,* as the extraordinary extension of this word-stem in various languages which deserves our attention. First we observe certain sound-changes in American Indian names of the thunder and the thunder-god, *HURAC-an,* usually explained as *HU* (one) and *RAC-an* (leg). This is merely a fable convenue, for the name *HURAC-an,* source of our *HURRIC-ane* (introduced by Shakespeare in his *Tempest*) is one of the oldest words and is spread over the entire earth.

(199) *How the Name HURACAN Changes its Sounds in American Idioms.*

Quiché	Taino
HURAC-an	HURAC-ane, FURAC-ane
(god)	(thunder-god)

Terrava	Cariban	Brazilian
FRUC	UROG-an	POROK-o
(hurricane)	(hurricane)	(thunder)

In Europe we found the Lithuanian name *PERK-unas,* according to Procopius the highest deity of the Slavic tribes: O. Prussian *PERK-unis* (thunder), Latvian *PERK-uns* (thunder-god), Slavic *PIORUN* (thunder, thunder-god), O. Norse *FYORG-yn* (a god, connected with the thunder-god), Sanskrit *PARJ-anya* (god of thunder and rain).

(200) *PERKUNAS and FYORGYN Thunder-Gods in Europe and Asia.*

O. Norse	O. Prussian	Latvian
FYORG-yn	PERK-unis	PERK-uns
(a god)	(thunder-god)	(thunder-god)

Slavic	Asia, Sanskrit
PIORUN	PARJ-anya
(thunder-god)	(thunder-god)

The Semitic tongues possess this word-stem also: Babylonian *BARK-u*, Hebrew *BARAK*, Arabic and Phoenician *BARK*. In this linguistic group it means *lightning*. The Carthaginian general, Hamilcar, was known in history as *BARC-as* (the lightning), and the three relatives Hamilcar, Hannibal, and Hasdrubal were designated as Barcidae or 'the clan of the lightning', as if they were forerunners of a modern 'Blitzkrieg'.

We have already noted two different forms of this word-stem in America: *POROK-o* (thunder) and *FURAC-ane* (hurricane), starting once with a *P*, then with an *F*, (Ph). In the Semitic tongues we find an initial *B* instead of *P*, but it is still the same root. In Tibetan, the *B* and the meaning "thunder" is preserved in ABRUG, while in the Andaman island the *P* returns in o-*PARAK* (to thunder), as in Australian *POOROK* (thunder), *PARG-igi* (god), *PIRK-uir* (a demon), in Tasmanian *BURAK, BERIK* (demon). As the name of a deity, the thunder-god, we find in Togo, Africa, *BURUK-u,* and all over North Asia *BURKH-an, BURAKH-an, BURAG-an* in the Turk, Ural-Altaic, and Mongolian vernaculars.

(201) *The Name of the Hurricane in All Continents.*

America, Haiti	Europe, Lithuan.	Africa, Togo
FURAC-ane	PERK-unas	BURUK-u
(thunder-god)	(thunder-god)	(a god)

Asia, Yakut	Australia
BURKH-an (thunder-god)	PARG-igi (god)

When Christianity spread over Europe the Church in the earlier ages was very tolerant and, wishing to spare the feelings of the pagans in the North, ordered the bishops and priests not to change the old religious customs too suddenly. Thus the old and the new faith lived for a while side by side peacefully, just as we see it today in many places of South America. Later however the heathen divinities were transformed into demons and devils by the priests. Thus *Perkunas* from a god of the thunderbolt similar to Jupiter, turned into the devil.

(202) *Huracan, Furacane, Perkun Turn into Devils and Demons.*

Finnish	Esthonian	Lappish
PERK-ele (devil)	PERG-el (devil)	BERG-alak (devil)

Russian	Latin
BURYA (hurricane)	FURIA (fury)

When the Spanish conquerors mingled with the American Indians, such words as *canoe* were borrowed from the Indian languages and spread over Europe. Thus also *HURACAN* (thunderstorm) became the Spanish form, *HURRICANE* the English, and *OURAGAN* the French.

(203) *Hurricane (Tempest) in Many European Idioms.*

Spanish	English	German
HURACAN (tempest)	HURRICANE	ORKAN (tempest)

French	Russian
OURAGAN (tempest)	URAGAN (tempest)

Behind these words stand other names, figures of mythology, such as Basque *ORK-eguna* (day of the thunder-god, Thursday, Thor's day), in the Groeden valley (Austrian Alps) *ORC-o*, the giant of hurricanes, and Latin *ORC-us* (hell). We find here the very source of German *ORK-an* (tempest), and its connection with Old Greek *ORG-ê* (fury) and *ORGia* (orgy). Fundamentally speaking, what is wrath and anger, fury and orgy?

(204) *German ORKAN* (hurricane) and Greek *ORGY.*

Basque	German	Austria, Groeden
ORK-eguna	ORK-an	ORK-o
(Thursday)	(tempest)	(giant of tempests)

Latin	Greek
ORC-us (hell)	ORG-eia (orgy)

It is the inner hurricane of the soul, a tempestuous out-
break of passion and greed. In the Mysteries of the North the
neophyte was led from observation of the outer tempest to
the experience of the divine, while in the Mysteries of the
South the pupil had to dive into his own soul, experience the
inner hurricane, the orgy, and by penetrating beyond that
region of fury, meet the godhead within his heart.

To a superficial observer it may appear that the French
OURAGAN (tempest) is a word borrowed from the American Indians, just as *hurricane* and German *Orkan* (thunderstorm), yet side by side with it stands French *ORAG-e* ,an-
other word for the tempest. This word antedates the rediscovery of America by Columbus, and still older is the name
of the Alpine thunder-giant *ORKO,* of the Basque thunder-
god *ORK-* (in *ORK-eguna,* Thor's day) and the Latin *ORC-
us* (hell). Even Huracan himself is not a new-comer in the
Old World. The Brocken Mountain Country in Central Germany which from time immemorial was considered the gathering place for the Witches' Sabbath, the Walpurgis Night in
Faust, in the Roman epoch was called *HERCYN-ia Silva,*

(205) *HURACAN in Old Europe and Ancient Asia.*

America	Europe, Old Germany	Asia, Persia
HURACAN	HERCYN-ia Silva	HYRCAN-ian Sea
(thunder-god)	(Huracan's Forest)	(Huracan's Sea, Caspian)

Huracan's Forest. *HYRCAN-ia* in the Northern part of Persia
was a country and likely the seat of an old religious mystery
centre on the shores of the Caspian Sea, since the old name
Caspi means *magic* in Babylonian, Hebrew and other Semitic
idioms. A last trace of the path of migration followed by the
peoples who carried this old god-name from continent to

(206) *Huracan's Name in Different Continents.*

America, Quiché	Europe, Germany
HURACAN (thunder-god)	HERCYN-ia Silva
	(Mt. Brocken, Harz)

Caucasus	Asia, Persia
HYRCAN-ian (dialect)	HYRCAN-ia (country)

continent is found in the Caucasus Mountains where one of the Caucasian dialects is still called *HYRCAN-ian*.

We set out to compare words which could be found on both shores of the Pacific, and we discoverd quite a number of them. However, instead of proving the usual theory that America was peopled from across the Behring Strait, from northeastern Siberia, or — according to other scholars — from Polynesia and the Malayan Archipelago, we came into close contact with mythology and the mythological age of humanity. *Gods* — not merely prehistoric periods — suddenly faced us. Today we describe the most dramatic events in Nature, thunder, lightning, tempest, snow and hail in a very unconsciously vague manner. We say, *it* thunders, *it* is lightning, raining, snowing, hailing, storming. Thus we admit that the elements are battling when *it* is thundering, but this was different in the Greek, Latin and Teutonic Epochs, and is still different today among such peoples as the Lithuanians or Andamanese, where the thunder-god is called *PURUG-a* (*PULUG-a*).

(207) *The Wrath of Gods Manifests in Thunder-Storms.*

Latin	Lithuanian	Asia, Andamanese
Jupiter tonat	Perkunas griauya	Pulug-a-la garawo-ke
(Jupiter is thundering)	(Perkun is thundering)	(Puruga is thundering)

Jupiter throws the thunder-bolts at the unfortunate mortals whom he wishes to destroy, according to the Hellenic conception. In India it is the Parjanyas who cause the rain, in Greece it is Zeus, in Rome Jupiter, among the Lithu-Slavic tribes Perkun or Piorun, in Scandinavian mythology Thor (or German *DONNER,* thunder) who threw his hammer *MYOELN-ir,* the "lightning". In modern Russian the lightning carries its old mythological name *MOLN-iya,* 'the crunching one'.

The 'heart of the heaven', Huracan, came down to earth

(208) *Mythological and Modern Names of the Lightning.*

Scandinavian	Russian
MYOELN-ir (Thor's hammer)	MOLN-iya (lightning)

and turned into a *hurricane,* Typhon, the hellish demon, became a *typhoon* and is known in Chinese as *Tai-Fung* (big wind). *Taranis,* the Celtic storm-god, was changed into Spanish *Trueno* (thunder), and *Turomi,* the Great Spirit of the Iroquois tribe, was transformed into the German *Sturm* (tempest), just as *Torom* or *Torm,* the god of the Ostyak and Vogul tribes, appears in modern English as *Storm.*

It is true that there are a few words which are the common property of tribes who lived on both shores of the Pacific or in Polynesia and in America and which are not found elsewhere. However these are very few in number, while the great preponderance of words are the common property of all peoples in all Continents. They are not products of recent creations, but witnesses of secret connections between the nations of the world, uniting them all. Thus we face the irrefutable evidence of language. For the first time the surviving witnesses of remote epochs of human history speak to us clearly revealing old secrets, old mysteries, old connections establishing the primal unity, the original oneness of the peoples of this world.

CHAPTER FOURTEEN

A LINGUISTIC BRIDGE IN THE ATLANTIC

THERE IS a strange fact which can be used as a strong objection to any theory built upon the foundation that the American Continent was peopled from the West, from Polynesia or from the southern coasts of Asia. The Galapagos Islands were found unpeopled at the time of Columbus' rediscovery of America. For several centuries these islands of the Pacific had been uninhabited. On the other hand we find in Rapanui, the Easter Island, those big stone-heads with peculiar features, long noses and ears, emerging from the soil as strange-looking representatives of some bygone stone-epoch. They must have been carved and erected many millennia ago, for the style of this kind of sculptures dates from a remote antiquity.

If there were any migrations from Asia to the American West Coast: Chile, Peru, California, then the words which we find in Araucan, Quichua and some of the more or less extinguished Indian dialects of California (Esselen, Yokuts, Yaudauchi, Klamath, Modoc etc.) ought to resemble Japanese, Chinese, Polynesian, Australian, Chukchee, Kamchatkan terms and so on. It is true that there are some particularly close linguistic relationships between Alaskan and other northwestern American idioms and those of northeastern Asia, such as Greenland *IGN-ek* (fire) and Chukchee *EGN-ek* (fire). On the other hand however, farther south the situation is completely reversed. We had good reason to call Araucan (Chile), Quichua (Peru), Mayan and Mexican (Central America) the *classical tongues* of America. As a matter of fact, we find in them words which sound similar to Latin, Sanskrit, Hebrew, Egyptian or Babylonian, and thus we can conclude that there must be secret connections between all these nations and tongues as a result of some community life in a remote past, and in distant places. The same applies to the shores of the Atlantic also, though — perhaps partly because the European and Western Asiatic tongues are more familiar to us — we find more and more intimate relations between the languages of these countries.

One question however is still to be answered: Are the islands of the Atlantic or Pacific not only remnants of former land-connections between the adjacent Continents, but also a kind of linguistic land-bridges between them? What is the nature of the languages spoken on those islands? Tenerife, the largest of the Canary Islands in the Atlantic, offers a good opportunity for such an investigation. Until the Fifteenth Century, before the Spaniards conquered these islands, the people called the *Guanche* lived in Chinerfe (Tenerife). They had their own civilisation which Boccaccio described in the Fourteenth Century after he had visited their homeland. According to the French anthropologist *Topinard,* the Guanche were handsome people, tall, blond and blue-eyed, valiant warriors, far advanced in neolithic culture. They had pyramids and obelisks, mummified the bodies of the dead, had a strange religion with vestals, temple-dances, and old rituals and customs.

The Canary Islands extend toward the West similar to the Azores. The last vestiges of the Guanche language, some hundred words in all, have been preserved by some British and Spanish scholars. They show a certain connection with the North African tongues, Berber, Hamitic and Old Egyptian. Schuchardt-Graz, Nikolai Marr and other linguists have proven this side of their relationship, and also their affinity with the Basque tongue. The Basque vocabulary is close to the Hamito-Semitic family of tongues, while its grammar (syntax) is related with the American Indian dialects. This fact is characteristic not only of Basque but of other related idioms and may be illustrated by one example, the title *NEG-us* of Abyssinia. We find its relatives in Basque *NAG-*

ushi (prince), Hebrew *NOG-esh* (ruler) and Hindoo books mention *Deva NAH-ushi* as a ruler of the universal empire of the Atlanteans extending beyond the pillars of Hercules and deep into the Mediterranean basin, to Hellas in the North, and the Egyptian border in the South.

(209) *Basque NAG-ushi (Prince) a Link With Africa and Asia.*

Atlantis	Europe, Basque	Africa, Abyssinia
NAH-ushi	NAG-ushi	NEG-us
(emperor)	(prince)	(emperor)

Asia, Hebrew	Mongolian
NOG-esh	NOY-on
(ruler)	(chief)

This old title is a short form of *INC-a,* Greek *ANAK-s* (ruler, prince), the post-diluvian name *INACH-os,* the *NOAH* of the Bible. It shows the deep connection of the Hybernian centre of culture with other parts of the world. What however is of a far greater interest to us, is to know whether Guanche actually connects the East and West, the Old with the New World, and what we can learn from the few remnants which are left of the Guanche civilisation after the Spanish Conquerors extinguished it as they partly exterminated old American Indian vestiges of culture. Let us examine a few important Guanche words.

(210) *A Small Guanche Vocabulary.*

JARC-o	(mummy)	HAR-i	(people)
ALI-o	(sun)	MAGUAD-a	(maid, vestal)
AMEN	(sun-god)	GUAN-oth	(people)
CORON	(lord, God)	TEYD-e	(peak)
MENC-ey	(lord)	TCHAP-a	(peak, ridge)
HUERAH-an	(God)	CANCH-a	(dog)
HU	(greatness)	PET-ut	(father)
GUAN	(son)	GUANAC	(people)
BEN	(son)	AFAR-o	(grain)
MAN-ya	(landing place)	CEL	(moon)
ATAM-an	(sky)	AN-a	(sheep)
EC	(I, Ego)	ADAR-a	(mountain)
T	(thou)	AR-a	(goat)
GUIRR-e	(vulture)	AR	(behold)
		AR-an	(farm)

What a strange collection! It appears as if several classical

nations of antiquity had met on that island of Chinerfe shortly
after the Confusion of Tongues: Phoenicians, Greeks, Romans, Hebrews, Hindus and others, and each had left the
Guanche tribe a linguistic heritage which still characterizes
that ancient idiom. *Helios* and *Selene, Ammon* and *Huracan,
Kronos* and *Manitoo,* all are represented in the solemn names
used in that region.

Who is that sun-being *ALI-o* if not the Greek *HELI-os,* in
Homer *AELI-os* (the sun-god), Hebrew *EL, AEL* (god), in
Assyrian *IL-u* (god), and in Arabic *ALL-ah* (god). In Sumer
the gods were called *IL-an,* in Babylonian *IL-ani,* and in Old
America, in Peruvian, the connection with this word-group
is established by *IL'-a* (splendent, shining). In the Hybernian region the Breton dialect contains *AEL, EAL, EL* for
angel, and far away in the Pacific, in Samoan and in Hawaiian,
ALI-i means *chief.*

(211) *The Sun-God HELI-os, AELI-os on Tenerife Island.*

America, Peru	Tenerife	Europe, Breton
IL'-a (splendent)	ALI-o (sun)	AEL (angel)

Greek	Asia, Hebrew	Samoa
HEL-ios (sun-god)	EL, AEL (god)	ALL-i (chief)

Side by side with the same name of the sun we find in
Guanche *CEL (SEL)* for moon, quite assonant to Greek
SEL-ênê (moon). As the Greek word *HEL-ios* (sun) alter-
nates with the Latin word *SOL* (sun), so does *Selene* shift
to *Helene,* a very frequent interchange of consonants in language. Sun and Moon have identical names in Guanche and
classical Greek. This certainly is not the result of mere accident.

(212) *Helios and Selene, Sun-God and Moon-Goddess in
Tenerife.*

Greek	Guanche
HEL-ios, AELI-os (sun-god)	ALI-o (sun)
SEL-ene (moon-goddess)	CEL (SEL) (moon)

When we keep in mind the phonetic interchange between
S, H, K, G (or Y) we discover this old word-stem *SEL, HEL*
for the moon spread over all the earth. In some tongues an-

other synonym has replaced *Selene* as an appellation of the moon, but *SOL* in Munda, or *ZAL* in Sumerian still preserve the original meaning *splendor*. Thus we can link the following words into a chain.

(213) *Guanche CEL (SEL) and Other Related Moon-Names.*

America, Peru	Guanche	Europe, Basque
KILL-a	CEL	HILL
(moon)	(moon)	(moon)

	Africa, Bantu	Asia, Arabic
	EYEL-i	HIL-al
	(moon)	(moon)

Let us keep in mind that in most tongues the moon is feminine, while the sun is masculine. Thus in the Quichua dialect of Peru the moon is worshipped as *Mama Killa* (mother moon) and is represented as the sister and wife of the sun.

In early times the Atlantic Ocean was called *Mare Cronium,* the Cronus Sea, of the Greek god Cronus who dethroned his father Uranus (the heaven) and was dethroned by his own son Zeus. According to old legends the lost continent supposed to be located in the centre of the Atlantic was ruled by Cronus, so that the whole region had a sort of Cronian aura. Now *CORON, ACORON* in the Guanche vernacular was the name used for *the Lord,* for *God,* and was connected with god-names. As we have noted, the priests and priest-kings in early American religions took the names of their divinities, (compare page 180) and thus we realize why the vice-kings of Cuzco in Peru had the title *KARAN.* They were initiates or high-priests of Cronus or Saturn, the deity of very ancient religions.

(214) *CORAN, ACORAN in Guanche Was the God Cronus of Hellas.*

America, Aymara	Guanche	Europe, Greek
KARAN	CORON	KARAN-os
(vice-king)	(lord)	(prince)

	Albanian	Asia, Hebrew
	KREN	KERAN-im
	(prince)	(princes)

In Manchu, the royal family is called *KURUN*. This name is related to the royal *CROWN*, Latin *CORON-a*, French *COURONN-e*. Many other similar evidences of parallelism confirm these relations between the names of priests and kings, e.g. Hebrew *KOHEN* (priest), Crimean *CAGAN-us* (prince, king) or in Turkish and many other Asiatic tongues, *KHAN* (king, ruler).

While the Guanche names *CORON, ALIO,* and *CEL,* appear as remnants of the Greek Olympus, of *Cronus, Helios,* and *Selene,* or of the mysteries of Saturn, the Sun, and the Moon, another name of a planet and the divinity who dwells on that planet, Guanche *AMEN,* points to the countries and cults of the classical Orient. *Amen* is the sun, and *AMEN Acoran* — the sun-god. It is not difficult to recognize in this holy name the appellation of the Egyptian sun-god *AMEN* (*AMOUN*) or *Ammon,* Sumerian *AMN-a,* Hebrew *HAM-MON* (sun-pillars upon the altar of Astarte). Again in Sumer *UMUN* meant *lord, king* and at the same time was the invocation of the sun-god *Bel.* In Babylonian cuneiform tablets we encounter the name *Abd-i-Himunu* (servant = priest of Ammon). According to Tavera-Acosta, *Venezuela Pre-Coloniana* (Pre-Columbian Venezuela, p. 45) *CAMUN-atzi* meant light among the Yabitero Indians.

(215) *Guanche AMEN (Sun) and the Egyptian Sun-God AMMON.*

America, Venezuela	Guanche	Africa, Egypt	Asia, Sumer
CAMUN-atzi	AMEN acoran	AMEN=AMMON	AMN-a
(light)	(sun-god)	(sun-god)	(sun-god)

In Egypt a deep mystery stands behind the name *AMEN*; *Hamon* means *eight,* Coptic *Shemûn,* Phoenician *Eshmûn* (the Eighth), and Hemenû designated the totality of the primeval eight gods of *Hermopolis,* of the seven Cabiri and *Eshmûn,* their eighth, their leader. This reminds us of the seven Elohim of the Bible, the Gospels, who as a totality were called *Pleroma* (the fullness). The Elohim, as we know from Genesis, were the gods of creation. Here again we find a strange parallelism in California (Müller, *Ur-Religionen Americas,* pp. 106, 134, 178): the Great Spirit, the Creator is adored there as *CUMON-go,* while the Caribans call him *GUAMOAN* or *HUAMOAN ocan.* In Peru the name *Ammon* is lacking except for one word: *HUAMAN* (falcon). Is there any connection between *HUAMAN and HAMON, AMEN?*

(216) *The Falcon — an Old Symbol of the Sun-God.*

America, Cariban	Africa, Egypt
HUAMOAN ocan (Great Spirit)	AMEN (sun-god)
Peru	**Egypt**
HUAMAN (falcon)	HEMEN (a hawk-god)

Thus in Old Egypt not only was the sun represented by its old symbol the phoenix bird (eagle, falcon, hawk), as Horus wore the head of a falcon as his symbol, but the symbol itself was designated with the same name as in Peru, *Huaman* (falcon). This is by no means an isolated coincidence, but a parallelism which opens an insight into the work-shop of language and the principles of its creation.

(217) *Sun Gods and Their Symbolic Birds (Eagle, Falcon).*

Egypt	AMEN	Peru	HUAMAN	(falcon)
"	SOKAR-is	Arabic	SAKR	(falcon)
"	HOR-us	German	AAR	(eagle)
"	SERAPH-is	Latin	SARP-a	(heron)
Hebrew	SERAPH-im	Maya	SARP-on	(eagle)
Chile	QUETAL	Mexico	QUETZAL	(Trogon)
Egypt	(H)ANUK-et	Arabic	(H)ANK-a	(phoenix)

We can add the sun-god *Quetzal-coatl* to Chilean *QUETAL* (sun), and the Peruvian *ANK-a* (eagle) to Egyptian *(H)AN-*

(218) *The Eagle or Falcon, a Sun-Symbol in Both Hemispheres.*

America, Peru	Europe, Lithuanian
ANK-a (eagle)	WANAG-as (falcon)
Africa, Egypt	**Asia, China**
BON-u (phoenix)	HUANG (phoenix)

UK-et (a hawk-headed goddess, doubtless a sun-being) and to Arabic *(H)ANK-a* (griffon, phoenix), a mythological bird,

as well as Chinese *HUANG* (the female phoenix), even
Lithuanian *WANAG-as* (falcon) and Irish *FAING, FANG*
(vulture).

The Egyptian word *BON-u* does not sound very like phoenix, but it is probably the same word, since *BEN-U* also means
palm-tree, called *Phoenix* in Greek. Let us now go back to
the Guanche Olympus. We find there two well-known, even
familiar American deities: *Huracan* and *Manitoo. Manitoo*
of course is not difficult to understand: it is the Great Spirit,
the *MIND*, or *MENT-ality*, whose annoucements and oracles
were called in Sanskrit *MANT-ram*, visions, cosmic thoughts,
MANIT-oos themselves.

(219) *Guanche MENC-ey (God) and American MANIT-oo.*

America, Algonquin	Europe, Engl.	Guanche
MANIT-oo	MIND, MENT-al	MENC-ey
(Great Spirit)		(God)

	Asia, Arabic	Sanskrit
	MANAT (god of Destiny)	MANAS (spirit)

Another divinity which we meet in Tenerife is *HUERAH-an*
(god). To recognize in this slightly changed word the name
of *Huracan* is not too difficult either. After all, Huracan was
first considered to be a god corresponding to Jupiter or Zeus,
the father of Gods and men, thus a beneficent being. He could
well be regarded as the divine ruler of the cosmos, at a certain
epoch, and thus the mysterious chain connecting the Old with
the New World can be extended further.

(220) *Guanche HUERAHAN (god) and Mayan HURACAN.*

American, Quiché	Guanche
HURAC-an (heart of heaven)	HUERAHAN (god)

Europe, Germany	Asia, Persia
HERCYN-ia Silva (Mt. Huracan)	HYRCAN-ia (Huracan's land)

We already have mentioned the Hyrcanian dialect spoken
in the Caucasus mountains by a tribe which probably migrated there either on the way East, to Central Asia, or West,
to Europe. Among the words contained in Table 210 we find

two which are connected at least with the cult of Gods: *hari maguada* (a vestal? a priestess?) and *Jarco* (a mummy). We can add yet a third: *Ahu*, a word of reverence, used particularly in early epochs as a prefix of god-names. *Huerahan* (Huracan) in Guanche was also called *Ahu-Huerahan* (revered or venerable Huracan!).

Hari-Maguada (vestal, priestess) is a compound word which sounds as if it were Anglo-Saxon or Old-German: *HAR-i* (people, army), Modern German *HEER* (army, crowd), Greek *KOUR-os* (young man), Sumerian *GUR-ush* (man), Munda *HOR-o* (man) and even Peruvian *KAR-i* (man).

(221) *Guanche HAR-i (People) and Old German HAR-i (People).*

America, Peru CAR-i (man)	Guanche HAR-i (people)	Europe, O. German HAR-i (people, army)
Asia, Munda HOR-o (man)		Sumerian AR-i (Amorite)

Maguada sounds even more familiar, for it is our *MAID*, *MAIDEN,* Anglo-Saxon *MAEGEDH* (virgin), Gothic *MAGATH-s,* O. German *MAGAD* (maid). Thus the meaning of *Hari-Maguada* is *folk-maiden* or *vestal*. It is related to Hebrew *MEGED* (fruit, offspring), and to many words in other tongues.

(222) *Guanche MAGUADA (Maid) and Anglo-Saxon MAEGEDH (maid).*

America, Peru MACT-a (young man)	Guanche MAGUAD-a (maid)	Europe, Gothic MAGATH-s (maiden)
O. German MAGAD (maid)		Asia, Hebrew MEGED (fruit)

We realize that this term of a vestal used in Chinerfe could as well be linked with American as with Old World tongues, in spite of its close resemblance to Teutonic words. The same applies even in a higher sense to *JARC-o* (mummy). We mentioned that the Guanche people had pyramids and obelisks. They also employed strange pointed stones, so similar to Celtic or Druidic Menhirs (long stones), as a decoration in places devoted to the memory of their dead.

We found the sun-god *Amen* in Tenerife and in Egypt. We noted that pyramids and obelisks were known and were erected in both countries. Now we find the practice of mummification on the lonely island of the Atlantic and in the land of the Nile. To conclude from this however that the Guanche were docile pupils of the old Egyptians and had taken from them the institution of mummifying their dead, would be a grave mistake. First of all, the technique of handling the mummies was different in these two regions. Mummies to such people as the Guanche meant simply dried flesh. Nations of old who lived in the vicinity of the Mediterranean Sea used different ways of disposing of the corpses of their dead: they buried or cremated them, they mummified them or dried them in the air.

This drying of corpses was practiced in those parts of the earth up to the Middle Ages and even later, e.g. in Italy. When crossing the Appenine Peninsula, we may enter some cathedral in a city of the south, and be guided by a young monk to certain large rooms where the bodies of very famous people well known in history, perhaps from Dante's *Divine Comedy*, are hanging on the walls entirely dessicated, clad in their ancient, costly and beautiful costumes, pale and faded, shrunk to the stature of dwarfs. Dukes and duchesses, counts and princesses, bishops and governors, generals and scholars, this is a whole exhibit of a once important, yet now dusty and dried-out world. Once in a while the monk in his brown cowl might approach one of the members of that large family of past grandeur, tenderly touch the dry body with the tip of his finger, gaze at him or her with a kind of melancholy stare, and say with amazement: *Ben conservati!* (Well preserved!), as if he had expected them to have fallen to pieces a long time ago. It was in this manner that the bodies of dead were dried in the air and thus preserved for centuries. A procedure similar to the Guanche treatment of corpses was applied in ancient America, all derived doubtless from a common source.

"These Guanche mummies," says Lewis Spence in *The Problem of Atlantis* p. 172, "many of which have been discovered in the Baranco de Fataga in Grand Canary, bear a close resemblance to both those of Egypt and America. They usually have a profusion of red hair, and are buried or placed on the left side. The body is often in an advanced state of dessication, wrapped in goatskin, with the hands crossed over the breast in the manner of some of the Peruvian mummies. They are generally discovered in caverns in the rock-face, in a crouching or sitting position, like that of the mummies of Mexico or Peru and the earlier interments in Egypt, rather than stretched out in the later Egyptian manner. That the method was fundamentally the same in origin as obtained both in Egypt and America no careful observer can doubt."

(223) *Guanche JARC-o (Mummy) and Its Extension.*

America, Peru	Guanche	Europe, Basque
CHARK-i	JARC-o	SARRASQU-ia
(dried flesh)	(mummy)	(corpse)
Greek	**Greek**	**Assyrian**
SARK- (flesh)	TARIKH-os (mummy)	SHARK-u (bloody)

The Guanche not only used methods of mummification similar to those of the Peruvians, but the same word for the mummy, and strangely enough this word is identical with that used in Greece in post-Homeric times, and is even the same which modern West-European peoples still apply for the *Sarco-phagus* and the *coffin* in general.

(224) *Greek SARKO-PHAGOS (the Mummy-Eater) in Both Hemispheres.*

America, Peru	Guanche	English
CHARQU-i	JARC-o	JERK-ed
(dry flesh)	(mummy)	beef
O. French	**Breton**	**German**
SARC-ou (coffin)	SERCH (coffin)	SARG (coffin)

German *SARG* and French *SARC-ou* (Twelfth Century)

are usually derived from Latin *SARCO-phagus* and considered an abbreviation of it. Yet the existence of *JARC-o* (mummy) on Tenerife, long before Columbus landed in the Antilles, and also found in Basque and in Breton in its brief form, points rather to ancient relations between Old Europe and America in the dark ages of unrecorded history.

The Egyptians do not possess the same word for mummy, although they used a name for the *bandages* which they wrapped around the bodies that is related to the Peruvian term. There is no doubt that the Egyptian, Gaunche and American method of mummification developed from the same original source, but later their technique changed and the common names for mummy used by the Peruvians and Guanche prove closer connections between these nations than with Egypt. It seems that obelisk-like stones were used in Old Peru also as a sort of tomb-stones. For in his *Origen de los Indios* (Origin of the Indians, Valencia 1607, p. 96) Gregorio *Garcia* writes: "All over the sierra of Peru there are fields full of graves in the form of little towers which now are filled with corpses and bodies of those Gentiles which on account of the homogeneous temperature and the thin air are dry and hard."

In Guanche we find a prefix *Akh, Ahu* before god-names such as *Ahu-Huerahan* (venerable Huracan), or *Ah-Amen* (revered Ammon). In Celtic a similar prefix was used in connection with the name of the highest god *HU-Aeddon,* assonant to the Hebrew *Adon-ai.* The same prefix as in Guanche exists in the Mayan vernaculars of Central America *AH* (high), related with Mexican *ACH-to* (the first): *OSH* or *AH* in Mayan designates *the highest rank,* as *AH-kin* (the high-priest of the sun), or *AH*-May, a true Mayan, used for the highest priest of the Mayan hierarchy. In Quiché *AKH, AH* means a *lord,* so strangely similar to the Turkish *Agha,* and the Greek *AGA-* in *Aga-Memnon* (alongside the simple name Memnon). We may even link with this group the names of the three divine beings of the Cabiri Mysteries, *Axio-Keres, Axio-Kersos,* and *Axio Kersa,* for AX-ios in Greek means *highly estimated,* as *ACH-ten* in German and probably our word *AWE.* In Assyrian too, *AKH* meant *highest.*

(225) *The Guanche Prefixes AHU or HU Mean AWE.*

America, Maya AH, AX (high)	Guanche AKH, AH, HU (high)	Europe, Celtic Hu-Aeddon (highest)
Greek AX-ios (reverent)		Asia, Assyrian AKH, AH (highest)

Most significant are the personal pronouns of the first two persons, *I* and *Thou,* in Guanche *EC* and *T. T* reminds us of the Egypto-Semitic nations (Hebrews, Phoenicians etc.) and their consonantic writing: it is identical with *Thou,* Latin *TU,* and Slavic *TY* (thou). Guanche *EC* (*I*) can unmistakably be linked with Latin *EG-o* and Greek *EG-ô* (I).

(226) *EC and T* (*I and Thou*) *in Guanche and Other Tongues.*

Guanche EC (I) T (thou)	Anglo-Saxon IC (I) THU (thou)	Latin EG-o TU	Greek EG-ô SY
Slavic YA TY		Asia, Sanskrit AH-am (I) TVA-m (thou)	

Such terms as the personal pronouns *I* and *Thou* are usually not transmitted from nation to nation alone. They doubtless are part of the original stock of words of each tongue. The Guanche terms are related with most Indo-European words for I and Thou, yet we can extend this relationship to Egypt and Asia, and thus point to a word-chain which certainly belongs to the oldest section of human speech and to a very remote antiquity.

There is however a still more fascinating word-chain particularly important for the problem of how the American Continent had been peopled. We have noted how *CAN-oe,* which the American Indians, the Caribans, have in common with several highly civilized peoples of the Old World, is to be found in the Egyptian *Book of the Dead.* Now we can add to this another enigmatic vestige, the name of a *landing-place, a harbor;* Guanche, *MAN-ya.*

(227) *Guanche MAN-ya (Landing-Place) in Different Continents.*

Guanche MAN-ya (landing-place)	Africa, Egypt MAN-yut (harbor)	Asia, Arabic MIN-at (harbor)

Japanese MIN-ato (harbor)	Syriac MAN-a (to reach the goal)

MAN-se in Guanche means *shore,* and *MIN-i,* in Egyptian, *to land.* It is probable that the Japanese *MINA-to* (harbor) is related with the Arabic *MIN-at* and the Egyptian *MAN-yut* or *MIN-yut* (landing-place). This word-stem can serve as an evidence of prehistoric sea-traffic between Europe, Western Asia and Egypt and, on the other hand, the Far East and that part of the West which is close to Africa. We shall find other words linking the Old World's navigation with the American Continent.

Among the other words mentioned in Table 210 there is *GUAN* (son) related to *GUANOTH* (people) and *GUA-NAC* (nation). All three are familiar to us, for they all stem from the root of Latin *GEN-us* (kind, generation), *GENT-es* (peoples) preserved in *GENT-le* and *GENT-iles,* and in Sanskrit *JANAK-a* (man, prince), related to Hawaiian and Polynesian *KANAK-a* (man), a word-stem extending over the whole earth. What is of particular interest is the appearance of the word *GON-e* (child) in French slang in Lyons and its vicinity. Side by side with *GUAN* (son), Guanche contains *BEN* (son).

(228) *Guanche BEN (Son) in Semitic Tongues.*

Guanche BEN (son)	Europe, Polish PAN (man)	Asia, Hebrew BEN (son)

Moabite BEN (son)	America, Calif. PAN-a (son)

Both *BEN* and *GUAN* (son) can be connected in Guanche with the name of the sun-god *Ammon,* and *BEN-Amana* as well as *GUAN-Amana* mean a *wizard,* a *medicine-man,* an *initiate.* The more we investigate the past, the more keys we find to the present. Why was the Chinese Emperor desig-

nated as the *Son of Heaven*? Why does the Japanese Emperor
bear the title *Son of the Sun*? Today such titles do not mean
anything to us: they are the dry leaves of faded and dusty
laurels. However, in ancient times a ruler was entrusted with
the spiritual guidance of his nation; he was a priest-king, an
initiate to whom the Sun-Mysteries had been revealed.

The connections between the Guanche and other nations
become increasingly clear if we point out two facts. First let
us examine a few animal-names (Table 210): *ANAH*
(sheep), *ARA* (goat) and *GUIRR-e* (vulture). Second, a
very characteristic name: *AR-an* (farm). *AR-a* (goat) is by
no means unfamiliar to us. Those interested in the stars know
the zodiac-sign *AR-ies* (ram), a constellation between Pisces
and Taurus . . .

(229) *Guanche AR-a (Goat) and Its Relationship.*

America, Peru	Guanche	Europe, Basque
UR-ku (male animal)	AR-a (goat)	AR-i (wether)

Latin	Africa, Ethiopic
AR-ies (ram)	AR-us (wild animal)

In Asia, we could add the Arabic word *AR-wi* (ibex).
Even if we were certain that the Peruvian word *URK-u* does
not correspond with the Greek name *ORYX* (antelope) instead of the Greek *AR-en* (wether), Guanche *AR-a* is in its
outer form so close to the Basque *AR-i* (wether) and the
other Eastern links of this chain that we would rather look
East than West for its relations. This applies equally to *ANAH*
(sheep), though the Peruvian relative *HUANAC-o, GUAN-
AC-o* (sheep-like animal) is somewhat phonetically closer to
the Guanche form.

(230) *Guanche ANAH (Sheep) and Its Relations.*

America, Peru	Guanche	Africa, Egypt
HUANAC-o (sheep)	ANAH (sheep)	(H)ANAK (sheep)

Asia, O. Phoenic.	Chinese
ANAH (sheep)	YANG (sheep)

Even in Babylonia, *UNIK-u* meant *goat*. To *GUANAC-o*
we can add the Greenland word *KENNEK* (sheep). There

is no doubt that *GUANAC-o* and *HUANAC-o* sound similar to Guanche *ANAH*, but identity of sounds can be stated only in the Old Phoenician form, *ANAH* (sheep) going back as far as 1400 to 2000 B.C. Perhaps forms of the Old Phoenician dialect of *Ugarit* in Syria have survived in the Punic dialect of Carthage, and Phoenicians who had pushed beyond the Pillars of Hercules had visited the Canaries, even settled there as colonists and thus imported such names as *ANAH* (sheep) into the island of Chinerfe.

There is the Guanche word *ATAMAN* (sky), so similar to the Sanskrit *ASMAN* (sky), and to Japanese *ATAM-a* (head). How shall we explain the existence of this word in the Canaries? And how the term *GUIRR-e* (vulture)?

(231) *Guanche GUIRR-e (Vulture) and GER-falcon.*

Guanche	Europe, O. German	German
GUIRR-e (vulture)	GIR (vulture)	GEIER (vulture)
Albanian	**Asia, Tibet**	**Manchu**
JAR-a (vulture)	KHRA (vulture)	KER-u (swan)

In Babylonian *IGUR-u* was the word for swan. If we consider also the prolonged form *AGOR* (eagle), a Semitic term used in Cyprus, we can easily extend this word-chain over the whole world, particularly to America. In any event, the appearance of this stem in Albania and in Tibet proves that we ought not to think only of a German origin.

Finally the word *AR-an* (farm) appears in Table 210. An important farm activity is ploughing, and *AR-o* in Latin means to plough.

(232) *Guanche AR-an (Farm) and Latin AR-o (to plough).*

Guanche	Europe, Spanish	Latin
AR-an (farm)	AR-ar (to plough)	AR-o (to plough)
Greek		**Slavic**
AR-oo (to plough)		OR-aty (to plough)

There is no link with American tongues in this case; everything points to the East. Why this? There is still another characteristic word contained in that Guanche vocabulary, and when we study its geographical extension we shall be led closer to an understanding why certain words are found chiefly in the Eastern parts of the world, while others can be encountered in American Indian vernaculars as well. This word is *AFAR-o* (grain, corn). It cannot come from Spanish, for the Latin word nearest to it, *FAR* (*wheat, spelt, flour*) does not exist in Spanish, and another word, *FAR-ina* (flour) in most Romance tongues fell a prey to sound-shifting and appears as *HAR-ina*. However there are many more relatives in other languages, first of all Latin *BAR* (spelt) related to *BAR-ley*.

(233) *Guanche AFAR-o (Grain) and Its Relatives.*

Guanche	Europe, Latin	English
AFAR-o (grain)	FAR (wheat, flour, grain)	BAR-ley

Slavic	Asia, Hebrew	Korean
BAR, BUR (millet)	BAR, BOR (wheat)	POR-i (barley)

Then we can conclude from these few instances that Guanche *AR-an* (farm) and *AFAR-o* (grain) can only be connected with the Eastern, not with the Western Hemisphere, that farming and agriculture came from the *Orient*, not from the *Occident*. This is in complete agreement with the findings of other fields of knowledge.

Are certain islands in the Atlantic linguistic land-bridges between the shores of this Ocean? There can be no doubt of this fact! The discovery of names of divinities which the ancient inhabitants of Chinerfe had in common with the American Indians, of words for mummies, for animals and other objects show it quite clearly. Were we to examine the complete vocabulary of the Guanche tongue and not only a small, all too small section of it, this conviction would certainly be much stronger. On the other hand however, there is another group of Guanche words that unmistakably points to the East rather than to the West for related words, but not for its origin.

Still we are not yet able to declare with sufficient certainty where was the cradle of mankind, the source of its language and its whole civilisation. However, in silhouette-form some unknown continent is emerging, located between both hemispheres. This was the centre where humanity grew up in the age of its childhood, developed its common language to a certain degree, evolved its culture in various fields of life and reached a level in its evolution which must be regarded as an everlasting foundation of Man's present development and existence. The investigation of land-bridges located in the Pacific and the comparison of languages spoken on the shores of this ocean will help us to determine with certainty that region of the world from which our ancestors started their and our present world-career.

CHAPTER FIFTEEN

LINGUISTIC BRIDGES IN THE PACIFIC

As PRIMEVAL Man who evolved his language by creating more and more new words and forms of speech had to be an *artist* rather than a thinker, a poet or painter endowed with great imaginative power, so the modern investigator of tongues who intends to rebuild bridges between vernaculars and words, various nations, continents, and epochs, to reunite the earth that broke asunder, needs a like *creative power of imagination.*

The Guanche of Chinerfe were a people that belonged to an epoch entirely different from ours. The speech remnants left behind by them seem on the one hand classical, but on the other hand are extremely original. Classical gods of Greek and Egyptian antiquity appear at the same time in the Canaries as medicine-men and wizards as we find them among the Indian tribes of Old America. Mummification, pyramids, menhirs, temple-dances, and vestals or priestesses with Teutonic names in an entirely non-Teutonic surrounding — how can we account for all this?

When we move from the Canary Islands to Hawaii, from the Atlantic to the Pacific, we must realize one fact. The Asiatic Shore of the Pacific as well as the Polynesian Islands located in this ocean contain tongues such as Chinese, Japanese, Hawaiian, Samoan, Tocolowan, Tahitian, the vernaculars of the Marquesas, the Easter Island, Tonga, Rapa, Maori (New Zealand) and the Cook Islands whose consonantic keyboard is and for a long time probably has been more or less defective. Chinese is all but a primeval or perfect language as far as its consonantic system is concerned. The words of the so-called 'Mandarin dialect' are cut to pieces. Almost all initial and final consonants are missing today in that tongue.

This means not only that it is very hard to compare any word of it with any related word in Hebrew, Babylonian, Latin, Greek, English or Russian, but it is hardly possible that classical word-forms such as are contained in Peruvian, Chilean, and in Mexican could stem from a vernacular such as Chinese. Besides, Chinese is lacking the L-sound and all compound consonants. There are no such words in Chinese as STAY, PLAY, TRY, SLY, SKY, still less such words as STAND, BRAND, FRIEND, SHRINK, CLING, BRING. *Stay* would be cut down probably to *TA, Play* to *LA, cling* to *LING, bring* to *LI* or *LING.* And in Hawaii we find a continuation of this extended zone of the Eastern side of the Pacific where *L* is lacking. This zone embraces a great part of the Pacific Islands. There are three groups of islands according to the keyboards of their consonants:

(1) Tongues without an *L,* but possessing an *R. R-Tongues.*
(2) Idioms without an *R,* replacing it by *L.   L-Tongues.*
(3) Vernaculars lacking both *L* and *R.   L- and R-less Tongues.*

This lack of *R* or *L* or of both, and their replacement by one another is one of the most mysterious phenomena of

(234) *Pacific Islands Lacking the R- or L-sound or Both.*

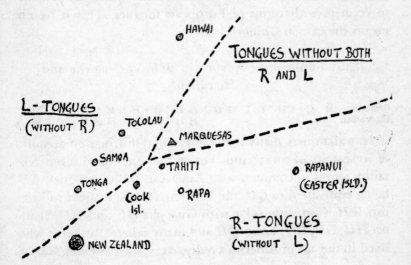

speech. There are in every continent and in almost every important group of tongues whole idioms which lack *R* or *L* or both, or have a strange relation to them, and also we find in many, if not most tongues parallel word-stems containing once an *L* and another time an *R*, such as *CLAMP* and *CRAMP*. We must realize that such phonetic differences are in part an evidence that not very many exchanges could have occurred during the last millennium or earlier between both shores of the Pacific, at any rate less than between the Atlantic coasts.

Guanche and Hawaiian, the latter related to Maori and Samoan, are different as far as their vowels are concerned.

(235) *Vocalic Keyboards of Guanche and of Hawaiian.*

Guanche	A	E	I	O	U	AE	EY	UE
Hawaiian	A	E	I	O	U	—	—	—

Still more different is the extension of their consonantic keyboards. Hawaiian contains (if we disregard combinations such as *KU and HU*) only seven consonants; Guanche has over twenty of them, and belongs to the idioms best equipped in consonants. In Hawaiian there are many words consisting of vowels only as *O-O-O* (to crow as a cock) which are difficult to connect with terms of European tongues. This is by no means the case in Chinerfe.

(236) *Consonantic Keyboards Both of Guanche and Hawaiian.*

Guanche	B	C	CH	D	F	G	GU	H	HU	K	KH	L	M	N	P	R	S	T	W	Y
Hawaiian								H	HU	K	KU	L	M	N	P				W	

Hawaiian uses many inevitable sound-shiftings on account of its scarcity of consonants. Yet on the other hand it has certain features in common with American Indian tongues, *KU* being equivalent to *QU* and besides *HU* (equivalent to English *WH*, Germanic *HV*) with Guanche *GU* and *HU*, Spanish *HU, GU, CU*, Latin *QU* and many others. Linguists who lived in the age of America's rediscovery, such as Peter *Martyr* and Theodorus *Bibliander* considered such consonants as typical of the Western Hemisphere vernaculars.

The name *GUANCHE* (people) contains the characteristic sound *GU* and so do other words as *GUAN* (son), *GUANAC* (nation), *GUANATH* (people), *GUIRRE* (vulture), *HUERAHAN* (heaven). They correspond with such American Indian words as *GUARINI* (battle)— so assonant to *GUERRILLA*—*GUANACO* (sheep), *GUALIO* (lightning), *GUARASI, CUARASI, HUARASI* (sun), *HUASI* (house) and others. In Hawaiian we can link with such forms *KUAI* (to buy, sell), *KUALAP-a* (a ridge), *KUAM-oo* (backbone), or *HUAM-oa* (egg), *HUAPAL-a* (sweetheart).

(237) *GU, CU, HU sounds in words of Guanche, Hawaii and America.*

Guanche	America	Hawaii
GUAN	GUANACO	KUAI
GUANAC	GUARINI	KUALAPA
GUANATH	GUALIO	KUAMOO
GUIRRE	GUARASI	HUAMOA
HUERAHAN	CUARASI	HUAPALA
	HUARASI	
	HUASI	

This combination *GU, CU, HU* seems to have been characteristic of ancient idioms. The same sound-combination *GU* appears within the Semitic branch in Abyssinian, a tongue separated for a long time from its main stock and having been altered but little by its African surrounding.

While the consonantic element in the Hawaiian instrument of speech is thus reduced, its vocalisation is so much the more rich and beautiful. Who could ever forget such sonorous words as *ALOHA* (love), *AETO* (eagle), *HEBEDOMA* (week) or *PALENA* (bread)? The more we become familiar with this strange Pacific idiom, compare its terms with words of other tongues and investigate them more thoroughly, the more we notice another fact: Hawaiian is far less informing than Guanche. The idiom of Chinerfe disappeared about the Fifteenth Century, thus being spared the modernization which the Pacific vernacular underwent during the last century.

(238) *Modernization of Hawaiian by European Loan-Words.*

Words borrowed from:		Transformed in Hawaiian into:	
Spanish	iglesia (church)	ekalesia	(church)
English	ink	inika	(ink)
"	hymn	himeni	(hymn)
"	bible	baibala	(bible)
"	hebdomadal (weekly)	hebedoma	(week)
"	broom	pulumi	(broom)
"	palm	puulima	(palm)
"	cook	kuko	(cook)
"	pin	pini	(pin)
"	captain	kapena	(captain)
"	moon, month	*mahina	(moon)
"	club, clap	*koilipi	(axe)
"	plough, plow	palau	(to plough)
"	hammer	amara	(blacksmith)
"	handkerchief, hanky	hainaka	(handkerchief)
"	sheep	hipa	(sheep)
"	hour	hola	(hour)
"	inch	iniha	(inch)
"	coal	koala	(cook, lay on coals)
"	coffee	kope	(coffee)
"	corn	kulina	(corn)
"	man-of-war	manuwa	(warship)

*May be indigenous Hawaiian.

In other cases a change of consonants had to take place there where certain sounds were lacking. We see *COAL* reappearing as *KOALA* yet with a somewhat different meaning, not as *coal*, but to *cook*. Here we may even doubt whether this word has been borrowed from English at all because the word-stem *KAL* (warm) is by no means confined to the Germanic or Indo-European tongues.

(239) *The Word-Stem COAL in All Five Continents.*

America, Peru	**Europe, Latin**	**Africa, Egypt**
KILL-u	CAL-or	ma-KAR-u
(hearth)	(heat)	(hearth)

Asia, Mongol	**Australia**
KAL- (fire)	KALL-a (fire)

In Babylonia *KAL-û* meant *roasted cereals,* Hebrew *KAL-a* means *to roast, burn,* Arabic *KALL-a,* Ethiopic *KAL-au,* Syriac *KALL-a — to roast,* Sabaean *KAL-at* means *heat.* Thus it might well be possible, though it is not likely, that Hawaiian *KOAL-a* (to cook) might be an indigenous word-stem. The same applies to *MAHIN-a* (moon) and *KOILIP-i* (axe), particularly to the latter; for the consonantic scheme *K-L-P* (clap, club) is a very widespread root meaning *to knock, to beat, to cleave,* and was used in oldest times by several linguistic families to designate *an axe, a mace, a club.*

(240) *The Word-Stem CLUB in Different Continents.*

America, Mexico	Europe, Greek	Africa, Egypt
ILP-itza	KOLAP-to	me-YENEB
(to blow)	(to beat)	(axe)

Asia, Assyria	Samoa
KILAPP-ati (axes)	LEP-eti (destroy)

Egyptian has no letter for the L-sound and replaces it either by *R* or by *N* or other letters (as we changed *BALUSTER* into *BANISTER*): thus 'axe' is likely me-*YELEB* in Egypt, similar to Russian *KELEP* (stick with hammer), Ukrainian *KELEP* (battle-axe). And as to Mexican *ILP-itza,* to blow, we notice a similar loss of the initial *K* in Latin *ALAP-a* (a slap, box on the ear), The other word *MAHIN-a* (Moon) — marked by an asterisk — may be an indigenous Hawaiian word-stem also; for we find the name *MOON* in almost every continent, generally used for the Moon, and in some ancient tongues for the planet Venus.

(241) *The Name Moon in Both Hemispheres.*

America, Cariban	Europe, Anglo-Sax.
MON-a (moon)	MON-a (moon)

Africa, Egypt	Asia, Hebrew
MIN (moon-god)	MEN-i (Venus)

Doubts about the relationship of some words may arise in certain cases, and we can drop each doubtful word-chain. Compared with the enormous abundance of material left, these few instances are almost insignificant. Yet even if we were not to drop such names, there would be a good reason to believe that some of the names of planets and of gods were indigenous, since we find Old World god-names in Polynesia and in America. One of them is the Hawaiian *AO* (daylight) which together with *EU* (to rise) reminds us of the Greek morning-goddess *EO-s;* another one is *LA* (sun). Who is *LA*? The Egyptian *RAH,* the old sun-god!

(242) *The Name of the Egyptian Sun-God Rah in Most Continents.*

America, Peru	Europe, Latin	Africa, Egypt
RAY (flame)	RA-tio (vision)	RAH (sun-god)

Asia, Sumer	Polynesia
RA (bright)	RA (sun)

Imbelloni in his *Esfinge Indiana* (p. 210) quotes *RA* as the original form of the sun-name in Polynesia, and there are good reasons to support this opinion. In the Easter Island *RAK-o* means a light, bright color, as in New Zealand *RA-RAK-o* means *albino,* and in the Caucasus vernaculars RAGH, REGH (sun). As has been indicated, 'sun' in its picture value was depicted as the *eye* of God. In Mayan *RU* designates the eye.

(243) *The Sun-Name RAH Applied in Language For "to See."*

America, Peru	Europe, Lithuanian	Asia, Hebrew
RIK-uni (to see)	REG-eti (to see)	RAH-a (to see)

In Egypt *RAH* was one of the oldest names under which the sun-god was worshipped, and Augustus Le Plongeon in *Sacred Mysteries Among the Mayas and Quichés* (p. 54) reports that the Chaldaeans, according to Pythagoras, Democritus and others, adored a superior deity, *RA,* so far removed from their first triad that they did not know how to worship it. Their historians did not even understand the meaning of this old name; they asserted that it means God. In Egypt *RA* was the name given to the Sun particularly, the life-giver and source of all things that exist on earth. *LA* in Mayan means "That which exists for ever. The eternal Truth".

There is a group of Hawaiian words such as *HIMENI* (hymn), *BAIBALA* (bible), *HEBEDOMA* (week) which are purely Old Greek in origin. The introduction of these words into Hawaii is connected with the Christian Church and its terms, thus it is almost certain that missionaries introduced these expressions into Polynesia.

(244) *Greek Words Introduced by Modern Missionaries.*

Greek	English	Hawaiian
HYMN-os (hymn)	HYMN	HIMEN-a (hymn)
BIBL-on (book)	BIBL-e	BAIBAL-a (bible)
HEBDOM-as (week)	HEBDOM-adal	HEBEDOM-a (week)

In a case such as the Hawaiian word *BAIBAL-a* (bible) this fact is obvious; for the pronunciation of this word is English, modern English, not Greek. And the Far East with its surrounding regions shows other influences of religious movements upon its tongues also. Buddhism penetrated into Japan in about the Sixth Century A.D. Still today we find in Japanese the word *BIK-u* (mendicant) from Sanskrit *BHIKSH-u* (mendicant), related to Hebrew *BAKASH* (to beg), Arabic *BAKSH-ish* (gratuity) and English, *BEGG-ar* from the Old French *BEG-ard* (mendicant).

(245) *The Word-Stem of Beggar in the Far East.*

Japanese	Sanskrit	Hebrew
BIK-u	BHIKSH-u	BAKASH
(mendicant)	(mendicant)	(to beg)

Arabic	English
BAKSH-ish (gratuity)	BEGG-ar (mendicant)

These facts are neither solitary nor new. They repeat themselves in history, and the introduction of Christianity and Mohammedanism were accompanied by a sort of linguistic revolution in many tongues, adding a new layer of religious words to their vocabularies, as in England *chalice, cross, ab-*

(246) *Old Greek Words in the Hawaiian Tongue.*

Hawaiian		Old Greek	
AET-o	(eagle)	AET-os	(eagle)
NOO-NOO	(thought)	NOU-s	(thought)
MAN-ao	(to think)	MAN-thanó	(to learn)
MEL-e	(to sing)	MEL-os	(MEL-ody)
LAH-ui	(people)	LA-os	(people)
MEL-i	(honey)	MEL-i	(honey)
KAU	(summer)	KAU-ma	(heat)
MAHIN-a	(month)	MEN	(moon)
KI-a	(pillar)	KI-on	(pillar)
NOH-o	(sit, live)	NAI-ó	(dwell)
HIK-i	(to come)	HIK-anó	(to arrive)
AM-a	(carry on shoulder)	OM-os	(shoulder)

bott, Messiah, angel, Satan and devil. Most European vernaculars abound in such names.

On the other hand Hawaiian contains old Greek words
which have nothing to do with religion or the Church. The
eagle is called *AET-o,* almost identical with old Hellenic
AET-os (eagle). Was it necessary to import a foreign name
for this bird? There are still scores of other Greek-like words
in Hawaiian where the same question arises.

Hawaiian *MEL-e* (to sing) is so assonant to Greek *MEL-os*
(song, *MEL-ody*) that we are induced at first glance to take
it for a Greek word imported to the Pacific and not for an indigenous stem. The same applies to *MEL-i* (honey) identical
with Greek *MEL-i* (honey), Latin *MEL. Hawaiian KAU*
(summer) and Greek *KAI-ô* (to burn), *KAU-ma,* (burning),
the same stem as contained in *CAU-stic* (burning), seem also
intimately related, and the Hawaiian word borrowed from
Greece. But when? And who introduced it? It is imaginable
that some missionary may have suggested the old Greek word
MEL-i found in Homer's Illiad as a name for honey. Yet no
missionary would take the Greek word *KAI-ô* (to burn),
select a form of it as *KAU-* (burning), create from it a noun
KAU (summer) and add it to the Hawaiian vocabulary. We
may also doubt whether Hawaiian was lacking such a name for
the summer season, for primitive tribes live in closer contact
of Nature than modern town-people do.

There is a way of checking such a problem and solving it.
Certain names are known from literature. All who read Homer and other Hellenic authors in the original are familiar
with the word *AET-os* (eagle), and not knowing of its existence in Oriental and other tongues are inclined to consider
it a name typical of Hellas. Yet Greece had by no means any

(247) *AET-os (eagle) Contained in Different Tongues.*

America, Maya	Europe, Anglo-Sax.
KOT (eagle)	CYT-a (kite, falcon)
Asia, Hebrew	Samoan, Hawaiian
(H)AYIT (hawk, eagle)	AET-o (eagle)

monopoly of the word. It is part of other idioms as well, and corresponds to English *KIT-e*.

The Hebrew word (*H*)*AYIT* (eagle) is spelt in such a way that it shows that it once had a *K* as its initial sound. The same applies to Polynesian *AET-o* and Greek *AET-os*. There are also words of the same stem and meaning found in the vicinity of Samoa and Hawaii, namely in China, Japan and Annam: China *HU* 4998 (falcon), Canton *KUET, UET*, Annam *KOUT*, Japan *KWATS-u* (for *KUAT-u*), *KOTS-u* for *KOT-u*, *GETS-u* (falcon). Many links could be added to this chain, particularly in such American vernaculars as Quiché, Poconchi, Tzutuhil, Cacchiquel, Pocoman, *COT* (eagle), Californian (Yokuts, Yaudaucht) *WIT-c* (condor), *WAT-c-WAT-c* (Falco columbarius), O. Norse *GY-ODH-r* (white tailed eagle), Anglo-Saxon GEAT, GEOTH (eagle, vulture), Cymric *CUT, CUD* (falcon), in the Caucasus vernaculars Andi *UEZ-u, UETZ-o* (cock), Georgian *KOT-am* (cock). The main conclusion we can draw from this material is that the word is probably indigenous in Hawaii and Samoa, and that it is found on both shores of both the Atlantic and Pacific.

(248) *KIT-e* (*Falcon*) *on Both Shores of the Atlantic and Pacific*.

Both shores of the Atlantic		Both shores of the Pacific	
America, Maya	Europe, Cymric	Asia, Japan	America, Quiché
COT (eagle)	CUT (falcon)	KOTS-u (falcon)	COT (eagle)

Let us select another word: *MAN-ao* (to think). This again is by no means isolated, for we find it in our *MEAN-ing* (sense, logic), Anglo-Saxon *MYN-e* (sense), German *MEIN-en* (to think), Greek *MAN-thanô* (to learn), Egyptian *MAN-û* (monument, from remember), Sanskrit *MAN* (to

(249) *Hawaiian MAN-ao* (*to think*) *in All Five Continents*.

America, Peru	Europe, English	Africa, Egypt
MAN (to think)	MEAN-ing (thought)	MAN-u (monument)

Asia, China	Hawaii
MIEN (consider)	MAN-ao (think)

think), Chinese *MIEN* 7889 (to reflect), Peruvian *MAN* (to think).

Most of the words mentioned in Table 246 could be represented in a similar way extending over vast territories. How careful we ought to be against too rashly accepting the idea that assonant words found in primitive languages, as we like to call them, are borrowed from "civilized" idioms, we can learn from an instance such as Hawaiian *MEL-i* (honey) and Hellenic *MEL-i* (honey). Both are identical, and everything seems here to point to a loan made from Greece to Hawaiian.

(250) *Greek MEL-i* (*honey*) *and Hawaiian MEL-i* (*honey*)
in Korea.

Europe, Latin	Greek	Asia, Korean	Polynesia, Hawaii
MEL	MEL-i	MIL	MEL-i
(honey)	(honey)	(honey)	(honey)

Yet we find in China *MI* 7834 (honey), Canton *MIT,* the same stem as our *MEAD* which is a product of honey. Korean *MIL* (honey, wax) is by no means a loan-word from Greek, but is a close relative of Chinese *MI, MIT* (honey) with a change of *T* into *L* as it occurs in Latin *LINGU-a,* older *DINGU-a* (tongue) and Germanic *TONG-e,* and as Latin *MEL,* Greek *MEL-i* (honey) are but variations of a common word-stem *MET, MEAD* etc., Sanskrit *MADH-u* (sweet, honey, wine), extending over the whole earth. The few instances

(251) *The Root Mead* (*Originally Honey*) *in Both*
Hemispheres.

America, Peru	Europe, Lappish	Asia, Mordvin
MISK-i (honey)	MITT (honey)	MED (honey)

Korea	Samoa, Hawaii
MIL (honey)	MEL-i (honey)

mentioned here are a small part of this very large word-chain. Thus it is clear that the apparent Greek influence is due probably to a few modern missionaries who imported some church-terms, and most of the other names are common to both Greek and Hawaiian — daughters of common parents, of the primeval tongue. A similar impression however as by words assonant to Hellenic sisters arises by the obvious occurrence in Hawaii of some words seemingly *Semitic*. Here too we are at first inclined to believe that some travelers may have imported them to the little Pacific Island.

(252) *Semitic Word-Stems in Hawaiian.*

Hawaiian			Semitic	
KAUHAL-e	(village)	Hebrew	KAHAL	(community)
NAHES-a	(snake)	"	NAHASH	(snake)
AMAN-a	(authority)	"	AMEN	(sworn, true)
KAHIN-u	(to anoint)	"	KOHEN	(priest)
KUHIN-a	(high officer)	Arabic	KHAN	(prince)
LAU	(leaf)	Hebrew	LU-LAU	(branch)
MOK-e	(to fight)	"	MAK-a	(to fight)

Are these words borrowed from Semitic sources, or are they indigenous Polynesian names? This is a hard question to answer; even if we consider all the material available, there are reasons pro and con each eventuality. *KAUHAL-e* (village) consists of the same three radical consonants as Hebrew *KAHAL* (community), *K-H-L,* and thus appears rather to be a loan-word. The meaning of both words varies however and the word-stem occurs in different continents: this rather points to the root being indigenous to Hawaii. We find assonant words in Swiss German *K-CHILL-e* (church), Irish *CILL-e* (church, house), as *CILLe-Di* (God's house) almost entirely corresponding with Mexican and Mayan *TEO-Calli* (God's house), Greek *KAL-ia* (hut, house,), Latin *CELL-a* (cell, small room), with Sumer *EGALL-u* (temple), Assyrian *EKALL-u,* Hebrew *HEKAL* (temple). In Alaska we find *IGL-oo* (snow-hut).

(253) *The Word-Stem CELL (room, hut) in Both Hemispheres.*

America, Maya	Europe, Greek	Asia, Hebrew	Polynesia, Hawaii
CALL-i	KAL-ia	KAHAL	KAUHAL-e
(house)	(hut)	(community)	(village)

What supports the idea of the indigenous character of the Hawaiian word *KAUHAL-e* (village) is another similar Hawaiian word *HAL-e* (house), and in Northern Siberia, Vogul *KOL,* Samoyede *YEL-e* (house), Chuvash *KIL* (house).

We could even link with this chain Egyptian *KAR* (for *KAL*) "chapel, shrine, divine dwelling-place", and thus extend it over all five continents. Again we are dealing with but a small part of this wide-spread root. There is however another word in Table 252 which is of a far greater interest: *KAHIN-u* (to anoint), *KUHIN-a* (the highest officer next to the king), and *KAHUN-a* (an expert, a scribe).

We compared these with the Hebrew word *KOHEN* (priest) and Arabic *KHAN* (prince) considered to be of Turkish origin, yet probably going back to a far older source. The older form of *KHAN* was identical with Hebrew *KOHEN* (priest), and Hawaiian *KUHIN-u* (highest officer), for we find in Turkish *KAHAN* (prince) earlier, and *KHAKAN* alongside, but only later *KHAN* (sovereign, emperor). *CHAGAN-us*, of Mongolian origin, appeared first in history in the Seventh Century as "princeps Avarorum", the ruler of the Avarian tribe, and was used in the Crimea as a title for the king of the Khazar tribe, Russian *KAGAN, KOHAN*. Another parallel word-form of this stem is *KING*, Scandinavian *KUNG*, Samoyede *KONG*, Africa, Mandé *KUNG* (chieftain), Chinese *CHÜEN* 3169 (sovereign, prince), Foochow *KUNG*, Korea, Japan *KUN*. No doubt it is one of the oldest designations of an initiate-ruler or priest-king, particularly of a "son of the Sun" like the Biblical Melchizedek, initiated into the Sun-Mysteries. For *CON* was the name of the supreme godhead in Peru, and *KAN-il* in the *Popol Buh* of the Quiché Indians of Guatemala was the god of fertility, of propagation, in a word of the etheric life forces of the Sun. The eighth day of the calendar was devoted to him and was called *Kanil*. On that day the Quiché people prayed for everything necessary to preserve life. Indian tribes of New

(254) *The Word-Stem KING in All Five Continents.*

America, Peru	Europe, Anglo-Sax.	Africa, Mandé
CON (sun-god)	CYN-e (king)	KUNG (chieftain)

Asia, Hebr.	Australia
KOHEN (priest)	KUNK-a (head)

England used the word *CON-e* or *CAN-ec* for the sun.

In Hebrew, *KHANAK* means *to initiate,* the same in Egyptian and other vernaculars. The vast extension of this word shows that it must be a very old name, used long time before the establishment of a merely worldly royal power. In Annam, *QUAN* means *king, prince,* a name whose close relationship to *QUEEN* can hardly be overlooked.

As to the word *AMAN-a* (authority) we are inclined, in spite of its resemblance to Hebrew *AMEN* (true), to consider it an indigenous Hawaiian stem on account of the great difference of the meaning of both words. The Greek word *OMN-ymi* (I swear) certainly forms part of this group, as well as Latin *OMEN*. Strangely enough, the Hawaiian term strictly resembles the Swiss word *AMMANN* (mayor of a small community), a word corresponding however with German *amt-mann* (man of office, official). We would rather like to connect this whole word-chain with *AMON, AMEN* (Egyptian sun-god).

(255) *Hawaiian AMAN-a (authority) connected with*
AMON (sun-god)

America, Cariban	Guanche	Africa, Egypt
HUAMON ocan	AMEN acoran	AMEN
(Great Spirit)	(sun-god)	(sun-god)

Asia, Sumer	Hawaii
UMUN (lord, king)	AMAN-a (authority)

This derivation is confirmed in Hebrew where the name of the sun-god *BAAL* is used for "lord", and that of the sun-god *ADON-is,* Hebrew *ADON-ai* became the denomination for a leader, a lord also. The principle of authority was predominant in that remote epoch when spiritual initiation and knowledge were the main condition for any guidance of or within a nation. Hence the custom that leaders and important officers had to be sworn into office, and the word *JUR-y* (from Latin *JUR-o,* I swear) is a remnant of that old institution. We can therefore link the Greek *OMN-ymi* and Hebrew

AMEN with this word group, and thus extend it over all five continents.

The word *NAHES-a* (snake) on the other hand seems rather of Semitic origin, for it is entirely assonant to Hebrew *NA-HASH* and Arabic *NAHAS* (snake). There is no doubt that

(256) *Hawaiian NAHES-a (Snake) in Both Hemispheres.*

America, Calif.	Europe, Latin	Asia, Hebrew	Hawaiian, Polyn.
NAHAAT	ANGU-is	NAHASH	NAHES-a
(otter)	(snake)	(snake)	(snake)

the outer appearance of this word-chain points to Hawaiian *NAHES-a* as a loan-word from the West (Asia), since the Mohammedan and thus Arabic influence in the Malayan Archipelago is so intense that still today Malayan and many related dialects use the Arabic alphabet in writing. Yet mythological facts point also to another direction, toward a remote past. We already mentioned the Hindu tradition according to which an emperor of Atlantis was called *Deva NAHUSH-a* (the divine Nahusha). This name reminds us of another name for ruler (a priest-king) developed in Table 209 namely Basque *NAGUSH-i* (prince), Abyssinian *NEGUS* (emperor, king).

(257) *Hawaiian NAHES-a (Snake) and Abyssinian NEGUS related.*

Atlantis	Europe, Basque	Africa, Abyssinia
Deva NAHUSH-a	NAGUSH-i	NEGUS
(emperor)	(prince, king)	(emperor, king)

Asia, Hebrew	Hawaii
NOGESH (prince)	NAHES-a (snake)

What kind of relation is there between a 'snake' and a 'prince'? At first glance it sounds utterly strange to link these words. However *snake* was used throughout all antiquity for a certain kind of education as a symbolic expression: a person who had been initiated into the 'hidden wisdom' was considered to have been lifted up and become a *Serpent*. Thus we read in the Gospel of St. John (3, 14) 'Just as once Moses lifted up the Serpent, even so will the son of Man be lifted up'. The way of initiation had become simplified since the incarnation of Christ and rendered accessible not only to a few elected ones, but to every 'son of Man'. The symbol of a snake has been used in China for the emperor whose emblem contained a dragon (the snake) in the same way as it is used in the Bible.

(258) *Native Words in Hawaiian Related to Names of Other Families.*

HAWAIIAN	OTHER FAMILIES		ENGLISH
KAN-i (to sound)	Latin	CAN-o (I sing)	CAN-tor
KANAK-a (man, people)	Guanche	GUANAC (people)	KING
UIL-a (lightning)	Chile	GUAL-io (lightning)	?
ALOHILOHI (shining)	German	LOH-e (fire)	LUC-id
NAH-u (to bite)	German	NAG-en (to bite)	NAG, NICK
KUA-i (to buy)	German	KAUF (buying)	CHAP-man
HOOL-a (consecrate)	German	HEIL-ig (holy)	HOL-y
NAK-ii (to bind)	Latin	NEC-to (I bind)	con-NEC-tion
ILI-o (dog)	O. Norse	YLG-r (she-dog)	?
NAM-u (speak)	Latin	NOM-en (name)	NAM-e
LANALANA (spider)	Latin	LAN-a (wool)	LIN-en
ULAN-a (to weave)	Slavic	VLUN-a (wool)	WOOLEN
AN-u (air)	Hebrew	AN-ah (sigh)	AN-imal
HAN-u (breathe)	Hebrew	AN-ah (breathe)	AN-emo- (wind)
KALO-KALO (to pray)	Latin	COL-o (worship)	CALL
WAHIN-e (female)	Japan	WOMIN-a (woman)	WOMAN
IK-e (to see)	A. Saxon	EAG-e (eye)	EY-e
PELEH-u (turkey)	Greek	PELEK-an (pelican)	FALC-on
CHUM-u (murmur)	Hebrew	HOM (humming)	HUM
KUN-i (kindle)	German	KIEN (fire-wood)	KEEN
HAK-i (to break)	German	HACK-en (break)	HACK
LA' (sun)	O. Norse	LOK-i (LUC-ifer)	LIGH-t

Until now we have turned our attention to Hawaiian words which possibly could be borrowed from foreign tongues, Greek, Hebrew or others. There are however scores of Hawaiian names which hardly can be considered loan-words and yet are related to terms found in many other linguistic families. Here we realize that they probably are indigenous or native names.

How can we place the word *KING* beside Hawaiian *KA-NAK-a* (man, people) and Guanche *GUANAC* (people)? *JANAK-a* in Sanskrit meant *man* and *king,* just as in Anglo-Saxon *CWEN* meant *woman, wife,* and *queen.* In olden times the king was the ancestor of the tribe, and thus up to our century in certain countries the king was called *father* and the queen *mother* of the country, as in German songs, *Landesvater.*

We must further consider some difficult phonetic changes such as the transition from Hawaiian *WAHIN-e* (female) to *WOMAN.* In the Bentan dialect of Indonesia *WAHIN-e* is spelt *WAWIN-ei* (woman), in Buru, Indonesia *(U)EM-PIN-a* (woman), and in Samoan, a sister dialect of Hawaiian, *FAFIN-e* (woman). The transition from *B, P, F,* to an *M* is very frequent in language. We have it in English between *SLEEP* and *SLUMB-er,* or *DEAF* and *DUMB.* Hence side by side with Indonesian forms such as *WAWIN-ei* we find in Old Japan *WOMIN-a* (woman), not as the current name, but one of the most ancient terms used in the oldest mythological text, *Kojiki,* quoted by *Noburhiro Matsumoto, Le Japonais et les langues austro-asiatiques,* Paris 1928, p. 52 (Japanese and the Austro-Asiatic Tongues).

(259) *The Word Woman in Four Continents.*

America, Brazil	Europe, English	Latin
BOEMAN	WOMAN	FEMIN-a
(wife)		(woman)

Asia, Japan	Polynesia, Samoa
WOMIN-a (woman)	FAFIN-a (FAMIN-a) (woman)

The current explanation of the word *WOMAN,* seemingly isolated in Anglo-Saxon, is *WIF-MAN* (female + human being). Webster quotes a whole chain of evolution of this word-stem in Middle-English and Anglo-Saxon:

(260) *Evolution of the Word Woman in Anglo-Saxon and Middle English.*

A.S. WIFMAN, WIMMAN
M.S. WOMAN, WOMMAN, WUMMAN, WIMMAN, WIFMAN

Since *WIFMANN* already appears in Anglo-Saxon and later on in Middle English, Anglicists are inclined to see in it the original form of this word-stem. When we extend the investigation over all continents we realize that the Anglo-Saxon *WIMMANN* and Middle English *WIMMAN, WUMMANN, WOMMANN* were actually the more ancient forms of this word, and that A. S. *WIFMANN* and M. E. *WIFMAN* are nothing but attempts of early scribes and students to explain this enigmatical word when most people no longer knew about its source and original meaning.

Such attempts, called folk etymologies, are very frequent and appear very early in literature. When the Egyptian priests no longer understood the derivation of the name *HATHOR* (Venus) from +*SATHOR, ESTHER, ASTAR-te, ISHTAR* and *STAR,* they explained it as *HAT HOR* (house of Horus), no doubt a plausible interpretation. Likewise when the wise men of India forgot about the origin of the miraculous bird of speech *SIMURGH,* a frequent figure in Indian and Persian legends, they simply interpreted his name as *SENA-MURGHA* (bird of the jungle). Further, when Greek linguists discovered in some Hellenic dialect the mysterious word *BOKAR-os* (spring), how could they connect it with the corresponding Hebrew word *BOKER* (early season) and the Aino term *BAIKAR, PAIGAR* (spring)? They tried to

(261) *The Greek Word BOKAR-os (spring) in Hebrew and Aino.*

Europe, Greek	Asia, Hebrew	Aino, Japan
BOKAR-os (spring)	BOKER (early season)	BAIKAR, PAIGAR (spring)

explain it out of their own mother-tongue and the result of

such an attempt was: hoti *BIO KHAR-in* ekhei (because it brings *charm* to our life). Thus folk etymologists may sometimes appear naive, and very charming, but they generally lead us astray. The English word *WOMAN* is an old name which we discover in most continents, and is not a *WIFE-MAN*!

In certain cases it is not difficult to discover the indigenous character of a Hawaiian word at first glance. Names such as *ALOHI-LOHI* (shining) or *KALO-KALO* (prayer) or *LA-NA-LANA* (spider) are doubtless native and ancient on account of their duplication. In tongues such as Sumerian and today in Japanese the plural of nouns was and is formed by duplication, and in most idioms duplication appears in the oldest layers of speech, all over the world. In this behalf classical languages are closer to so-called primitive vernaculars than we imagine. It is necessary to stress this fact, since it shows that relationship of most tongues does not only consist of a resemblance of nouns or words but of a common development of their structure and syntax up to a certain point. The example of Hawaiian *KAN-i* (to sound, sing) can prove it. This word sounds familiar to us: we recall it in *CAN-tor*, *CAN-tata* and *CHANT*, in French *CHAN-son* (song) and Latin *CAN-o* (I sing), Irish *KEEN* (dirge), originally *CA-OIN-e* (funeral song), Hebrew *KIN-a* (dirge), Breton *KIN-ed* (singer). We find it in Egypt as *KHAN-u* (musician), Ethiopic *KEN-é* (song), Chinese *YIN* (sound), Peruvian *KEN-a* (flute).

(262) *The Hawaiian KAN* (Sing) *in All Five Continents.*

America, Peru	**Europe, Irish**	**Asia, Hebrew**
KEN-a KEN-a	KEEN	KIN-a
(flute)	(dirge)	(funeral song)

Africa, Ethiop.	**Hawaii**
KEN-e (song)	KAN-i (sing)

Yet what matters more than this word-chain to which we can add many more links, is the doubled form in Peruvian

KENA-KENA (flute), and again duplications in the Latin and Hawaiian conjugation of the verb Latin *CAN-o* (I sing) and Hawaiian *KAN-i* (I sing).

(263) *The Duplication of KAN-(Sing) in Latin and Hawaiian.*

Hawaiian
KAN-i (I sing)
KA-KAN-i (I sang)

Latin
CAN-o (I sing)
CE-CIN-i (I sang)

We can discover similar verb-duplications in the New World also; they go back to the very origin of speech, and are a vivid expression of the predominant rhythmic feeling in language and its intimate relationship with music when both were at their start. Let us close this chapter with the last instance in Table 258, the Hawaiian word *ILI-o* (dog).

(264) *Hawaiian ILI-o (Dog) in Both Hemispheres.*

America, Peru
ALC-o (dog)

Europe, O. Norse
YLG-r (she-dog)

Slavic
WILK (wolf)

Finnish
YILG
(wolf)

Asia, Arabic
YILK-a
(wolf)

Korea
ILK-ai
(dog)

Hawaii
ILI-o
(dog)

ALC-o designated in the Western Hemisphere the *Canis Magelhanicus Incae,* and was the name common to the vernaculars of Mexico, Peru and Chile. We find it, again as a term for the dog, on the other side of the Pacific, in Korean *ILK-ai,* and the linguistic land-bridge, in Hawaii. It is thus imaginable that this name could have reached the shores of Chile, Peru and Mexico across the Pacific, either from Korea or from Polynesia, yet hardly from Kamchatka or north-eastern Asia, since we find there no clue of this stem. On the other hand it could have come across the Atlantic to Mexico, from Scandinavia, perhaps even imported by Vikings; for *YLG-r* meant a *she-dog* in the Edda.

Yet who knows anything about direct crossings of the Atlantic from Norway to Mexico, even from Iceland or Greenland to Mexico, in the time about 1000 A.D. or earlier? Moreover, how can we account for the fact that no trace of this word has been left in North America, particularly on the Atlantic coast, but also in the vicinity of Behring Strait? Further, what about the other examples? What about Slavic *WILK* (wolf), Finnish *YILG* (wolf) so close to O. Norse *YLG-r*, and the most mysterious link of all, Arabic *YILK-a* (wolf)? What about Sumerian *LIK* (dog), a word of a language which ceased to be used in general speech about 5000 years ago? And what about the Greek link *LYK-os* (wolf)?

We see relationship everywhere, on both sides of the Atlantic and Pacific. We see relationship even amidst these oceans, on islands which appear as linguistic bridges. Because of these multiple and various relations and resemblances we cannot possibly make up our mind and reach a definite decision about the question from which corner of the world words of the Eastern Hemisphere could reach the Western half of of our globe or vice versa. We even begin to doubt whether both hemispheres so long practically severed from one another have mutually fructified their tongues. Still less are we certain about the other problem: how the American Continent has been peopled.

This lack of certainty however does not mean that we are not able to answer all these questions in a reliable way. We observe the earth, humanity and its nations, their tongues and dialects more and more closely, and go on collecting and presenting new material: words and thoughts which represent living evidence. All these word-chains are more than mere objects to look at. They have something in common with living human beings; *for they can tell us their story!*

CHAPTER SIXTEEN

AMERICAN TONGUES AND UNIVERSAL HUMAN SPEECH

A struggle in the late Nineteenth and early Twentieth Centuries which found its climax in extremely one-sided racial theories was centered around one basic question: Was Europe or Asia, the East or the West, the primeval dwelling-place of those mysterious tribes whose ancestors allegedly spoke a common tongue called Indo-European or Indo-Germanic? It may sound strange, yet it is called a fact that this confusion brought about a great part of the tension which led to the catastrophe of the Second World-War. The rivalry between the East and the West is connected with the legend of the Tower of Babel, and concerns the Bible and the Hebrew tongue. In Chapter XI of Genesis we read:

1. And the whole world was of one language containing words of one kind (debarim akhadim).
2. And it came to pass as they journeyed from the east that they found a plain in the land of Shinar (Sumer). And they dwelt there.

Then follows the story of the building of the Tower of Babel and of the Confusion of Tongues. After all, the tower of Babel is a symbol, a picture that hides a reality, the former unity of speech and its destruction. The mention of Shinar, usually translated *Sumer*, but possibly *Dsungary* near China is doubtless an addition made in the time of Ezra and Nehemiah, after the Hebrew people returned from their Babylonian captivity. It would be naive to think of Babylonia or Mesopotamia and Sumer as the original home of mankind, for in this case we could find no solution of the great question of how America was peopled. No one ever will be able to prove that the American Indians came from Babylonia to the Western Hemisphere.,

227

Yet, what about the passage in Chapter XI, 2: "as they journeyed from the east"? Was the original home farther East in Asia? Perhaps in Tibet or in the Malayan Archipelago? If we confine ourselves to this translation of the Biblical legend we will get into trouble. Always the difficulty of America and the American Indians will arise. We begin to realize the fact that America is the *key* to the problem of the common speech and other questions connected with it. This is why it seems not only justified, but inevitable that one put the American Continent foremost in linguistic research. Can the difficulty concerning the Western Hemisphere be removed? Indeed it can, and easily too. The critical passage "from the east" is the translation of Hebrew *KADM-ah*. Yet strangely enough, in Hebrew *KADM-ah* can mean both "*from* the east" and "*toward* the east", and the correct translation in this case is: "As they journeyed *toward* the East." It is from the West that the nations migrated at that time.

There is a deep secret around the name of Babel. 'Therefore is the name of it called *Babel*; because the Lord did there confound the languages of all the earth and from thence did the Lord scatter them about upon the face of the earth' (Genesis XI, 9). — According to this Biblical passage, the name Babel is derived from the Hebrew word *BAL* (to blend, to confuse), but the Babylonians had a more complimentary interpretation of this name: *Bab Ilu* (the door of God). However, language seems to follow the Biblical conception, for in many tongues of both hemispheres the name *Babel* is connected with *Babble*.

(265) *Babel and Babble.*

America, Mexico	Europe, English	French
PAPAL (talkative)	BABBL-e	BABILL-er (babble)

German	Magyar	Asia, Hebrew
PAPPEL-n	PAPOL-	BABEL
(babble)	(babble)	(babble)

We may also add *FABL-e,* Latin *FABUL-a,* and besides Spanish *HABL-ar* (to speak), from Latin *FABUL-are.* Thus

Hablar became mere babbling and the whole tragedy of language is expressed in the transition from one of these words to the other.

If there is a reality behind the legend of the Tower of Babel, there must be a reality behind the Confusion of Tongues also. From a scientific point of view, what does this confusion mean? *Dante,* who believed in the reality of an original tongue, thought the confusion represented the oblivion of primeval speech *(Confusio linguarum nil nisi oblivio veteris)*. All those who work creatively in the field of language know that speech resembles a tree which developed from a common root, raised its head like a giant stem spreading its branches more and more, and covered itself with numberless leaves. But the leaves are not always green; they fade and die, and are replaced by others. Thus words fall away and are replaced by others, in a ceaseless transformation.

What the Bible calls Confusion of Tongues is a deep process of transmutation of all the elements of speech in the course of ages. The vocabulary changed, structure, grammar and syntax changed, the sense of the words was altered and a great displacement took place. A sort of revolution occurred, a kind of violent volcanic eruption, in the course of which the different layers or strata of the vocabularies were transferred from one place to another. To discover and to reconnect the different parts and fragments is more difficult than to reassemble a mosaic picture which has fallen into pieces.

Throughout the Middle Ages many European scholars sought for a language which, as they believed, had survived as a kind of remnant of the primeval speech. Some believed Hebrew was the tongue used in Paradise by Adam and Eve. Others, in the Nineteenth Century, chose Chinese as the primitive tongue because of its monosyllabic character. All such ideas were mistaken, because they did not take one important factor into consideration: *evolution in time.* Human speech is no exception to this universal cosmic principle, since our language undergoes changes in common with everything in this mortal world. Thus it is naive to expect that we can discover any language on earth which would sound today as it sounded at the time of its creation. Neither Hebrew, Chinese, Sanskrit, Turkish nor any of the American vernaculars can be regarded as the primeval tongue. They all had to pay tribute to time and evolution, since life and growth, decay and death play their eternal part in the existence of language as in that of any other living thing.

However this does not prevent us from approaching imaginatively that original tongue which still haunts us like a shadow in every word and every sentence to which we listen today. It emerges little by little before our mind's eye when we observe the numberless word-chains which still connect the various vernaculars that broke away from the one mother-tongue. It was in the beginning of our present century that a great scholar, *Dr. Rudolf Steiner,* (1861-1925), in his book *Spiritual Guidance of Man and Mankind,* clearly pointed out that there actually has been a common tongue upon earth, and that every idiom, whether living or dead, was and is but a dialect of that lost primeval speech. At the same time he stressed the fact that languages such as Sumerian or Hebrew were closer to that original tongue than are most of our modern idioms. It was Rudolf Steiner who connected the problem of the former unity of speech with the problems of the unity of the human race and of the common cradle of mankind. To him these three questions could only be solved together. We shall see that by this combination Rudolf Steiner pointed to *America* as the keystone of the whole problem.

We must realize that many questions emerged at once when the Western Hemisphere was re-discovered, questions that have remained unsolved even today. At the end of the Fifteenth Century European scholars were stirred by the sudden extension of the geographical and anthropological horizons. They searched the Bible to find out about the new continent and its inhabitants. What was this mysterious American hemisphere in the light of the Bible? Was *Ophir,* the gold country whence Solomon's fleet brought immeasurable treasures for the Temple of Jerusalem, actually *Peru?* Was *Yucatan* in Central America the land of *Yoktan* the brother of *Peleg* — "for in his days was the earth divided" (Genesis, X, 25)? *Peleg* is a very interesting name, for it means *to split* and at the same time a *folk,* a *nation,* thus indicating the epoch when mankind split up into nations and peoples. Whether we accept such interpretations or not, at any rate the thousands of years during which the Western and Eastern Hemispheres were separated from one another could well coincide with the age of Peleg!

Who were the Indians? To which of the Biblical branches of classification of humanity did they belong, to Shem, Ham, Japhet? Were they aborigines of the new continent? This was an impossible conjecture in an age in which the authority of the Bible was still respected by scholars. Were they the Lost Ten Tribes of Israel who never returned to Palestine from their Babylonian captivity? The mysterious destiny of those tribes has been always a fascinating and attractive subject of human speculation, particularly to Anglo-Saxons. In the Eighteenth Century and after when North America was more and more peopled with British settlers, a strong movement was started in the British Isles by Richard *Brother* (1757-1824) which began to spread the idea that the British people were the descendants of those lost tribes. He called himself 'Brother of the Almighty' and was regarded as the first apostle of Anglo-Israelism after having issued his *Correct Account of the Invasion of England by the Saxons, Showing the English Nations to be Descendants of the Lost Ten Tribes* in 1822. The deep influence of Anglo-Israelism (compare British Encyclopedia, *Anglo-Israelism*) upon Great Britain and the United States can be seen in the fact that at a certain time this movement is said to have included about three million followers. When one of their leaders, Edward *Hine,* published a book *Identification of the British Nation*

With Lost Israel in 1871, a quarter of a million copies are said to have been sold.

Far earlier, however, the Mormon Movement took up the same idea and *The Book of Mormon* is based upon it to a great extent. Anglo-Israelism extended to other countries, among them Germany. In 1878 *Backhaus* issued a book in Berlin, bearing the title *Die Germanen ein Semitischer Volksstamm* (*The Germanic Nations — a Semitic Tribe*). It seems that it did not impress the Germans very deeply, and was so little known in 1933 that it apparently escaped the literary holocausts that took place in Germany under the National-Socialistic régime.

These facts are worth mentioning since this movement for its ideas was based upon linguistic facts: the English language was considered to be derived from Hebrew. R. *Govell* in *English Derived from Hebrew* mentions the following instances:

(266) *Examples from R. Govell English Derived from Hebrew.*

English	Hebrew	
BERR-y	PER-i	(fruit)
KID	GED-i	(goat)
SCAL-e	SHEKEL	(scale, weight)
KITTEN	KATAN	(small)

We shall not discuss the truth or untruth of Anglo-Israelism, but Govell's examples are correct. We can greatly extend them by adding more words of both the Germanic and the Hebrew tongues, in a methodically exerted research. However in spite of their correctness these instances by no means can prove the thesis of Anglo-Israelism. Such writers of the years following the rediscovery of America as Malvenda, Garcia, Charlevoix, Thevet, Emanuel de Moraes and others, after dealing with the Lost Ten Tribes as the ancestors of the Indians, suggested the possibility of deriving the Indians from the *Phoenicians*. They suggested that Phoenician sailors in remote epochs had journeyed beyond the Pillars of Hercules and may have landed in the Western Hemisphere.

Let us consider such a theory in the light of linguistic comparison between American Indian and Hebrew words.

Were it possible to prove the descent of the Anglo-Saxons

(267) *American Indian and Hebrew Words Identical or Similar.*

	AMERICAN	HEBREW
Botocudo	COUP-o (ape)	KOP (ape)
Tarahumara	POCHOT-e (plant fibre)	PESHET (cotton)
Lule	LAIL-a (night)	LAIL-a (night)
Chepeway	TSI (ship)	TSI (ship)
Cora	KUSHAT (rainbow)	KESHET (bow)
Mundurucu	PI (mouth)	PI (mouth)
Brazil	USH-et (woman)	ESH-et (woman)
Galibi	TOP-o (conflagration)	TOPH-et (conflagration)
Huazteca	CHALL-o (sand)	CHOL (sand)
Peru	KOTSHOR (wreath)	KETHER (wreath)
Peru	POKPUK (bottle)	BAKBUK (bottle)
Cariban	AP-a (father)	AB, AV (father)
Cariban	AM-a (mother)	AM (mother)
Californ.	AKH-ika (brother)	AKH (brother)
Chaques	CAZAR-e (peccary)	KHAZIR (pig, swine)
Quiche	QUETON-ec (fur coat)	KITON-et (coat)
Brazil	GUELEM-inen (feather-dress)	GELIM-a (coat, dress)
Cacchiquel	CHUTIN (small)	KATAN (small)
Californ.	PAN (son)	BEN (son)
Brazil	CUAPAR-a (mate)	KHABIR (mate)
Kumanagoto	HUOPER-i (cedar)	GOPHER (Cypress tree)
Chile	MAN (right)	YEMAN (right)
Aymara	MALLC-u (king)	MALK-i (my king)
Chile	ELP-a (family)	ELEP (family)

Omaha	ESHK-a (to desire)	HASHAK (to desire)
Brazil	TAPIR (deer)	TSAPIR (deer)
Peru	MALLC-u (sun)	MOLOCH (fire-god)
Peru	INC-a (king)	HANAK (initiate)
Peru	TUS-uni (to dance)	DUS (to dance)
Maya	HUNAC (a grandee)	(H)ENAK (a giant)
Mexico	MASH-tli (girdle)	MEZEG (girdle)

or of the American Indian tribes from the lost Ten Tribes of Israel on the basis of such a small group of words this table 267 would provide us full evidence of such a bold thesis. From the foregoing tables and those that will follow it becomes clear that scores of words could still be added, yet this would not prove either the descent of the Indians or that of the Anglo-Saxon nations from the Lost Ten Tribes of Israel.

The Hebrew name *GOPHER* (Cypress tree) appears only once in the Bible (Genesis VI, 14) when gopher wood was used for the building of Noah's ark. In California, between Carmel-by-the-Sea and Monterey, we find an isolated grove of cedar-trees the like of which only exists in Palestine. Indeed this is a very startling coincidence. In addition the same name — evidently a very old one — is found in the Old Testament and in Venezuelan, yet, all this and numberless other coincidences do not prove the Ten Tribes thesis. If we extend the search beyond these two fields (Table 267) we find the same word-stem in the Greek word *KYPAR-issos,* Latin *CUPR-essus,* German *KIEFER* (Scotch fir).

(268) *The Word CYPR-ess in Both Hemispheres.*

America, Venezuela	Europe, German	Latin
HUOPER-i (cedar)	KIEFER (fir)	CUPR-essus (cypress)

Greek	Asia, Hebrew
KYPAR-issos (cypress)	GOPHER (cedar)

Thus we could examine one word of Table 267 after the

other and find that most of them are not only common to the
Indians and the Hebrews, but to the Indians and to other
nations as well. We can illustrate this in several cases. Let us
suppose we were to believe that the Phoenicians had crossed
the Atlantic in ancient times and had settled in Venezuela or
some other American country. In such a case we would look
for linguistic ties between the Phoenician and American Indian idioms. Most of the words contained in Table 269, if
not all, are Old Phoenician; they stem from texts dug up
since 1929 in Ras Shamra, Syria (near Minat el-Beida), a

(269) *Old Phoenician and American Indian Words Related.*

PHOENICIAN		AMERICAN		
ANAKH	(sheep)	Peru	HUANAC-o	(sheep)
KIS-e	(purse)	Chukchee	KUISS-u	(purse)
ANAK	(king)	Peru	INC-a	(king)
KAR-t	(town)	Chile	KAR-a	(town)
OKEL	(store-house)	Maya	HACAL	(house)
*AGN	(fire)	Greenld.	IGN-ek	(fire)
*KHARUS	(gold)	Guarani	CUARAS-i	(sun)
*AR	(light)	Brazil	AR-e	(day)
*MESEK	(wine)	Peru	MISK-i	(sweet)
*YIN	(wine)	Peru	HVIN-apu	(liquor)
*KAD	(jar)	Chile	GUID-i	(pot)
*LAK	(to send)	Maya	LAC-u	(leg)
*DAK	(to bite)	Cariban	TAGH-uhe	(to eat)
*SHAPASH	(sun-god)	Klamath	SHAPASH	(sun)

*Words marked by an asterisk are Old Phoenician names contained
in cuneiform tablets of the Mystery Centre of Ugarit (Syria).

Mystery Centre called Ugarit, that flourished between 2000
and 1400 B.C. This Centre was conquered and destroyed
about 1400 B.C. All the tablets with their inscriptions in a
cuneiform alphabet were buried beneath the sand of the
Syrian coast, until the year 1929 when an expedition of French
scholars, archaeologists and linguists (F. A. Schaefer, Charles
Virolleaud and others) succeeded in excavating them after
they had been hidden for at least 3300 years. However in the
city of Carthage in Africa, people spoke a Semitic dialect
closely related to Phoenician, and containing most of these
words. Thus up to the Third Century B.C. sailors from Carthage and even from its colonies in North Africa, Spain and

France may possibly have journeyed beyond Gibraltar, reached the American Continent and imported some Phoenician words. But in spite of this theoretical possibility there are cases where such a conclusion would be excluded.

There are indeed certain words found in the texts of Ugarit (such as the name of the sun-god *Shapash*) which belong to a remote antiquity and to most ancient religious cults, and

(270) *Egyptian 'Vestiges' in American Indian Vernaculars.*

EGYPTIAN		AMERICAN
BAIT-i (king)	Apinages	PAIT-i (king)
SER-et (hand)	Guarani	ZIR-i (hand)
ANT-a (sun)	Chile	ANT-a (sun)
KEB (earth-god)	Maya	CAB (earth)
ATON (sun-god)	Mexico	ATON-a (sun-god)
UNG-a (son of the Sun)	Peru	INC-a (emperor)
TEP (top of a hill)	Maya	TEP-eu (hill)
KHAM (to burn)	Brazil	COOM (to burn)
HAP-a (to seize)	Peru	HAP-i (to seize)
HENT-i (ends)	Carib.	ENAT (to end)
KHAN-u (barge)	”	CAN-aoa (canoe)
MAKH-i (to be in water)	Peru	MOKK-a (wet)
MIY-u (water)	”	MAY (water)
KAP (hand)	Maya	CAB (hand)
BAKH (inundation)	”	PAC (river)
KHEPER-a (beetle)	Carib.	CUPAR-i (insect)
KAP (smoke)	Peru	KAP-a (smoke)
SEK-eu (to till)	Brazil	SIC-a (to till)
HARF (to wrap)	Peru	KIRP-a (to cover)
+MOUT-e (to speak)	Guato	MOUT-eu (to speak)

+ Coptic (daughter of Old Egyptian).

which did not pass from Ugarit or Phoenicia to the West, or

to subsequent ages. They were unknown to Carthage. If we discover them however in the dialects of the Klamath or Modoc Indian tribes of California, long before the landing of Columbus in 1492, we are puzzled by their presence. Who could have brought them from Syria to California, and at what time? It must have been before 1400 B.C., for the god-name *Shapash* vanished after that time. This is a difficult problem indeed.

Some archaeologists believe in certain religious and artistic connections between Old Egypt, Mexico and Peru. Obelisks and pyramids are found in all three countries. Mummification was practiced in Egypt and in Mexico, Peru and even North America. Sun-gods were worshiped on the Nile River and in the New World as well. In addition there are artistic relationships, architecture, painting, sculpture and the like between the Old and New Worlds. Many Americanists are thus inclined to admit certain unknown relations between the Egyptian and the Old American civilisations. The 'savage' Indian tribes cannot possibly have been the teachers of the Egyptians. Thus the current opinion is that the highly civilized nations of the Old World, such as the Egyptians, brought a part of their civilisation to the Western Hemisphere. Now the question emerges: can language confirm such a theory? Are Egyptian words found in America?

This list contains three god-names, *ANT-a* (sun) assonant to *Indra, ATON,* the sun-god, one of the oldest in Egyptian religion whose cult had to give way to that of *Ammon,* yet was for a few years revived by the modernist Pharaoh *Ekh-n-aton* (the splendor of Aton), and finally *KEB*, the earth-god, again one of the ancestors of the Egyptian Olympus. Then there appear two names of priest-kings, of servants of godheads, of initiates, *BAIT-i* (king), in the Apinages dialect of Brazil *PAIT-i* (king), in Lithuanian *wiesz-PATI* (lord of the house or village), Russian *gos-PODI=hos-PODI* (lord, god). It is sufficient to point out that these same word-stems can be found in other languages too, not only in Egyptian. The Vikings as well as the Egyptians could have brought some of the words of Table 270 to the Western Hemisphere. The meaning of the Viking word *BEKK-r* (brook) is even closer to Mayan *PAC* (river) than that of the Egyptian *BAKH* (inundation.

(271) *Zoque (Maya) PAC (River) and Old Norse BEKK*
(beck, brook).

America, Zoque	Old German	German
PAC (river)	PACH (brook)	BACH (brook)

English	O. Norse	Egyptian
BECK (brook)	BEKK-r (brook)	BAKH (inundation)

Before we discuss the Vikings who preceded Columbus by some 500 years in reaching Old America, we must investigate another problem. More than a century ago *Alexander von Humboldt* traveled across the American Continent and came to Mexico. When he first saw a Maya pyramid temple and heard that in the native Maya tongue it was called *Teocalli,* he was told that *TEO* means *god* and *CALL-i* — *a house!* Humboldt was startled. "This is pure Greek!" he exclaimed. The Maya word *TEO* is the Greek word *THEO-* and the Maya word *CALL-i* is the Greek word *KAL-ias* (hut, house). Even Homer himself might have called a temple *THEOU KALIAS, God's house.*

In the latter part of the Nineteenth Century, *Augustus Le Plongeon* spent four years in studying the Maya language of Yucatan, and he said: "One third of this tongue is pure Greek. Who brought the dialect of Homer to America? or who took to Greece that of the Maya? Greek is the offspring of Sanskrit. Is Maya? Or are they coeval? . . . The Maya is not devoid from the Assyrian". Le Plongeon's first impression that Maya words were assonant to Homeric names is completely correct, but he is mistaken in believing that Greek is "the offspring of the Sanskrit". This is no more true than would be the assertion that American Indian vernaculars were offspring of Egyptian, Hebrew or Phoenician. However there seem to be so many Greek words not only in Maya, but in Peruvian,

Mexican, Brazilian and Chilean also, that sometimes we cannot help thinking that these American Indian vernaculars are the classical idioms of the Western Hemisphere.

(272) *Hellenic Words in American Indian Vernaculars.*

GREEK		AMERICAN
OMBR-os (rain)	Yagua	HUMBR-a (rain)
PELAG-os (ocean)	Eyeris	BALAGU-a (ocean)
KEP-os (garden)	Chile	KEP-u (garden)
KAR-os (deep sleep)	Brazil	KER (to sleep)
LIN-on (flax,linen)	Chile	LUN (bast)
OIK-os (house)	Brazil	OK-a (house)
OUK (not)	Galibi	OUC-a (not)
ORG-e (rage)	Eyeris	URAG-an (rage)
APOLL-o (sun-god)	Nutka	UPEL (sun)
TOP-os (spot)	Brazil	TYB-a (spot)
GYN-e (woman)	"	CUN-ya (woman)
DAKR-y (tear)	"	DICR-u (water)
PTER-na (heel)	"	PYTER-a (sole of the foot,
OUS, OT-os (ear)	Carajas	OUT-ai (ear)
POL-y (much)	Cauixana	PEL-e (many)
LEUK-os (white)	Apache	LAK-i (white)
NEM-o (to dwell)	Huazteca	NEM-i (to dwell)
NOM-os (pasture)	Brazil	NYUM (pasture)
CHOIR-os (boar)	Botocudo	KUR-ek (boar)
HETAIR-os (fellow)	Huron	YATAR-e (fellow)
KAT-a (near to)	Pehuelche	KAT-a (near to)
CHITON (garment)	Quiché	QUETON-ec (fur coat)
HEKYR-a (mother-in-law)	Carib.	AKIR-u (mother-in-law)
KARAN-os (prince)	Aymara	KARAN (vice-king)
THIB-e (basket)	"	TIP-a (basket)

POR-os (travel)	**Aymara**	PUR-ini (to travel)
OMICH-le (cloud)	**Mexico**	MIX-tli (cloud)
ORYX, ORYCH-os (antelope)	**Bororo**	OROG-o (fallow deer)
ANAX, ANAK-os (prince)	**Peru**	INC-a (king)
PALM-ys (king)	**Chile**	PULM-en (noble man)
CHELID-on (swallow)	**Maya**	QUELETZ-a (bird, swallow)
HALK-yon (auk)	**Peru**	ALLC-a Mari (holy falcon)

Humboldt and Le Plongeon were correct when they spoke of Greek stems existing in American Indian languages, particularly since the list of these words could be greatly enlarged. We find here the name of a sun-god assonant to that of Apollo as well as names of kings, vice-kings and princes, spiritual guides of their nations, priest-kings and initiates, *Inca, Karan, Pulmen,* names of water, sea, clouds and rain, of house and garden, of animals, plants and so on. Who introduced them into the New World?

This is not an idle question, for many fine students were of the opinion that Greek or Hebrew words found in American dialects must have been imported from Hellas or Palestine. *Vicente Lopez* in his book *Les Ariens du Pérou* (*The Aryans of Peru*), Paris, 1871, and *Thomas Stewart Denison* in *Mexican Linguistics,* Chicago, 1913, saw in Peruvian and in Mexican the daughters of Sanskrit, "Aryan" tongues. They rightly felt that such linguistic coincidences prove some real contacts must have taken place in an unknown past between those nations. Today there is no doubt whatever that about the year 1000 A.D., Vikings from Norway, Iceland and Greenland had landed on the east coast of the United States between Boston and Labrador. The Younger Edda contains reports about their adventures with the so-called *Skrallinge,* probably the American Indians. They did not establish any lasting settlements, and vanished after a few years, probably being exterminated by the Indians. Did they leave any traces in the tongues of America? It seems so.

(273) *Viking Words in American Indian Vernaculars.*

OLD NORSE		AMERICAN
MARK (march)	Peru	MARC-a (march)
BIKAR-r (beaker, cup)	Eskimo	POAGR-e (vessel)
WIF (wife)	Shoshone	WEP-ee (wife)
NOS (nose)	Californ.	NUSH (nose)
FUGL (fowl, bird)	Taino	BOGIAEL (bird)
HECL-a (coat)	Chile	ICL-a (woman's dress)
BEKK-r (beck, river)	Maya	PAC (river)
HRIM (ice)	Quiché	HOROM (cold)
BY, BO (dwelling)	Taino	BO (dwelling)
YLG-r (she-dog)	Mexico, Peru, Chile	ALC-o (dog)

There are Old Norse words found in American Indian dialects, yet whether they stem from those anonymous Vikings who less than a thousand years ago landed in North America, appears highly improbable. Out of the ten words selected at random and given above only one is found in the North among the Eskimo, while the other nine belong to Central and South American vernaculars. Further, most of them can be found in other languages, and some of them were mentioned in the foregoing tables. Let us examine word No. 8 of Table 273: Old Norse *HRIM* (ice, hoarfrost), our *rime*. In Europe we find some of its relatives.

(274) *The word RIM-e (frost), Old Norse HRIM, in Europe.*

English	Anglo-Sax.	O. Norse	Breton
RIM-e	HRIM (ice)	HRIM (ice)	FRIM (hoarfrost)
French		**Greek**	**Related to**
FRIM-as (hoarfrost)		KRYM-os (frost)	CREAM (crust)

The vocalisation here is weaker than in the Quiché word *HOROM* (cold), and the meaning also varies somewhat. The impression completely changes when we examine related words found in other continents.

(275) *The Word RIM-e (frost) Found in Different Continents.*

America, Quiché	Europe, Basque	Africa, Nuba	Asia, Hebrew
HOROM (cold)	HURM-a (rime)	OROM (cold)	KAROM (crust)

HURM-a or *URM-a* in Basque is similar to Quiché *HOR-OM* (cold), yet the African form *OROM* (cold) is identical with it in sound and meaning. Some Americanists such as *Leo Wiener* believe that African tribes peopled the Western Hemisphere, and he uses language extensively to prove his thesis. However since he generally limits his investigation and does not include other than African linguistic families omitting other continents and peoples, particularly of remote ages (Egyptian, Sumerian, Babylonian, Hebrew etc.), his evidence is inconclusive. We note further, that even the Hebrew is more similar to Quiché (*KAROM* : *HOROM*) than the Viking form (*HRIM*), not because words have been imported from the Asiatic continent to the American but because some of them belong to an older word-strata with a more ancient vocalisation.

Thus we realize that language can be considered a kind of chronometre, indicating the age of words, tongues, and things. So long as we remain within the Indo-European ('Aryan') linguistic circle, the span of time embraced by its historical records is comparatively short: it hardly goes back farther than 2500 years, mostly to the first millenium B.C., and cannot be of a great help to us, when we wish to fix the age of unrecorded facts or things. However the moment we extend our investigation to Sumerian, Egyptian, Babylonian, Old Phoenician, Hebrew and — last not least — Old American, we extend recorded history by at least 3000 years further, and we begin to realize the true age of words and things.

Let us illustrate this by one example. Let us take the English *PIT-A-PAT* (to move in a flutter) and compare it with Egyptian *PET-PET* (to move, to jump) and Manchu *PATA-PATA* (sudden falling of fruits from a tree). In England and Europe this word appears very late in records, not earlier than the Second Millennium A.D., while in Egypt it is to be found in records of thousands of years earlier. Thus we learn how old it really is.

(276) *Egyptian PET-PET Recorded Long Before English PIT-A-PAT.*

Europe, England	Africa, Egypt	Asia, Manchu
PIT-A-PAT	PET-PET	PATA-PATA
(to move)	(to move, jump)	(fall from a tree)

Another advantage of the comparison of words with relatives in Egyptian, Sumerian or like languages, involves the disappearance of these oldest witnesses of human civilisation in later epochs. When in America we find a word which resembles another which lives in a modern tongue, the objection can always be raised that such a name may have been imported to America after 1492. If however, we discover in American vernaculars words of a tongue that ceased to be spoken some 5000 years ago (as is the case with Sumerian), then, of course, no one can speak of a word as borrowed from another contemporaneous idiom. This new method can be used as a way of finding out how and why the American Indian vernaculars are related to the oldest recorded tongue:*Sumerian.*

(277) *Old Sumerian Words in America.*

SUMERIAN			AMERICAN
LUL		Peru	LLULL-u
	(a lie)		(a lie)
SUG		"	SOC-o
	(reed-bank)		(reed)
KURUN		Panari	KURN-é
	(mead, wine)		(honey)
SABAR		Chaques	ZAPAR-a
	(net)		(fishing net)
A		Mexico	A-tl
	(water)		(water)
MAGH		Taino	MAG-u
	(great)		(great)
SIM		Peru	SIM-i
	(to call)		(speech)
ID		Californ.	ID-ik
	(water)		(water)
AR-a		Brazil	AR-a
	(shining)		(daylight)
UR, KUR		Venezuela	UR, KUR
	(mountain)		(mountain)

SAG	Peru	TAK-e
(house)		(shelter)
MASH	Mexico	MASH-atl
(antelope)		(deer)
EGALL-u	Alaska	IGL-oo
(house)		(house)
IG-i	Maya	IC
(sun, light)		(sun, light)
DAM	Calif.	DAM
(husband)		(man)
MUSH	Carib.	MUSIK-o
(a flie)		(an ant)
TAG	Calif.	TOK
(to hit)		(to hit)
SAG	Peru	SAK-tani
(to kill)		(to kill)
GUB-i	Cabecara	CAB-e
(snake)		(snake)
GIN	Calif.	XIN
(to go)		(to walk)
GAN	Mexico	CON-otl
(to bear)		(son)
BUR	Brazil	BYR-a
(son)		(son)
SHUG-a	Peru	ASUK-a
(fisher)		(a seal)
MULG-e	”	MALLC-u
(sun-god)		(sun-god)
BAL	Chile	BAL
(axe)		(axe)
KASHER	Peru	KUSUR-u
(basket)		(basket)
URUM	Carib.	URUM-i
(man)		(son, boy)
ILD-ak	Chanabal	ALATZ
(offspring)		(child)
GUR-ush	Peru	CUR-aca
(Lord)		(chief)
RA	”	RAY
(bright)		(flame)

Some of these words, of course, are found in many other tongues as e.g. *MAGH* (great), a word-stem which most linguistic families have in common, related to *MUCH* and *MIGH-t,* and contained in *MAG-nitude.*

(278) *The Word-Stem MIGHT in Different Linguistic Families.*

America, Taino	Europe, Greek	Latin
MAGU-a (great)	MEG-as (great)	MAG-nus (great)

Asia, Sumer		Sanskrit
MAGH (great)		MAH-a (great)

If the American vernaculars had borrowed this name, they

could have taken it equally from the Teutons or Greeks, as from the ancestors of the Hindus, and not necessarily from the Sumerians. But the case is completely different when certain of the Sumerian words are found nowhere else in the world except in Mesopotamia and in pre-Columbian America. This applies to instances such as *LUL* (lie) or *MASH* (antelope).

(279) *Sumerian LUL (a Lie) and Peruvian LLULL-u (lie)*
Isolated.

America, Peruvian	.English	Anglo-Saxon	Asia,Sumer
LLULL-u (a lie)	a LIE	LYG-e (a lie)	LUL (a lie)

We could consider Peruvian *LLU-LLU* and Sumerian *LU-L (U)* as doubled forms since duplications as we have mentioned are typical of very ancient vernaculars. In that case we could try to link with them to *LIE,* as the simple form of the stem. According to a comparison of the Anglo-Saxon, the older form of English *LIE,* the form *LYG-e,* German *LUEG-e* (lie) shows however a G-sound as the final consonant of the stem and it is doubtful whether the Peruvian or the Sumerian words, *LLULL-u* or *LUL,* had such an end-consonant. Thus we must admit that both the Peruvian word *LLULL-u* and the Sumerian word *LUL* doubtless have been related for more than 5000 years and that both nations must have met somewhere in some place which was neither Mesopotamia, nor the American Continent.

This becomes still more lucid in the case of the Sumerian word *MASH* (antelope) and the Mexican word *MASH-atl* (deer). Both are absolutely identical except that the Sumerian word shows the pure word-stem (as is usual in Chinese words) while the Mexican name contains the root plus the ending -atl, as in *TEO-tl* or *TE-otl* (god). In *Huazteca* another form of the word is used as the name of an Aztec god of hunting *MIX-coatl* or *MISH-coatl.* In Nicaragua the old Indian god of hunting is called *MAZ-at,* and in Algonquin the deer is called *MOOS-e,* while *MEES-e* in Lappish means a reindeer, with a similar vocalisation as in the Californian word *AMIS-a* (deer). This word-stem is one of the oldest and found in many tongues.

(280) *Sumerian MASH (antelope) and Mexican MASH-atl (deer).*

America, Mexico	Europe, Lappish	Asia, Sumer	Sanskrit
MISH-coatl	MEES-e	MASH	MESH-a
(god of hunting)	(deer)	(antelope)	(sheep)

The Aztecs and the tribes of Nicaragua prayed to *MISH-coatl* or *MAZ-at* for a successful chase. The Mexican word *MASH-atl* thus is identified to a very distant past, to the mythological age. We may rightly conclude from this fact that it is older in its meaning than even its far earlier recorded Sumerian cousin. It may be as old as 15,000 years, if not more. The same applies to another name of a divinity, *MULG-e*, the sun-god of the Sumerians, and *MALLC-u*, the sun or sun-god in Peru. This is a strange coincidence, for does not the Sumerian god-name *MULG-u* remind us of the Biblical *MOLOCH*, Hebrew *MOLECH*, a Semitic deity whose worship was accomplished by the sacrifice of first-born children who were burnt on his arms? This Semitic deity exists before the appearance of the Semites, among the old Sumerian nation of Mesopotamia, and — what matters more — in pre-Columbian America, in Peru *MALLK-i* (mummy, the soul of a dead, spirit), and *MALLK-i Villak* (the name of a priest who was able to speak with the dead).

According to *Saavedra, El Ayllu,* Paris 1914, *MALLC-u* was the title of very high ranking caciques, and *Villka* was the term used for a high priest of the Sun-god. Since in Hebrew and in other Semitic idioms (Babylonian) *MELEK* or the Assyrian *MALK-u* meant a king (a priest-king), there can be no doubt about the religious nature of the Peruvian name *MALLC-u* and its connection with the sun. In Magyar *MELEG* means *warm*, the Tungus tribe calls the *fire MILG-an*, the Chukchee *MILG-in*, while in the dialects of the Caucasus mountains *MALKH* means the sun. *O'Connor* in his work *The Chronicles of Eri*, London 1882, cites the Irish word

MOLC (a constant strong fire), as the earthly type of the god *BAAL.* The relationship of *MOLOCH* and *BAAL* is a well-known fact.

(281) *The Sun-God MOLOCH and the Relationship of His Name.*

America, Peru	Europe, Irish	Asia, Caucasus
MALLC-u	MOLC	MALKH
(sun-god)	(fire, Baal)	(sun)

Chukchee	Sumer
MILG-in (fire)	MULG-u (sun-god)

We obtain here the same impression as in the case of the Mexican hunting-god *Mix-coatl*: a deep grounded connection between the names and the words of various idioms whose great antiquity we realize, and which cannot be explained by any recent transition from nation to nation. These are mysterious links pointing to a time of life on earth when the human family was not yet scattered, but lived far from the present continents yet in some connection with them, in a time unknown, evidently removed from ours by ten thousands of years.

One thing is clear: it is a mistake to limit the relationship of speech to a few tongues or even groups of tongues, be it Sumerian, Egyptian, Indo-European or Semitic. From whichever language we may start and whichever idiom we may choose for a comparison, we shall always meet with relationship. It does not matter from which continent we may sail and to which corner of the world we may journey, the tongues of these parts of the earth will always show themselves connected and related. There is no such thing as related and non-related languages: there are only tongues which are more or less closely related, more or less transformed in the course of their separation and isolation.

No part of the Continents in existence today contains the cradle of mankind, the place where humanity spent the years of its childhood and youth in common evolution, common speech, common spiritual and social life, common approach to the same godheads and spiritual beings, common religion, art and science. The northern regions of the present world, of America, Europe, Asia, were not that common home, for those parts of the earth lay beneath the surface of the oceans, or were covered with ice and snow. No human beings, no plants and hardly many animals existed there. Those parts of our planet emerged only later from beneath the waters, beneath the Seven Seas.

Why do we speak of Seven Seas today? Does the captain of a modern ocean steamer realize that the holy books of India used this expression thousands of years before him and that he — a representative of our Twentieth Century, who does not believe in lost continents or legendary islands — repeats what he should shun? The Seven Seas were connected with the Seven Continents. From the most ancient times up to the days of Columbus our Western World knew only three Continents: Asia, Europe and Africa, and these three parts were still connected. In the meantime two more had to be added: America and Australia.

However, of the Seven Continents of the ancients, two remain to be accounted for. An ancient tradition tells about a Lemurian Continent located south of Asia, extending from Ceylon, or further west, to the Malayan Archipelago, which was destroyed by a volcanic catastrophe. Egyptian temple archives together with Greek tradition and such a great authority as Plato, describe a lost continent called Atlantis submerged in the floods of the ocean that bears its name.

The one-time existence of Lemuria has been officially admitted by leading natural scientists. Is it not time to decide whether the last of the former Seven Continents of the world, *Atlantis,* was not a reality too? Perhaps, if we solve this riddle, we shall discover the original home of mankind and the cradle of its civilisation.

CHAPTER SEVENTEEN

THE LOST CONTINENT OF ATLANTIS

LIFE TURNS into legend much faster than we imagine, and the great spirits of the past, were they to be resurrected in our present day and hear and read what we are saying and printing about them, would probably call our prosaic age a legendary one. For in spite of our scientific soberness we are weaving legends around many people and events. Even the history of the discovery of the Western Hemisphere by Columbus has become legendary to some extent in the short span of 450 years.

Who was Columbus? Where was he born? What was the real purpose of his voyage? Did he wish to discover a western route to India, the land of spices, the gold treasures of the Biblical Ophir? Why did he not search for such treasures? What he brought back upon his first return to Spain were no hoards of gold, but a few Indians, some parrots and similar attractions. In the eyes of Ferdinand and Isabella who had sent him out for gold he must have appeared more of a Don Quixote than a genuine explorer.

Why did the admiral not sail directly west when he left the little port of Palos in Spain? According to his log-book Columbus steered his three caravels south, then south-west, during the first weeks. When he approached the Canaries the rudder of his second vessel, the 'Pinta', broke. He stopped at Tenerife for three weeks for repairs. During this delay, Columbus spent much time in reading, and what interested him most was the story of *Atlantis* as described in *Plato's* dialogues *Critias* and *Timaeus.*

Was it Atlantis which Columbus had in mind when he undertook his voyage of discovery? He obviously made certain concessions to his sponsors and was searching for a western seaway to India also. He named the Antilles, where he first landed, *West-India*, and the American natives *Indians*. Yet such reliable students as the great philosopher and humanist *Luis Vives* have stressed the fact that it is first of all Columbus' belief in the story of Atlantis to which we are indebted for the discovery of the American Continent.

Plato relates that he had learned about the Lost Continent of Atlantis from his own grandfather, a close friend of the great Athenian legislator, *Solon*. Solon, following the custom of his time, went to the Orient and later to Egypt, to the mystery-centre of Sais in the Nile delta region. The priests of Sais were Solon's teachers and initiators and they told him the story of Atlantis as recorded in their secret archives. They spoke of the catastrophe which destroyed Lemuria in pointing to the legend of Phaethon who one day attempted to drive the chariot of his father the sun-god, Helios, but unable to control the wild horses, was thrown out of the orbit and killed while the fire which broke out burnt part of the earth. Atlantis, however, was destroyed by a flood-catastrophe. Nothing of these events has been preserved in the records of Greece, for the Greek were a comparatively young nation. The archives of Sais contained many stories about Greek achievements of which Hellas itself had no inkling, for all these facts had fallen into oblivion. Did Solon know anything about the victory obtained by his native town, Athens, over the Atlanteans some 10,000 years ago? The Atlantean armies had tried to conquer Greece, to expand their empire still further east and to subdue even Egypt. Thanks to the courage and power of the Athenians this onslaught was repelled and the Atlanteans defeated. They were driven back Westward to Atlantis, and there received the punishment of the gods for their misdeeds.

According to that Egyptian source the Island of Atlantis, one of the original Seven Continents, was located beyond the Pillars of Hercules, amidst the Atlantic ocean, between Europe and Africa on the one side and the *'opposite continent'* on the other. Islands, serving as land-bridges, connected Atlantis with the opposite parts of the earth and there was much traffic between both shores of the ocean. Let us keep in mind that by such a circumscription as 'the opposite continent' Plato must have imagined that part of the earth which now is called America. We encounter here about 3300 years ago the first indirect mention of America in recorded literature.

The Island of Atlantis was ruled by gods, by Kronos-Saturn and his sons. The people of Atlantis had developed a high civilisation; they were excellent navigators, had marvelous harbors for their fleets, built great cities with great stadiums and beautiful temples, whose walls were covered with pure gold. They extended their empire more and more by founding colonies, until it reached deep into the Mediterranean zone, on its southern shore up to Egypt, on the northern shore to Hellas. Italy whose name so strangely recalls that of Atlantis came under the sphere of their influence, yet Atlantis fell into decay, its spiritual and moral civilisation degenerated and similar to the Bible account and to most flood legends, the Gods decided to destroy that island. One day, Zeus convoked a meeting. . . . Here the dialogue *Timaeus* is suddenly interrupted. The story of Atlantis remained a fragment.

The Greeks were actually a "young", a modern people as the priests of Sais had expressed it. Many of them no longer understood Plato's report on Atlantis or believed it. Plato's most outstanding pupil, Aristotle, doubted his teacher's story and called it mere fancy. The mythological and religious age had come to an end; the community with the Gods had ceased and the Human Age was about to start, the Age of Man, Earth and Earthly Knowledge. Aristotle contradicted his teacher on three important issues: (1) he denied the spiritual creation of language and stressed its origin by mere convention, (2) he repudiated a common source of speech, and stressed the independent creation of various tongues, and (3) he decried the story of Atlantis and of a common origin and dwellingplace of all mankind as mere fantasy. Aristotle later became the leading thinker in the Occident and the official philosopher of the Church. His opinion was predominant, and his remarks about Plato were passed from generation to generation as a kind of slogan used to discredit Plato's ideas and works. Thus the idea of a lost continent called Atlantis became untenable, except for unbiased minds.

However the remembrance of the submerged island not only survived in the Old Testament and in Babylonian cuneiform records, but in legends, fairy tales and traditions among most peoples of the earth. Sometimes it appeared disguised as the story of a submerged city, as in the German legend of lost Vineta (Winida) allegedly located on the shore of the Baltic, or the old Breton tale of *Ker d'Ys* (the city of Ys), reflected in a legend of the *Cardigan Bay* in Wales and of *Lough Neagh* in Ireland, where, according to legends mentioned by Lewis Spence, *The Problem of Atlantis* (p. 223), at low tide the fishermen could see ruins of ancient buildings at the bottom. The Irish poet Thomas Moore sang:

> 'On Lough Neagh's bank as the fisherman strays
> When the clear, cold eve's declining,
> He sees the round towers of other days
> In the wave beneath him shining'.

There is something mysterious about the whole Atlantis legend. When Aristotle called it a product of mere fantasy, he overlooked the complete seriousness of the tone in which his teacher Plato had announced that tale. In *Timaeus* Plato had written, "Listen, Socrates, this is a marvelous story, and yet full of truth!" This is by no means the way Plato would have introduced a story which he had considered mere fiction.

Nevertheless Aristotle discredited it by his critique, but destiny played a strange turn to the Father of Logic. While his pupil, Alexander the Great, was on his expedition to India and had conquered Phoenicia, he ordered students of the city of Tyre to collect all types of ancient reports and legends, and he sent them to Aristotle. Among the records contained in the library of Tyre was an ancient report concerning a continent called *Antilia* located beyond the Pillars of Hercules. In some manuscripts the name *Antilia* is even spelt *Atilia,* closely assonant to *Atlantis.* This report was accepted by Aristotle, who thus threw the story of Atlantis out of the front-door only to take it in again by the back-door. *Antilia* thus became the traditional name used for a group of islands stretching from Florida and Yucatan to Venezuela, enclosing the Gulf of Mexico and the Caribbean Sea.

Antilia was known throughout the Middle Ages and at that time was mapped as an island located beyond the Pillars of Hercules in the Atlantic Ocean. It was even contained in the map drawn by Toscanelli, a geographer of Florence, in the year 1472. This map was given to Columbus. Thus Columbus did not start his journey haphazardly, but knew very well where he intended to go. On October 12, 1492, he set foot on the island of Guanahani which was part of Antilia — the Antilles, West Indies — already shown on his map.

Let us not discredit legends and history, for the one can easily turn into the other. Only four hundred and fifty years have passed since Columbus arrived in America, yet who can locate precisely that island where Columbus landed, and which was called *Guanahani* in the Indian vernacular? The landing-place of Columbus' three caravels has become legendary in an age noted for the accuracy of its historical research. Thus Atlantis appears to modern science more and more in the light of an historical reality. Aristotle acted out of a prophetic impulse when he introduced Antilia into European knowledge.

At the turning point of history which opened the Christian Era there was still another prophetic hint at the re-emerging of Atlantis and the discovery of America. Lucius Annaeus *Seneca,* the teacher of the Emperor Nero, announced in his tragedy *Medea* the re-appearance of a lost continent in the (Atlantic) Ocean, with the following words:

'Venient annis saecula seris,
Quibus Oceanus vincula rerum
Laxet, et ingens pateat tellus,
Tiphysque novos detegat orbes,
Nec sit terris ultima Thule!'

(In years yet to come will ages arise,
When the ocean shall loose the fetters of things,
The earth will then widen her far-reaching space
And a helmsman discover longhidden lands.
Then Thule will not be the bound of the world!)

After the re-discovery of the American Continent Spanish monks and writers as well as other students tried to answer the question of the origin of the American Indians. They thought of many possibilities as to how the western hemisphere was peopled, of the Lost Ten Tribes of Israel, of Phoenicians, of Egyptian, Greek people and others who had come to America from the Old World and settled here. At the beginning of the Seventeenth Century, at the Age of Enlightenment rationalistic theories began to replace traditional legends. It seemed as though the Bible did not contain direct information about America and the American Indians. Indians of the United States, of Canada and Alaska, with their high cheek-bones reminded some anthropologists of the inhabitants of northeastern Asia.

In addition certain relationships were found between the vernaculars of the Chukchees, Kamchadals, Siberian Eskimos and the Eskimos and other tribes of Alaska and other American Arctic Zones, especially Greenland. Thus in the Seventeenth Century certain European geographers supported the idea of the peopling of America from North-Eastern Asia across the Behring Strait. This idea appeared so much the more plausible as scholars began to doubt whether such primitive tribes as the ancestors of the American Indians could ever have crossed the Atlantic or Pacific in their primitive canoes. To cross Behring Strait seemed quite easy in comparison. Thus the Behring Strait theory became more and more the preferred opinion of North-American scholars. In Latin America however, the idea of Atlantis as the original home of all mankind became prevalent.

The admission of Atlantis as a serious scientific possibility of explaining the peopling of America, occurred in 1932 in the University of Leipzig. Dr. Bessmertny, a Russian student, obtained the degree of Ph.D. of that university with a doctor's dissertation titled *Das Atlantis-Problem.* (The Problem of Atlantis). In this dissertation Bessmertny refers to almost all the sources, both positive or negative, which have touched upon this deep problem. One of his chapters is particularly devoted to a description of Atlantis and its life as given by *Dr. Rudolf Steiner* in his book *Atlantis and Lemuria.* At several points Bessmertny stressed the deep knowledge and high scientific standard of Rudolf Steiner's description.

Another positive contribution to the question of Atlantis appeared somewhat later in the United States. Nelson's *American Encyclopedia* considers the existence of a continent of Atlantis and its submersion by a flood as a historical reality (Article *Atlantis,* Vol. II): "As a result of recent palaeontological research, geologists have concluded that in the Tertiary epoch such an island really existed. The Tertiary shells of the United States are identical with a whole series of fossils in the same beds of France. Also the Tertiary vertebrate animals in France have their analogues either in fossil creatures or in living species in America, justifying the conclusion that a land connection existed between the two continents." As sources of information Nelson's *American Encyclopedia* quotes Plato's *Critias* and *Timaeus* and Rudolf Steiner's *Atlantis and Lemuria.*

Thus this latter book appears to be not only informing but reliable. According to it there actually have been two continents lost; Lemuria, once located south of Asia, and Atlantis amidst the Atlantic. Lemuria was destroyed by a fire catastrophe, while Atlantis was submerged in a catastrophe which

Rudolf Steiner identifies with that event which the Bible and the legendary teachings of almost all nations, call The Flood.

The great Migrations of Peoples which took place in Antiquity were connected with the whole evolution of mankind and its relations to the Universe. There are different conditions affecting the growth and development of humanity in different corners of the earth, various astral influences and constellations, various earth-forces, various climates and relations with the watery element. When Lemuria existed, mankind that dwelt on that lost continent where still today anthropological expeditions are searching for the missing link between ape and man, had not yet perfected its bodily nature. The Lemurian type of man cannot be compared with the appearance of present-day humanity. After the destruction of that continent a small part of the Lemurians moved west to Atlantis and developed into Atlanteans. In the first phase of the Atlantean epoch the physical body of man had not yet reached the outer shape which it has today. It is in Atlantis that man developed upright walking, the bodily speech organs, language and the first roots of modern thinking. Thinking was developed upon speech and by speech.

The man of Atlantis evolved speech not out of an abstract consciousness or an abstract faculty of thinking, but out of a deep imaginative power and a kind of decadent clairvoyance. In sound and meaning speech in that remote epoch had a more artistic, picturesque and spiritual nature than it possesses today. Since the Atlanteans lived in closest connection with Nature, they not only understood her better than we do today, but in their language they could imitate her vividly, the rustling of leaves, the ruhsing of the wind, and the roaring of a hurricane, the seething of waves, the singing of birds and the like. Their language was far more musical than ours today. In a state of dimmed consciousness as that between sleeping and waking, the Atlantean people could use their mind's eye which we have lost in the development of our abstract thinking. They used what the French call 'la seconde vue' or 'second sight', a kind of spiritual perception as Swedenborg called it when he was in London and suddenly realized that a fire had broken out in Stockholm and had destroyed a good part of the old town. People in the Northern parts of the Old World, in Scotland, Ireland, Scandinavia, Finland, Siberia had and still possess partly this extraordinary gift.

The overwhelming majority of the Atlantean population were not far developed in education, hence the great part which their leaders and teachers, great initiates, later heroes and priests-kings played in their affairs. In many parts of the country there were Mystery-Centres where selected students, not only intellectually talented, but endowed with a pure and strong character, were trained and prepared for initiation. No one was admitted to initiation who had not passed through a probation of his soul and spirit forces. Self-knowledge and knowledge of nature, self-control and faculty of leading others were the conditions of any initiation. In the teacher, the initiator, the faculties needed may have been innate; but the adept had to acquire them through a training that little by little unfolded his soul and spirit, his character and will.

In the beginning the Mystery Wisdom embraced the entire field of knowledge, just as in the first ages after their foundation our universities were intended to embrace the *universitas literarum* or totality of human science. The principal original Mystery-Centres were institutions where the Sun Mysteries were taught. It was only later that the hidden wisdom was severed into various parts and Moon-Mysteries and Centres of Mars, Mercury, Jupiter, Venus and Saturn wisdom were created. According to the principle of initiation which prevailed in that epoch, the position of a spiritual or external leader was not transmitted simply from father to son. If the son of a king or a chieftain or priest-king was not capable of leading or being initiated, the office passed to another member of the tribe or nation. These precautions were necessary because the Atlanteans had an insight into the forces of Nature which went far beyond that of later epochs, and they could use those forces, especially the so-called life-forces more intensely than later generations. Hence they were aware of the grave danger of misusing them.

There are ancient oral secret traditions about the Atlantean epoch and its Seven Phases or Sub-Ages, each with one Sub-Race prevailing. The Seven Sub-Races followed one another in this sequence: Rmoahals, Tlavatli, Toltecs, primeval Turanians, primeval Semites, primeval Accadians and Mongols. Rudolf Steiner accepts this sequence, and though we know the story of Atlantis only in dim outline, we realize that in the first three phases, those races developed who — as the Tlavatli and Toltecs — seem to have reappeared later in the American Continent, in Mexico and in other countries. In the later phases of Atlantis however we meet primeval Turanians, Semites, Accadians and Mongols as forerunners of nations who in historical epochs have played an outstanding part in Asia. Two of the present continents, *America* and *Asia,* were most closely connected with the Atlantean Race and civilisation, but this does not preclude the fact that on the edges of the entire Old World, Europe and Africa included, were Atlantean colonies. Thus at an early epoch, Atlantean civilisation spread to various quarters of the earth.

Characteristic of the Atlantean mind and its close connection with the forces of Nature was their phenomenal *memory*. In an epoch when the art of writing had not yet been invented every content of an historical or literary nature had to pass from generation to generation by oral tradition. Until the Age of History, such texts as Homer's *Iliad* and *Odyssey*, or the *Vedas,* or the *Old Testament* and the *Gospels* were passed orally from father to son. Only such a prodigious memory as primeval man possessed enabled him to perform such a difficult task, but it was rendered easier by depicting in pictures what anyone intended to convey to posterity. History, mythology, the life of the community, of great heroes or of leaders was presented in grand tableaus which by their beauty and power deeply impressed the minds of the audience. Myths, legends, fairy tales and magic poems were the first literary and historic fruits of the spirit of Atlantis, and symbols such as a cross, a star, wave-lines, animals such as a bull, a lion, an eagle to express man's earthly nature and connection, the rhythmic current of breathing, the light and flight of thoughts were used as hints to call back to memory the words of the teacher. Symbols were the only written expressions of images or ideas used in oral presentation.

One Sub-Race of Atlantis, the primeval Semites, first developed the germ of abstract thinking, of moral principles and of laws, of a pictureless cognition of the Divine by pure thought. The following Sub-Races began more and more to acquire and use the knowledge of magic forces, chiefly for selfish purposes, for the sake of obtaining power and wealth and of subduing other people. Thus the Atlantean civilisation fell more and more into decay and lost its pure moral foundation. The Atlantean Race had achieved its mission on earth, had developed all the necessary qualities to enable the following ages to further man's tasks upon earth. Now the Atlantean people as a whole were ripe to disappear from the scene of history, in a great flood-catastrophe.

The destruction of Atlantis was not the result of a single act, of a sudden single inundation, but took centuries in accomplishment. Part after part of the island broke away under the rushing of the waves. What we call the drowning of the Atlantean continent is but the last act of that great tragedy and only this is described in the Biblical legend of the Deluge as well as in the other Flood Legends of the different nations.

In those remote epochs of a dark past, when mankind was under the guidance of great spiritual leaders, these outstanding personalities were able to foresee catastrophes and to take necessary precautions against the destruction of all mankind, and to arrange for a survival of a small part of the human race who would be able to continue man's life upon earth. In the following chapter will be shown how a part of humanity survived the submersion of the primeval home, and how they were led to safety by a great guide, the patriarch of the Biblical Flood Legend.

CHAPTER EIGHTEEN

THE MIGRATION OF PEOPLES

Who was the great leader who for many years before the
end of Atlantis, foreseeing the catastrophe which was to befall
that mysterious island, did his best to gather a part of his
people and to lead them to safety across the ocean thus protecting a nucleus of mankind, of the future mankind against
inevitable death? The Bible calls that great spiritual guide
Noah, while in Greece and in other Old-European countries,
the name used for him was *Inachos,* the Inca, and in the holy
books of India he is called *Manu. Manu* means Man as far as
he is or is destined to become a *thinking being;* not just a
philosopher, but a thinker. Man-kind is the human kind, the
thinking kind, or the kind, the children of Manu. It refers to
his race, if we were able to use the term 'race' rightly after the
Atlantean epoch. For the blood forces and connections played
a vital part in the old age of Atlantis, during the childhood of
humanity. In the age of thinking Man that followed, blood
relations and races lost more and more of their original meaning, and their loosening has the purpose of strengthening
more and more conscious spiritual relationship and connections.

Manu not only had foreseen the catastrophe of Atlantis,
but realized also the task lying ahead of the nucleus he was
leading East. He split his group of Atlanteans into two parts,
and guided them with the aid of helpers upon two different
paths of migration to the centre of Asia, the desert of Gobi
and the country of Tibet. The two streams of migration were
a Northern and a Southern one. Both had landed on the
Western shore of France, in the region of the Hybernian Mystery-Centres. Before they separated, the Atlantean pilgrims
were trained in Hybernian wisdom and initiated, thus com-

260

ing into touch with Ireland and the British Isles, with Brittany and the Basque country, with the region of the Franco-Cantabrian Caves, and with Spain. Many decades passed, before the northern wave of migration continued its pilgrimage to the East across northern France, Germany, Scandinavia, Russia, the Caucasus, the Near East toward Gobi. The southern wave of migration went southward to Spain, then along the North-African coast, through Egypt, Palestine, Mesopotamia to the desert of Gobi. There the junction of both waves took place.

For several centuries Manu and his successors trained the 'seed of future mankind' in spiritual wisdom, thus creating a new humanity able to become the bearers of a new civilisation. After this common training and education had been achieved, ages of great migrations followed. The new seed of humanity had multiplied and was now under the supervision of initiated wise men who were directed westward again to people the countries of Western Asia, Northern Africa and Europe and to introduce there the new civilisation. First the pilgrims went to India, then to Persia, afterwards they settled in Mesopotamia, Palestine and in Egypt, then in Greece, Italy and — wave by wave — in the other countries of Europe. We must imagine that many, many waves followed one another even into the same part of the Old World. For example there were at least five migrations of Semites to Mesopotamia, Phoenicia, Palestine, Arabia and Abyssinia, and several branches moved into Egypt. A new Age, which is not to say a new race developed: the *Aryan Age*.

Old tradition and especially Rudolf Steiner never use the term *Aryan* in the narrow and erroneous sense of nations who speak today an Indo-European tongue or are part of a blue-eyed and blond human type. Aryans, in the sense of Rudolf Steiner, are all those nations who founded and developed the civilisation of our present epoch, the Aryan Epoch. Thus the people of India, the Persians, the Sumerians, Babylonians, Phoenicians, Hebrews and other Semites, the Egyptians,

Greeks, Romans, Celtic, Germanic and Slavic nations of Europe as well as several others, all belong to the true Aryan family.

To confine true Aryans to those nations of Asia and Europe who speak an Indo-European tongue today or to a still narrower racial group, and to exclude Sumerians, Egyptians, Babylonians and other Semitic peoples from the Aryan community meant no less than to suppress the first fundamental phase of the Aryan Age, namely the third or Sumero-Babylonian (Egypto-Semitic) stage of the Aryan era, that time which can rightly be called the *first historical epoch*. The art of writing did not start in the primeval Indian or primeval Persian Epochs, but later in Sumeria, Babylonia and Egypt. What we find today in the written or printed editions of the Holy Books of the Orient, the *Vedas,* the *Upanishads,* or the *Zend Avesta* are to an extent degenerated and partly distorted passages of the marvelous original texts which were primarily their genuine content. It may suffice to study the *Rigveda* and the conception of the idea of reincarnation as it is developed in it, in order to realize the deep decline of the teaching of these great holy works in the course of later evoltuion. They not only represent the shadows of the originals, but sometimes are their caricatures.

The question of races becomes more and more difficult, for several reasons. First of all, as we have stressed, the Aryan Age is an epoch where blood ties lose their importance more and more and spiritual connections come to the fore. Second: there are hardly pure races to be found in the post-Atlantean Epoch, because every nation then appears to be a kind of racial mixture; for there were Atlantean colonies surviving on all edges of the Old World, and the last Atlantean survivors of the main island who migrated East mixed with the groups of those colonists. The effects appear clearly in the ages which followed. Even a group such as the Jewish people who go through the ages of history with a strongly developed blood impulse appear first with a stock of about twenty percent

blond and blue-eyed members and with a clear tendency to
blond individuals. There can be no doubt that the whole
spiritual development of the Aryan Age tended toward a predominant rôle of the individuality, and a recession of importance of the blood forces. The outer light of thinking consciousness and the inner torch of moral conscience were to
evolve, while the selfish tendency of a sympathy for one's own
children, one's own race and blood, one's own tribe and nation had to give way to an impartial and unbiased sympathy
for every one who was and is our 'neighbor'. In the Atlantean
Age Man liked his own likeness. In the truly Aryan Age Man
is to develop into a being who likes even those who are not
his likeness.

This required a deep change of human consciousness. The
old picture-consciousness was to disappear, and together with
it the dim, decadent power of clairvoyance. Both, but particularly our former Atlantean picture-consciousness, survived
today in our dreams. Here we see life in picture form, in a
symbolic way. A dream is not only an artist, a painter, but
a symbolist. To look for any principles of our daily logical
thinking, of the well-trimmed order of ideas in the unspeak-
able labyrinth of our dream pictures and their limitless possibilities, would be a hopeless attempt. In our dreams we are
submerged in a life which actually lies far, far behind us in
the day-time — ten thousands of years behind us!

Only when we are aware of this fact can we realize the long
path of evolution which our thinking had to follow in order
to develop into that faculty which it represents today. Mankind in the course of its development, had to migrate from
one part of the earth to the other in order to change the influence of forces that work upon our nature out of the spaces
of the surrounding Universe and make us grow and evolve.
At the end of the Lemurian Epoch humanity had to wander
from the East to the West, in order to acquire the faculty of
upright walking, of speech and the first germs of abstract
thinking. This part of our earthly development was success-

fully achieved during the Atlantean Epoch. Then, when that Epoch came to an end, mankind again had to migrate, this time in the opposite direction, from the West to the East, in order to develop the full power of modern thinking in the Aryan Age.

Thinking, as is known today, consists of two acts: *perceiving* and of *conceiving,* of *percepts* and of *concepts.* Through our senses we take in the outer world, its beings, its objects. We obtain percepts of them. Our thinking forces work upon these percepts and unite with them, transmuting them into ideas or precise, well-defined concepts. The Man of Atlantis had developed neither the faculty of perceiving nor that of forming concepts. His percepts even were as dim as his consciousness. He saw the world and its parts, animals, trees, rocks, rivers and woods not as we do today in clear-cut contours but as it were in a fog, in dim lines, pale and shadowy. In the same manner his thoughts grew; they were but silhouettes of our modern, logical, sharp ideas. Here the migration had to bring about a change. The two waves of those migrations, the Northern and the Southern, had a certain purpose and effect. The Northern wave brought the survivors of the Atlantean catastrophe into closer contact with groups of mankind who were still nearer to Nature, while the Southern wave of migration brought them into touch with peoples who had developed their soul forces, their inner life. Later these opposite tendencies turned into two different forms and methods of initiation, the *Apollinian* way leading across Nature and an exterior hurricane to the experience of the Godhead active behind it, and the other way leading across the passions and imperfections of our soul life, their inward tempest, towards the living up to the divine forces at work within our Self, the so-called way of the *Dionysian* Mysteries. A kind of cosmic polarity manifested itself in those opposite paths and principles.

The same polarity appeared in a general way, accessible to both the Southern and the Northern waves of migration, in the opposite directions of their migrations: once from East to West, from Atlantis to Gobi, then from West to East, from Gobi to Western Asia and Europe. On the way from Hybernia to Gobi the whole nucleus of the Atlantean survivors, the seeds of a new age and Mankind, acquired the faculty of *perception* and evolved it. Perception was particularly necessary for those who later wished to follow the Northern, Apollinian path of initiation. Later the new 'race', the children of Manu, who had been trained in the Mystery Centres of the Desert of Gobi for centuries, migrated from East to West, developed the complementary faculty of thinking, of forming *concepts,* abstract ideas, to free themselves from the remnants of the old picture-consciousness in order to experience the godhead inwardly, in a so-called Dionysian way. The development of perceiving and conceiving was a condition for the whole evolution of the Aryan Age.

The first period of the Aryan Age is called that of the *primeval Indians,* the forerunners of the historical Hindus. These first Aryans were still in a state of transition between two ages, the Atlantean and the Aryan, and were only at the threshold of a new kind of consciousness, the thinking consciousness. They were more closely connected with the Divine than with earthly life, more with the soul than with the senses, more with the soft and mild moonlight than with the powerful, for them too shrill rays of the sun. They and the people of the *primeval Persian* phase which followed, can best be characterized in the light of their polaric attitude toward agriculture.

The Vedas of India contain passages which make it plain that agriculture, farming and raising of cattle, were not in the line with the true Indian life conception. The earth was a holy being, and her symbol, the cow, was also holy. Today this attitude still prevails in the old custom of a kind of reverence toward a cow. In the streets of any town of modern India, a cow can move more freely than a human being. According to the feelings of the Hindu people the earth itself should be left untouched also. To approach the soil, living and sensitive, with an iron knife such as the plough, or even with a strong branch, meant hurting and wounding our mother. This was not merely a sin, — after all we are mortals and are compelled to eat bread — yet to them it was and is an evil. Obviously it could not be entirely forbidden, or the people would die. However such activity was prohibited for the higher castes, the Brahmins and Kshatriya, the priests and the warriors, and was tolerated only so far that the lower caste of the Vaishya, the farmers and merchants, were allowed to deal with it. Thus those forerunners of the modern Hindus lived still at a kind of distance from the ground, to which they had not thus far entirely descended.

Just opposite to the Vedas was the attitude of the *Zend Avesta,* the teaching of *Ahura Mazdao* containing the sunwisdom of Old Persia. In Persia, agriculture, farming and cattle-breeding was a virtue, nay one of the highest virtues. To till the ground was almost a religious duty. Persian wisdom was not concerned with hurting Mother Earth with a plough-share. This treatment was necessary to bring about the thriving, blossoming and productiveness of the soil. Thriving, growing, fruit bearing was not only a physical, but a spiritual manifestation of the earth from the Persian point of view. Where the soil thrives, and the fields thrive, the garden thrives, the trees and the bushes thrive, where the cattle thrives, the wife thrives, the children, the house and everything is growing and blossoming, there is happiness and bliss. The Persians had completely descended to the earth, they no longer stared back at the paradise lost — as did the pimeval Hindus — but stood upon the ground with both feet. They felt this earth is not the prison of our spirit, it is our home for the near future, here we must live, and here we shall try to get along.

It is no wonder that a nation such as those primeval Persians looked at farming and agriculture as the highest mark of human civilisation. This was the yardstick to measure other peoples and to judge their very nature. Hence the well-known hostile attitude of *Iran* (*Airiyana* or *the true Aryan land* was the ancient name of Persia) towards *Turan*. To the true Persian, civilisation started with agriculture, with an end of the nomadic life of hunters and fishermen, of wandering tribes, with the foundation of permanent settlements. Turan was the land of the savage Scythians of northern Asia, of Siberia, who moved about from one country to another, grazing the fields here and there, devouring like animals whatever Nature had to offer them, game, fish, berries and other plants, yet not paying their debt to Mother Earth, not adding anything to her treasures, but merely exploiting and robbing her. Modern agriculture did not start before the primeval Persian Period. It was a gift of the Divine world, acquired by initiation from the great leaders, and was considered a religious duty and activity, a cult: hence *agri-CULT-ure*. In China as elsewhere (we can learn it from Herodotus about the Scythians) it was always a divine being who threw a golden plough from the sky to earth, thus giving a nation the impulse to start agriculture.

The *third* Aryan Period is the *Sumero-Babylonian and Egyptian* phase. It is the first in which historical nations (not merely forerunners) appear in two branches of migration from Central Asia, one to Mesopotamia and to Palestine, the other to Egypt and Northern Africa. As a result of their activity great civilisations blossomed in the Euphrates, Jordan and Nile Valleys. Science, in a modern sense, begins to germinate, astrology is linked with astronomy, work in architecture and other fields of activity bring about the development of geometry and mathematics, the art of writing, however complicated, still linked with the picture consciousness of bygone epochs, turns little by little into a phonetic script, a simple alphabet. Still prevalent is the religious atmosphere of the whole epoch: pyramids and temples are erected to the gods, priest-kings are the rulers of the empires and smaller countries, while archives are established in the Mystery Centres, history is written, the light of human consciousness becomes brighter and brighter, so that the way is paved for the birth of human conscience and the growth of Man's individuality.

This evolution became the task of the *fourth* Aryan period, the *Greco-Roman,* embracing the central event of human history, the introduction of Christianity. In full awareness of the impact which it contains, humanity started a new era from that decisive moment on: the Christian Era. Hebrews, Greeks and Romans had for centuries prepared this development. Europe, which was to become the chief scene of the growth of Christianity, had begun to play an important part in the period when Christianity arose. The centre of historic gravitation had moved Westward, from Asia and Egypt to Europe. Greece appeared first on the scene, followed by Italy. Then the other peoples of the West and North of Europe, of Spain, Gaul and the British Isles, all Hybernia, then Germany and the Slavic East, rose from their Sleeping Beauty slumber.

While the Orient had played the first part in the orchestra of human development and history, those nations had kept silent. Now these young peoples took over the leading rôle. In Hellas and in Rome the *Mythological and Religious Age* had survived in part, but the *Philosophical Period* had begun. It had supported the development of both Christianity and its counteracting forces, the materialistic ideas. After Greece and Rome had finished their mission, in the *fifth Aryan period*, the leading rôle was transferred still further West, to Germany, France and Spain, and later, particularly after the discovery of *America,* to England and the Anglo-Saxons, the English speaking peoples, and to Russia. Our age, the *fifth Aryan period* indicates already the predominant part of the Anglo-Saxons and the Russians in the future, for two more periods a *sixth and a seventh,* will follow ours in which successively the Anglo-Saxons and Russians will not only be leading from a political and economic viewpoint, but from a spiritual one as well.

In early science a sequence of periods in time was usually expressed by a symbol, the number *seven,* a figure which even from a natural scientific standpoint has a certain importance e.g. in physiology; for after a period of seven years all cells of our body are renewed. Thus the Hindus speak of their seven Rishis or wise men, the exalted teachers of the *Vedas* and of Atlantean wisdom. Seven wise men of Old Greece assailed Thebes the colony of an ancient Oriental Mystery Centre, there were seven early philosophers of Greece and seven was the number of kings with whom Roman history started. One of them, *ANC-us Martius,* has a name which reminds us of an *INC-a,* just as the Scottish king's name *ANG-us* does. Two of these kings bore the name of *TARQUIN-ius.* *TARQU-in* is an Etruscan name, and according to Herodotus, the Etruscans, the inhabitants of Etruria (around Florence), had migrated to Italy from Asia Minor. This name *Tarquin* points distinctly to the East.

(282) *The Scottish Name ANG-us (king) and Roman ANC-us (king).*

America, Pehuelche	Europe, Scotch	Rome
HUANAC (chieftain)	ANG-us (king)	ANC-us (king)

Asia, Zend	China
ANKH-us (lord)	HUANG (prince)

These are but a few instances of the widespread name *ANC-us* and *ANG-us* (king) related with *INC-a,* with the name *NOAH* of the Bible (in Phrygian *HANAK*), and thus with the legend of the Deluge. The Phrygians celebrated the festival of the Flood in honor of *Hanac,* as in Argolis, Greece, the Deluge Festival was celebrated in memory of *Inachos* or *Noah.* Let us recall that in Egypt *UNG* or *UNG-i* meant 'son

(283) *The Roman TARQ-in Identical With Mongol TARKH-on (paladin).*

Europe, Irish	Rome	Etruscan
TORC (prince)	TARQU-in- (king)	TARC-na (prince)

Hungarian	Asia, Mongol	Buryat
TARKH-an (judge)	TARKH-on (paladin)	TARG-a (prince)

of the solar deity', thus an initiate into the Osiris Mysteries, or a priest-king (Pharaoh) devoted to the Sun-God.

There are many more interesting relations of this name in Europe and Asia. One is contained in cuneiform tablets of Asia Minor, *TARKH-un* (prince, king, god), and is probably the same name as the Biblical *SARG-on* (Babylonian *SARG-on*), a king who ruled Babylonia about 2870 B.C. or some 4500 years ago. *TARQU-in* is typical of the East-West migration, the more recent one, while the Roman name *ANC-us* and Scottish *ANG-us* are characteristic remnants of the migrations from Atlantis to Asia, across Europe and Africa. Thus a right conception of the name Aryan and of the Aryan epoch solves many of the riddles and contradictions which otherwise cannot be explained.

Once we understand the idea of a Lost Continent of Atlantis, and apply it to an investigation of our past, once we realize the genuine meaning of the name Aryan (post-Atlantean) and its complete extension, and are working with it in manifold fields of human knowledge, vestiges of bygone epochs begin to emerge more and more. Stone after stone of an antique mosaic picture of the early ages appears and links itself with its right neighbor, and the more we progress, the more its once-scattered parts re-unite and coordinate to show us a true and natural image of what actually happened.

Once again we can ask: who is *Manu?* Since we know that the Sumerians, Egyptians, Babylonians, Hebrews and Phoenicians, all the nations who helped create and develop our present culture are members of the great Aryan family of nations, we can open their ancient holy books as well as the *Vedas* and the *Zend Avesta,* and search for an account of their great common ancestor and leader. *Manu* was not confined to the *Vedas;* he was not only the ancestral guide of Old India. The Egyptians too called their first Pharaoh — *MEN-es, the thinking Man,* while the Cretans and Greeks called him *MIN-os,* that founder of their dynasty who had sponsored the building of the *labyrinth,* the symbol of the brain, the laby-

rinth-like instrument of thinking. *MANN-us* was the divine
ancestor of the Germanic tribes, according to Tacitus' *Germania*. And in Hebrew, *MAN-asse* reminds us of the same
name and probably is a close relative of the Sanskrit *MANUSH-a* (man), and the German *MENSCH* (man). Not only
can we link the name *MANCH-u* (man) with this group

(284) *MANU as the Ancestor of Many Classical Nations.*

Europe, Germanic	Greece, Crete
MANN-us (ancestor)	MIN-os (first king)

Africa, Egypt	Asia, India
MEN-es (first pharaoh)	MAN-u (great guide)

and Guanche *MENC-ey* (Lord), but probably even the name
Mos-es, since its root once was spelled M-N-S and still contained an *N-consonant,* sounding similar to *MANUSH-a*
(man). We open a new door to our knowledge by re-uniting
the great classical nations of the Near East with the Aryan
family. One of the greatest mysteries of ancient history begins
to unveil its secret: the *Table of Nations* (chapter X of
Genesis).

Science today uses the names which the Bible introduced
for the chief races of humanity. We are still calling them
Shem or Semites, Ham or Hamites, and Japhet or Japhetites,
simply because we cannot find any better than this Biblical
nomenclature. Does not Greek mythology include an echo of
Japhet (the widespread) in the name of *IAPET-os?* We find
repeatedly the Biblical name of *GOMER,* Babylonian *GIMIRR-i.* Are these *GIMIRRI* not Homer's *KIMMER-ioi*
(a nation dwelling in a remote region of mist and gloom),
the *Cimmerians* or *Cimbrians* of later writers, the *KYMRI* or
CYMRI of the British Isles? There are many more members
of that widespread Nordic family, e.g. *CUMBER-land.* Who
are the *MAD-ai* of the Old Testament if not the *MED-es* of
Persia and Media? Are the *JAVAN* not the *ION-ians,* the
Greek people, today called in Arabic, *JAVAN?* Are the *ELISH-a* not the people of *ELIS,* the Hellenes? Who are the *ASHKENAZ* if not the people of *SCANZ-ia,* the Scandinavians

and the Germanic tribes? Hebrew people use today this same name for the Germans. Finally is not the name of the *ARAM-aeans* completely assonant to the *ARM-enians?* Thus we find the names of nations which Moses used in *Genesis* as current names of outstanding European peoples, many centuries after the Bible had mentioned them in the Table of Nations One vestige after the other thus emerges out of the dark background of the Past.

CHAPTER NINETEEN

MAN, SPEECH AND CIVILISATION

More and more students today accept the one-time existence of an island-continent of Atlantis as a fact. In his novel *Joseph and his Brothers, Thomas Mann* adheres to this conception. "If then the days of an established language of signs are so unnumbered, where shall we seek for the beginnings of oral speech? The oldest, the primeval language, we are told, is Indo-Germanic, Indo-European, Sanskrit. But we may be sure that there existed a still older mother-tongue which included the roots of the Aryan as well as the Semitic and Hamitic tongues. Probably it was spoken in Atlantis. . . ."

As a matter of fact no serious modern linguist would consider Sanskrit or even the postulated Indo-Germanic or Indo-European primeval tongue as the oldest language spoken by humanity, nor would anyone who knows Sanskrit call it the 'mother-tongue' of Greek, Latin, German or Slavic. It is very misleading to use the term 'Aryan' in a narrow sense as a term including only Sanskrit, Old Persian, and most European idioms. Actually Aryans in the right sense of this name are the members of all the three Biblical groups, Japhet, Ham and Shem. This must be clearly understood, or no definite solution will ever be found for the whole problem of the common origin of mankind and its tongues. One question above all would remain unanswered: Where does America and its aborigines fit in this scheme? According to Plato America was the 'opposite' continent of Atlantis!

Who are the American Indians and from which part of the world did their ancestors migrate to America? Were they Semites, the lost Ten Tribes of Israel, as some writers had fancied, or were they Hamites, Egyptians, who in addition to their tongue, brought civilisation to the Western Hemisphere, pyramids, obelisks, temples, mummification and so on? Or were they Japhetites, perhaps Turanians, north-Siberian tribes, who crossed the Behring Strait and landed in Alaska?

What is it that induced many scholars, including many Americans, to cling to this strange Behring Strait theory? In the first decades after the discovery or re-discovery of America, the Spanish writers and students who took up the question of how America was peopled, pointed to a very important part of this problem: the question of *wild animals*! How did they migrate to the Western Hemisphere? Emigrants, settlers certainly did not bring with them tigers, lions, crocodiles, or boas when sailing to their new land of Promise. Thus, such animals must have found their way to the shores of America themselves, yet tigers, lions or alligators are not used to living in arctic regions of the earth, but in tropical countries such as Africa or southern Asia. Did they also cross the giant Asiatic continent, from the Persian gulf to Kamchatka, and from there traverse the sea, or cross the Behring Strait, when it was frozen? How could they survive the climate of Alaska and North America, before reaching the tropical southern parts of the New World? Thus it becomes very doubtful whether the entire Behring Strait theory can be supported at all. In addition, the most important adherents of this solution cling to the improbable opinion that American civilisations do not reach back further than to the year 400 or 600 B.C. This again is an untenable idea.

The whole Behring Strait theory which emerged in the 17th century in a scientific struggle between two outstanding Dutch scholars, *Hugo Grotius,* a humanist and jurist, and *de Laet,* a geographer, goes back to one basic question: Could the ancestors of the American Indians have crossed the Atlantic or the Pacific Oceans in their primitive small boats? Could they have come to America from Europe, Africa, Polynesia or the Malayan Archipelago? The adherents of the Behring Strait theory deny it. Hence the solution with the aid of the nearest point of the Behring Strait where both continents Asia and America are in closest touch with one another. Hence the strange idea that not only the ancestors of the American Indian tribes, but also of tigers, lions and alligators as well as most plants may have arrived in the Western Hemisphere via Behring Strait.

In the light of language this argument is simply melting away as snow in the sunshine, for as a matter of fact, the American Indians and most nations of classical antiquity such as the Egyptians not only used boats, but gave them the same name: *CAN-oe*.

(285) *The Word CAN-oe Common to Tongues of the Old and New World.*

America, Caribbean	Europe, Old Norse	Africa, Egypt
CAN-aoa (boat)	KAN-e (boat)	KHAN-u (barge)

This fact points to a very old connection between the ancestors of the Indians and those of the Germanic tribes and of the Egyptians. Where did they meet? In the Old World? Except for north-eastern Asia there is no other corner of the Eastern Hemisphere where there could have been any prehistoric contact between those nations, and even there, according to the Behring Strait theory, there was no contact. No, according to this conception tribes, probably Mongolian tribes, migrated from that corner to America and became the ancestors of the American Indians.

However the name *CAN-oe* common to the Caribbean vernacular, to Egyptian and to Germanic idioms shows that there must have been some contact *across the Atlantic*. Otherwise we could hardly explain the presence of the same name for boat in the New and the Old World. Further, the Egyptian word *KHAN-oo* (death-barge of the sun-god *Sokharis*) is contained in the *Book of the Dead* a text dating back as far as about 4000 to 5000 B.C. The contact between the ancestors of the Egyptians and Indians must have taken place some 6,000 to 7,000 years ago. Alexandria was not yet founded at that time, nor did Cairo exist: Thebes and Karnak may already, and so may some of the pyramids. Yet neither in the West nor in the East is there any reminiscence of such a contact preserved. It is as if the memory of such an event had been blotted out. Or did it never occur?

There is still another reason why an immigration across the Atlantic to the Western Hemisphere cannot be proved by the common possession of the boat-name *CAN-oe*. This name cannot be considered a conclusive argument, for we have another Indian boat-name in the Caribbean vernacular which the American Indians share with the Malayans: *PIROGU-e* (boat). It is identical with the Malayan word *PERAH-u* (boat), with Danish *FAERG-e* (ferry), French *FARGU-e* (boat), Munda *BORG-a* (raft) and Samoyed*e WORG-a* (boat), and contains the same word-stem as our *BARK, BARG-e,* and *FERRY.*

(286) *The Boat-Name PIROGUE and BARGE in Both Hemispheres.*

America, Caribbean	Europe, Danish
PIRAGU-a (boat)	FAERG-e (ferry)
Asia, Samoyede	Malayan
WORG-a (boat)	PERAH-u (boat)

This word proves that all nations who possess the name *PIROGU-e* for the boat or some related word, must have spent part of their life together in some unknown place at some unknown time, when they still used similar words for the same things. Yet their words extend so far and are related with so many tongues that it could be both: they could have been brought to America across the Atlantic as well as across the Pacific. Vikings could have imported their word *FAERG-e* (ferry, boat), or Malayans or Polynesians their native boat-name *PERAH-u,* and the Caribbean Indians might have transformed it later into *PIRAGU-a* (pirogue, boat).

When we consider both names, *CAN-aoa* (canoe) and *PIRAGU-a* (pirogue, boat) which are found in America only in the Antilles dialects, and observe the route they must have taken to reach this part of the Western Hemisphere, we wonder whether Vikings or Malayans or Egyptians could have imported them to the New World. The idea of Vikings importing the name *CAN-oe* would appear at least possible, if we were to explain only one thing: How did the name *CAN-oe* pass from Labrador to the Antilles, without leaving the slightest vestige on its way south? Much more difficult to answer is the other question: How could the word *PERAH-u* (pirogue) have come from Malay or Polynesia — across the Pacific — and again pass to the Antilles? Did it sail around Cape Horn and up the whole east coast of South America to the Caribbean Sea, or did the Vikings bring both words to the Antilles? Again we realize that the theory of the peopling of the Western Hemisphere by migrations from the Old World puts numberless dilemmas before us. Many students realize this fact more and more. We must think of another possibility, namely that the nations of both the Old and the New World had come to their historical dwelling-places from some common homeland which was located neither in the East nor in the West. Here the tradition of Atlantis, the submerged island, helps to solve the riddle.

If we accept this solution without paying attention to the traditions of those who became the successors of the Atlanteans in the following ages, we are faced with a new dilemma. How did the American Indians pass from Atlantis to their homes in America? Did they follow the northern or southern wave of migration? Did they perhaps reach the desert of Gobi with the northern half of the Atlantean nucleus and in the following centuries pass to the north-eastern corner of Asia and thence to Alaska? This would simply be a new version of the Behring Strait theory. Again the same objections would arise as have been mentioned.

Here the old tradition alone can help us in solving the riddle. According to tales and legends of the Indian tribes of Central America, their ancestors had come to their present dwelling-places from a country called *Tulan* or *Tollan*. Is this Seneca's *Ultima Thule*? Is it *Atlantis*? In Mexico, this part of the world is called *Aztlan* or *Atlan* and this name sounds precisely like *Atlan-tis*. And according to the *Annals of the Cacchiquel, Tulan* was the place *where the sun rises,* hence east of the American Continent, and this source adds another feature: Tulan is *ri chaka palo,* that is *beyond the sea.* The American Indians have preserved an old tradition of Atlantis as their original home where they lived in common with other tribes of mankind, just as they maintained the reminiscence of a great water catastrophe by which that ancestral home was destroyed.

Manu and his helpers had prepared the transfer of a small nucleus of Atlanteans from Atlantis to the Eastern Hemisphere, that nucleus which was to develop into the Aryan 'race'. However not all the Atlanteans who survived the catastrophe followed the guidance of Manu and went East. Part of them went *West* instead of East, landed in America and became the *ancestors of the American Indians.* Hence the physical resemblence, the relationship of tongues, and of the whole civilisation between the nations of the Old and the New World. We realize the existence of what we could call a continuation of Atlantean culture among the Mexicans, the Mayas, the Incas, the Indians of Chile and of Brazil. A degeneration in knowledge occurred in the American Mystery Centres and this is why we cannot regard the American Indian religions and rituals as pure reflections of Atlantean spirituality. One very remarkable symptom of a complete corruption of the American Indian civilisations is the rite of human sacrifice as it was practised in Mexico and Central America.

What happened to the Indians, the successors of the inhabitants of Atlantis? In Chapter Eighteen we learned that after the submersion of Atlantis, a migration took place *from West to East,* in order to develop a new faculty of mankind, *the power of modern thinking.* The surviving Atlantean nucleus, germ of the new humanity, the *Aryan* kind of Man, migrated East and developed *perception* to a higher degree, then went back West, particularly to Europe, and there acquired the faculty of forming *concepts,* of evolving *abstract* thinking, the sense of *philosophy.*

The American Indians however failed the mission of the new age and lagged behind. They still preserved the former Atlantean picture-consciousness to some extent, and were in no way the match of the new *Aryan* 'race'. The whole tragedy of this deep difference of the thinking power of both the red and white races was manifested immediately after that fateful day of October the 12th, 1492, when descendants of the same Atlantean ancestors, after having been separated from one another for more than ten thousand years, met each other for the first time again on American soil: brother did not recognize brother, and a terrible war of extermination followed.

Thus a few hundred Spanish soldiers under *Cortez* and *Pizarro,* conquered Mexico and Peru which were defended by millions of courageous Indian warriors. In other words, two European infantry companies conquered the wide Mexican Empire extending from Yucatan to California and from the Gulf of Panama to Canada; and less than one infantry company occupied Peru, the Empire of the Incas.

The truth of this conception of the peopling of the American Continent can be proved in a simple, direct way by studying the life, nature and culture of the modern American Indians. The Atlantean Civilisation is reflected in the modern American Indian culture in a distorted and decadent way, but wherever we approach that strange remnant of a remote past with sufficient knowledge and understanding, we can still discover beneath its surface some genuine features of the Atlantean Man.

In 1942 the author of this book was invited by the Indian Office of the United States, Department of the Interior, to spend a few weeks in New Mexico and Arizona, visiting Indian reservations and contacting Indian chieftains and various scholars and officials. In the course of this visit the author came in touch with Navajos, Hopis and other tribes, and collected interesting linguistic and mythological material.

Among other literature he obtained several papers issued by the Indian Office. Among them was a text-book on World History for the use of reservation day-schools, compiled in English and Navajo by *Robert Young*. In this text-book Young points out that we cannot talk to a child grown up in an American Indian surrounding in the same way as to other American school children of the same age. The Indian children have *a different kind of consciousness* than other pupils. For example, one cannot tell them that the Germans recently waged a war against the people of the United States. It would not mean very much to Indian pupils to describe German soldiers as we usually do in our class-rooms. The Indian boys and girls would not understand it. They need picturesque expressions, *images* such as *iron-head people,* as a term to characterize Germans. This image the Indian children easily take up and remember, and whenever it emerges again, they connect it with the German nation. No concepts — but images, says Young; for the Indians still have a sort of *picture-consciousness*. Thus, in an American text-book, edited by American authorities, we find the confirmation of the existence of a picture-consciousness in Atlantis, for this kind of consciousness has survived among the modern descendants of the Atlanteans.

Another characteristic feature of the survival of Atlantean institutions among modern American Indians is *initiation*. Still today the meetings of those members of a tribe who with the chieftain form its council, take place in so-called *KIV-as*. A *KIV-a* is an underground room to which the council members descend by ladders. It is a hidden place, difficult, sometimes even dangerous to reach, located among rocks, a place which in olden times contained many secrets, especially cer-

(287) *The American Indian Kivas Were Originally Caves.*

America, New Mexico KIV-a (subterranean meeting place)	Spanish CUEV-a (cave)
English CAV-e	Navajo Indian GA-ACH (kiva)

tain *acoustic secrets*. Such mysterious devices were known in antiquity as characteristic of Mystery Centres. In Syracuse, Sicily, is a spot near the ancient amphitheatre which is called *The Ear of Dionysius*. We know also from the location of the Franco-Cantabrian Caves and from sanctuaries and meeting places, hidden among steep rocks, that the American Indian Kivas must have been caves originally, for the word *KIV-a* itself is not an Indian word, but a Spanish term: *CUEV-a* (cave).

The indigenous Navajo name of a kiva is entirely different: Ga-ach! Every important person of the tribe had to be initiated into the Old Indian (Atlantean) mystery wisdom: the chieftain, the medicine-man, the members of the sachem and so on. The author of this book asked several Indian chieftains, some of them members of highly respected families recognized as outstanding people by the American Government, how the dignity of a chieftain was transferred from one chieftain to his successor. They told him that the successor had to be a tribesman capable of initiation by virtue of his intellect and character. If the son or some other relative of the late chieftain had such qualities, he could well be elected. If not, an entirely different person had to be chosen.

This old initiation knowledge is vanishing more and more, and is becoming a sort of professional secret. Ever fewer individuals in an Indian tribe are capable of fulfilling the duties of a chieftain, a medicine-man or a healer. Old times are gone, a new spirit is about to arise. The last remnants of the Atlantean race are dying out, carrying back their ancient knowledge to the world from which they came. Indians become more and more members of Christian churches, yet in many cases Christendom to them is but an outer varnish used to screen the old faith of their ancestors, even — as in Japan — the worship of their ancestors.

Many baptized Indians in Latin America celebrate their old Indian festivals before the church, performing old rituals, burning incense, wearing masks and so on, while within the church they later partake of the Christian service. Typical of the whole spiritual chaos, of the inner struggle of these pilgrims between two ages, between two worlds is an experience which the author of this book had with an Indian driver, a reservation employee, who drove him from Window Rock to Aztec, and then back to Gallup. There was but one interest this Indian had — food! All the other problems of life did not bother him very much. When he was asked about his faith, he said: "Well, up to my fifteenth year, I was brought up in my tribe, and believed in the teachings of our ancestors. Later, when I left my relatives and worked outside, I became a Catholic, then a Baptist, then a Presbyterian, and now, I am an atheist!"

Today a great number of Indians, even chieftains do not have any knowledge of the faith and the customs of their ancestors. On the other hand, much of the ancient Atlantean wisdom has survived. One of the most wide-spread fields of ancient Indian wisdom deals with the problem of *reincarnation*. Most Indians who have been initiated into their ancient knowledge consider life after death to be a fact. One day, in Isleta, New Mexico, the author had a long talk with two Indian chieftains about this question. He had asked them: "What happens to our souls after we die?"

"Well", said one of the chieftains "The body disintegrates, and the soul separates from it."

"How fast does it separate?" I asked him.

He looked at me thoughtfully, as if he were to penetrate into the whole depth of my mind to find out whether I asked merely out of curiosity, or was driven by some hidden knowledge about those things. Almost hesitatingly, he said: "The soul leaves the body behind it after three days."

"After three days? And what happens to it later?"

Again he gazed at me: "Later? The soul is in the shape of a duck, and flies far, far away . . . to California!"

A strange language, strange images. The soul leaving the body three days after death. We recall a passage in the Gospel of St. John (chapter 2, 18): "Then answered the Jews and said unto him, What sign showest thou unto us, seeing that thou doest these things? Jesus answered and said unto them: *Destroy this temple, and in three days I will raise it up.* Then said the Jews, Forty and six years was this temple in building, and wilt thou rear it up in three days? *But he spake of the temple of his body.*"

Certainly, this 'raising of the temple of his body' by the Christ does *not* mean the same as the *reincarnation* of a mortal. A deeper acquaintance with all these questions will show clearly that the Bible here uses the term 'body' (flesh) for 'substance'. Nevertheless we feel that there is some inner connection between the three days of the building up the temple of the body (as in St. John) and the three days before the soul abandons the dead body. We learn from such significant details that the religious conceptions of the American Indians must be related to conceptions of the classical nations of the Old World, and that both must stem from a common source, from ancient Atlantean wisdom. Hence the resemblence of American symbols with those of Egypt, Babylonia, Greece and Palestine.

Do we not recognize in the duck flying to California the same symbol of the soul as it is applied in the Egyptian *Book of the Dead,* some six to seven thousand years ago? What does *California* mean once we penetrate into its deeper sense? Viewed from New Mexico, California lies in the *West,* the region of the setting sun. The Egyptians also imagined *Amenta,* the land of Ammon (the god of death and of reincarnation) to be in the West, just as the Greek *Erebos,* the *Inferno,* was not only thought to be in the West, but even meant *West!*

(288) *The Greek Kingdom of the Dead, EREB-os Meant West.*

Europe, Greece	Asia, Hebrew
EREB-os (inferno)	EREB (sunset, West)

Arabic	Latin
ma-GHREB (sunset, West)	CREP-usculum (dusk)

Thus, the answer of the American chieftain to the author was the same as an Egyptian priest would have given to Solon or Plato, or a Greek priest of Apollo would have given to any neophyte, for it was drawn from the same source of knowledge.

Among many cultural and religious features which the New World has in common with the Old are *dances and masks*. Whoever has an occasion to observe or to study the performance of temple-dances in different continents, whether in America, in Africa, or in many Asiatic countries, will easily discover certain common characteristics among all of them. Sometimes even the costumes which men and women are wearing are similar. In the war dances of the Hopi Indians and of certain African tribes we discover the same kind of helmets as the Greek warriors wore in the Trojan war or as we find them at Cnossus or elsewhere in Old Crete. The way the dancers move, the rhythm of the accompanying music, in a word the spirit of these ancient performances appears to be the same. There is no doubt that these dances of a bygone epoch together with many other customs of the American Indians, can be traced back to the same source in Atlantis.

All these facts speak in favor of the conception that all mankind once lived in a lost continent which we may call Atlantis, that there is but one human race which split into different sub-races and nations. We must suppose that mankind spoke one language while living in close community on that island, and only later, after their separation, language was split into different idioms, single national vernaculars developed out of the common mother-tongue of all humanity. A similar split occurred in each part of our civilisation: in religion, in science and in art. All these differentiations are but the results of evolution in time.

We learned about another fact connected with the reality of Atlantis: this continent was originally peopled by settlers from Alantis and not by pilgrims from the Old World. It is possible that in later epochs migrations from Asia to America took place — perhaps across Behring Strait, from China, or from the Malayan Islands, across the Pacific. The close connection between the vernaculars of the Siberian, North-American and Greenland Eskimos and the Lapland idiom provides evidence of such movements, but until now we are not certain whether these migrations passed from Europe across the Atlantic to Alaska and hence to north-eastern Asia, or followed the opposite direction.

At any rate, those who study this particular problem must be aware of the fact that in this case we must think of migrations which took place across both the Atlantic and the Pacific. We must consider the fact that quite a number of islands beyond the western coast of South America — such as the Galapagos and others — were not peopled at the time of the rediscovery of America by Columbus. This may sound strange, yet the conclusions we can draw from this fact will be confirmed by the witness of languages. Peruvian, Chilean and Mexican are so similar in their vocabularies to certain classical tongues of the Old World such as Greek, Sanskrit, Hebrew and so on, that, if they were influenced by other idioms, this must have come from the East and not from the West. Those who brought such words to America, must have landed on the American coast of the Atlantic and moved to the Pacific coast, to Peru, Chile ,Mexico, California across the American, especially the South American Continent; for it is not likely that Latin, Greek, German, Egyptian or Hebrew words were carried East by an unknown people in an unknown age, and then reached Peru across the Pacific.

Yet another fact supports all these conclusions. Not only was *America* *s*eparated from the Old World for many thousands of years by the Atlantis catastrophe, and the memory of that part of the world lost, but the whole *eastern part of Asia* — including India — was severed in a similar way from the entire western part of the Old World, and remained unknown even centuries later, after Alexander the Great had first penetrated to the centre of Asia. The population of southern Asia and the Far East thus was cut off from America as well as from

Europe and Western Asia. The Chinese had established archives of recorded history at least 1000 to 1500 B.C., and certainly such an event as the landing in America of big Asiatic
groups would not have escaped the writers of Chinese history.

Thus shadows of the Past emerge and we discover unex-
pected links between those continents which were separated
from each other for innumerable centuries. Identical words,
resounding like echoes from one corner of the world to the
other, confirm unmistakably the original unity of mankind
and the unity of origin of human speech. Speech is one of the
greatest achievements of the human mind. The words and
word-stems were created in the beginning of Man's career in
order to enable him to form this world in the shape of his
language. It is as if the divine world created originally by the
celestial, the lost Word, had arisen for a second time in a human, earthly form, as a creation of God's noblest creature.

The primeval tongue has changed in the course of evolution, but never has vanished. Its remnants still live among us,
and each nation, whether conscious of it or not, still uses the
same elements of speech, the same stems and words as in the
first days of the creation of Man. Today we look at the world
with Adam's eyes, listen to all its noises and melodies with
Adam's ears, and name things in our environment, sun, moon,
hills and valleys, rivers and fish, plants and animals, with
Adam's names. The deeper we penetrate into the mystery of
speech, the more we realize that human speech is not a cha-
otic, accidental conglomeration of sounds and syllables and
words — as some people believe — but is built up of simple
elements according to a cosmic plan, just as everything else
in the world.

Just as the material elements of Nature are the same wherever we move upon the earth, so speech consists of the same
spiritual elements, the same roots and words wherever we find
it, in this or that nation, this or that hemisphere, this or that
epoch. Some changes certainly occurred in the course of many,
many thousands of years, yet in most cases words hardly

changed so essentially as to become unrecognizable. Those who deal with different tongues will soon recognize certain patterns — not 'laws', or rigid rules without exceptions, but certain ways — according to which changes occurred, thus enabling them to reunite brother with brother and family with family once again.

In the Nineteenth Century when the science of language was still in its infancy and students had only begun to coordinate a few linguistic families, various theories arose which represented Man as originally speechless. This was a grave mistake, due to an insufficient knowledge of the nature of tongues. The Twentieth Century has enabled us to learn more and more about the relationship of most, if not all linguistic families. The horizon of knowledge has widened and we know today that speech is a creation of humanity, not a fabric of nations or races. Speech is as old as the human race itself, and as far as we can trace history — whether recorded or unrecorded — we find all languages related and Man endowed with the faculty of speech. As far as speech is the very barrier between Animal and Man, that barrier has existed from the very first appearance of Man upon earth. This is a fact of the highest importance, not only for linguistics, but for anthropology and other fields of natural science.

Likewise we can recognize the importance of America and of American antiquities for science in general. Something is preserved in the Indian civilisation of the American continent which represents a kind of museum of Atlantean life to a certain extent. To study the life and language of the American Indians in the light of Atlantean civilisation is similar to witnessing the afterglow of the setting sun with all its flaming colors. American Indian vernaculars reflect the tongue used in Atlantis, and the words still preserved enable us to restore the stage of human development reached by the Atlantean race.

We can start with a study of the worship of gods, and will be amazed at the great number of names of divinities which both the Western and Eastern Hemispheres have in common, the names for temples and priests, for incense and libations and other religious terms. We pass to the celestial world, and find common names for the sun, moon, and the other heavenly lights, for air and wind, fire, water and earth. We learn common names of tools, weapons, boats, clothing, food, and recognize something far more than the mere relationship of numberless words, namely the close community between that part of human life which has survived as a remnant of a very remote period of history, and our life today.

Certainly, we find such common features in the Old World also, between Asia, Africa and Europe. As we mentioned, the Far East has been separated from Europe for almost as many thousands of years as America since the submerging of Atlantis. Yet many waves of migration rolled from one part of the Old World to the other. This was not the case between America and Europe. Thus if we find common features between America and the Eastern Hemisphere, we know that they stem from the Atlantean epoch. Fifteen to thirty thousand years as an average lie behind these connections, for language is not created and developed in a short time. Even in our present, swift-living age it takes thousands of years before a daughter-language such as Italian or French can develop out of a mother-tongue such as Latin. Thus, the common words found in the Old and New World must have existed some fifteen thousand years ago, when the ancestors of the American Indians brought them from Atlantis to the American Continent.

All these indications are facts. We can draw all these conclusions from the material submitted thus far. Until now our knowledge of prehistoric man and his life upon earth has been dependent upon the mute testimony of tools, weapons and other fragmentary remains of the Stone-Age. Today that silent Age has opened its mouth and speaks to us. Dead stones are replaced by living human speech, the darkness of matter is penetrated by the illuminating rays of the Spirit of Words.

CHAPTER TWENTY

LANGUAGE IN THE PAST AND FUTURE

Certain scholars in the middle of the Nineteenth Century compared what they termed the search for a Primitive Tongue with the squaring of the circle. It seemed to them a Promethean undertaking, but the idea of tracing all tongues to a common source, to one original language has always fascinated imaginative spirits.

It was in the last ten years of his dramatic life that one of these pioneers, the Swedish poet *August Strindberg,* took up this problem. Despite his advanced age he started studying Oriental tongues: Hebrew, Babylonian, Chinese and others, and his *Blue Books* contain a great number of essays dealing with this subject. "One need not know much of Hebrew to find in any Biblical Dictionary the echo of a tongue that probably everywhere was the same."

On many occasions Strindberg indicated reasons why the idea of a Primeval Tongue met with obstinate resistance in the Nineteenth Century. As early as 1910 he pointed to certain prejudices as the actual cause of that strange opposition. One event of his life which occurred shortly before he passed away, is of special interest.

In 1911 the poet had a strange correspondence with three Finnish people. In December of that year, Strindberg, then 63 years old, fell sick. On Christmas day he had an unusual experience which he described in January 1912, in a letter written to his translator *Emil Schering:* "I did not suffer any pains, but was pervaded by a great peace, felt indifferent towards the outer world, and had the impression that I had finally come to rest. Generally it was my habit to jump out of bed at seven sharp, take a stroll, and then, driven by a burning wish of activity, turn home. Now that restlessness was gone; I believed I had fulfilled the task of my life. I had said everything I had intended to say, and the unprinted manuscripts lay in well ranged files."

"But sleep failed to come, because, as I believed, the fever rose. Yet I must have slumbered a little, for I awakened. During my slumber—which I could not determine from waking or sleeping—I had before me a written dictionary containing all languages, and I saw at the bottom of each page the Swedish translation of every term. As long as I was slumbering, this seemed to me a complete reality. As soon as I awakened, the book had disappeared. Upon waking one time I held my right hand in the air, with a gesture of turning pages. This lasted for three days and three nights, and wore me out. I believed that my turning pages of many dictionaries during four years was haunting me now mechanically. Sometimes however I had a dim impression as if not it was I, but my Finnish friend W. A. who was searching, following me with his thoughts, and entering the vacuum left behind by my extinguished consciousness. Then all became still. . . ."

This was one of the greatest imaginations in human history.

A few months later, on May 14, 1912, Strindberg died.

Today such a work as Strndberg saw in his vision could become tangible, if we wished. We could publish an *Etymological Dictionary of Human Speech,* containing at the bottom of each page the corresponding term of our individual mother-tongue, yet certain, all too skeptical people would still produce objections.

One of the most frequent of these is the following: Words alone, mere vocabularies, are not sufficient evidence for proving affinity among languages. Words alone do not constitute a language. It is their connection and inner structure which characterize languages. If we wish to overcome still prevailing doubts, we must prove the identity of grammar and syntax in the various tongues.

The impressive force of this argument cannot be denied. Language, of course, is not a mere summing up of words. Its spirit is manifested in its architecture and the pattern of its tissue. This however does not mean that the forms of the Indo-European tongues can serve as a yardstick for general linguistic relationship. It does not follow that we can take features such as those presented in List 4, and make them into a touchstone. The languages of today are no longer the same as those of the Past; and speech in the Future again will appear different from that of today. Languages are living creations; they have changed and evolved, and still are changing and evolving.

Once we realize this essential fact, we shall change our methods of investigation, and we shall be astonished of what excellent results we shall obtain. *Grammar,* we shall discover, is a *younger* creation than words. Such word-endings as king-*DOM,* friend-*SHIP,* full-*NESS,* false-*HOOD,* beau-*TY,* nati-*ON,* etc., are not abstract syllables picked up haphazardly, but ancient *words* distorted in the course of their development. Today we do not recognize their original meaning. However, in a word such as friend-*SHIP* we may recognize the word *SHAPE,* and in king-*DOM* the word *DOOM* (judgment).

Some of them, as -*TY* in beau-*TY,* are very old and widespread; others such as friend-*SHIP* are comparatively modern and are confined to a very small group of tongues: the Germanic family. -*T* as an ending designating the *feminine gender,* and later an *abstract idea,* is already found in *Old Egyptian* and in many *Semitic* vernaculars, such as Hebrew, Aramaic, Phoenician and Arabic. Ancient *Hellas* and *Rome* used it as well: e.g. Greek orth-*OT*-es (righteousness), Latin civ-*IT-as* (city). Thus we see that the search for common structural (grammatical) forms cannot be made in a mechanical way, but must be based upon the age of each form. We must find and compare linguistic features which existed many thousands of years ago, long before the different nations separated.

This may be illustrated by a form of conjugation as frequently used as the Perfect Tense in *English* and in other

Western languages. It is formed with the auxiliary verb *I HAVE.*

(289) *The Past Perfect Formed with I HAVE.*

English	I love	I have	loved
German	Ich liebe	Ich habe	geliebt
French	J' aime	J' ai	aimé
Italian	Io amo	Io ho	amato
Spanish	Yo quiero	Yo he	querido

However, this way of forming the Past Perfect did not exist either in India, in Persia, or even in Greece and Rome. *It does not exist today* in the Slavic tongues, and we find that it was not used before the Christian Era in Germanic and Romance languages. Therefore it is not to be expected that it will be discovered in Egyptian, Sumerian, Semitic or Ancient American tongues.

Another interesting point concerns the *articles*. Today, English, German, French, Spanish and Italian, chief vernaculars of the world, use definite and indefinite articles.

(290) *Languages With and Without Articles.*

	INDEFINITE ARTICLE	DEFINITE ARTICLE	
Sanskrit	——	——	
Avestan	——	——	
Slavic	——	——	
Latin	——	——	
Greek	——	HO, HE, TO	HOI, HAI, TA
English	A, AN	THE	
German	EIN, EINE	DE-r, DIE, DA-s	DIE
French	UN, UNE	LE, LA	LES
Italian	UNO, UNA	IL, LA, LO	: I, LE
Spanish	UNO, UNA	EL, LA	LO-s, LA-s
Hebrew	——	HA, HE, HO	
Arabic	——	AL, EL	
Babylonian	——	——	
Japanese	——	——	
Chinese	——	——	
Peruvian	——	——	

In our modern world tongues, the articles are one of the most essential grammatical features, yet it would be a mistake to imagine that articles were an integral part of speech at its beginnings. Even within the Indo-European family, articles were not in use some 2500 years ago. Man of antiquity did not separate the individual beings and objects. As in our story of the creation of writing we are confronted with a type of consciousness which saw the Universe as a totality, as a Unity, and did not individualize things. In those epochs language did not discriminate between trees *in general, a* tree, and *the* tree; hence the absence of articles.

Thus all languages of antiquity, at their beginning lacked articles. *Homer* did not use them except in connection with personal names, with individuals. *Socrates* and *Plato* used the definite article. It is those modern tongues which developed in Central and Western Europe which introduced and extended the use of both the definite and indefinite articles. Latin contained no articles; it is its alleged daughter-tongues, the Romance vernaculars, which developed them at the end of the first millennium of the Christian Era.

The ancient languages and those of the so-called primitive nations did not use any articles. Hebrew and Arabic among the Semitic tongues do possess them. These facts are not only interesting but very significant. We recognize not only that the *definite article* is *older than* the *indefinite,* but also become aware of certain connections between the Hebrew and Arabic articles on the one hand, and the Old Greek and Romance definite articles on the other.

(291) *Similar Definite Articles in Indo-European and Semitic Tongues.*

| **Greek** | HO, HE | **Hebrew** | HA, HO, HE |
| **Spanish** | EL | **Arabic** | EL, AL |

The Hebrew language uses the same definite article as the Hellenic tongue, while the Arabic language shows a clear connection with Romance forms such as Spanish *EL* and Italian *IL* (the). Did the Arabs borrow this article *AL, EL* from the Spaniards after the conquest of the Hibernian Peninsula? No. This article is found in the Koran, long before the penetration of the Arab general, *Tariq* into Spain. On the other hand, did the Romance vernaculars borrow their definite articles from the Arabs? This is also very doubtful.

Still more complex is the relationship between the Greek

and Hebrew articles: *HO, HE* (the). Who originated these essential elements of grammar: the Greeks or the Hebrews? The article *HA, HO HE* (as in *HA-GAN-a,* the army, literally the *gun,* arm, weapon) appears in Hebrew in the earliest recorded texts, long before Socrates and Plato.

What is the definite article? What does this little, mysterious English word, *THE,* really mean? We can answer the question, when we experience what it means in *THE*-y, *THE*-n, *THE*-re, *THA*-t or *THE*-se. As every other definite article in any language, it consists of the stem of the *demonstrative* pronoun. We find this stem contained in ancient and modern tongues all around the world. In Hebrew too, *ZE* means *that.* Once we recognize this connection, we can continue our search, and shall find the stem of Greek *HO, HE* (the) not only in Hebrew *HA, HO, HE,* but in English as well: in *HE!* In Hebrew, *HU, HE* mean*s he,* as in Arabic *HU*-wa (he), *HI*-ya (she). The same relationship can be established between Spanish *EL,* (the), Arabic *EL, AL* (the) and such demonstratives. The Romance forms of the definite article *EL, IL,* are usually derived from Latin *ILL-e* (that, those). In the Semitic family, too, we can connect the Arabic article *EL* with Hebrew *EL-e* (that, those).

(292) *Connection Between the Definite Article and the Demonstrative.*

Greek	HO, HE (the)	English	HE (he)
Hebrew	HA, HO, HE (the)	Hebrew	HU, HE (he)
English	THE	English	THE-se
Greek	TO (the)	Hebrew	ZE (that)
Spanish	EL (the)	Latin	ILL-e (that, those)
Arabic	EL, AL (the)	Hebrew	EL-e (those)

Thus, the relationship of all tongues is by no means restricted to nouns only. We find adjectives, verbs, numerals, pronouns, prepositions, adverbs and conjunctions of the same stem in every continent and linguistic family. The common origin of languages is now a fact established beyond any doubt.

Yet did we not admit that Arabic *AL, EL* (the) is not borrowed from Spanish, and Spanish *EL* (the) is not borrowed from Arabic? If this is true, they must be independent creations of the spirits of each of these languages, originated in different places, at different times. How can we speak of relationship in this case?

This is a valid objection, yet it can be accounted for. We learned that both the Spanish (Indo-European) article *EL* (the) and the Arabic (Semitic) *EL, AL* (the) are derived from demonstrative pronouns, Latin *ILL*-e and Hebrew *EL*-e (that, those). These elements existed in both linguistic groups before their separation. The definite articles may be, and probably are, later creations which were formed after the split of the primeval tongue. This however does not exclude their relationship. The same applies to another objection: to *onomatopoeias*. Words can of course be imitations of noises in Nature, the rustling of leaves, the roaring of the wind, the breaking of waves, the barking of dogs. Does this indicate the period when such imitative words were created and introduced into speech? Were the first ancestors of mankind unable to imitate Nature in their language? Words can be onomatopoeias, yet nevertheless related, derived from a common source. It is the nations who in the course of evolution, undertook the task of enriching the national vocabularies by adding more and more newly coined words. However, in almost all cases, the metal out of which these new words were coined was and is property of all mankind, and not of the individual nations. *Humanity* yielded the *elements,* and the *nations* shaped these elements according to their individual styles, thus creating new *forms.* Hence the present difficulty to discover who owns the 'copyright' of our words.

We must emphasize that the Indo-European tongues, Sanskrit included, are comparatively young languages, a rather recent stratum. From study limited to them alone we cannot draw any definite conclusions valid for all languages or for these which belong to the oldest strata of human speech. It is true that some rather modern tongue may contain traces of the original structure, but such clues are not just to be found on the surface.

This fact can be illustrated by French examples already mentioned. It has been pointed out that if we draw a diagonal from the north-western part of France to the south-eastern part, we find, West of that line, in the Atlantic zone, a great number of localities with names ending in *-AC,* such as Carn-*AC,* Berger-*AC,* Luss-*AC,* Cogn-*AC,* Cavaign-*AC,* etc. We found names similar to *Carnac,* in England, Carn-*OCK,* in Egypt, Karn-*AK,* in India and Turkistan, Karn-*AK.* But this ending, *AC, OCK* seems to be a remnant of a very ancient state of languages, doubtless a heritage from Atlantis. Such endings as *-AK, -EK, -IK, -OK, -UK* were used in antiquity in almost all tongues, and have been passed down from the unrecorded to the historic epoch of human evolution.

(293) *Ancient Endings of Nouns and Names:*
-AK,-EK, -IK, -OK, -UK.

Swiss Patois	sér-AC	(cheese)
Alaskan	tad-AK	(daddy)
Greenland	ign-EK	(fire)
Hungarian	gyerm-EK	(child)
Californian	id-IK	(water)
English	pan-IC	
Peruvian	pint-OK	(bent-reed)
English	hill-OCK	(small hill)
Babylonion	Mard-UK	(Mars)
Eskimo	Nan-UK	(son)

Thus we discover that the English tongue is characterized by ancient endings which we can call Atlantean; for they refer to the earliest epochs of human speech. There is quite a number of words in English which are formed with the ending *-OCK,* which are about to be entirely replaced by the shorter original forms consisting of the pure word-stem.

(294) *Simple English Words and Their Parallels
Ending in -OCK*

HILL	HILL-ock
BULL	BULL-ock
BUN	BONN-ock
BIT	BITT-ock
MACE	MATT-ock
HUMP	HUMM-ock

Most of the parallel forms ending in *-OCK* stem from Scotland, or from regions where the Celtic and Hibernian elements once prevailed. In a limited number of cases the forms ending in *-OCK* are still in use in modern England, while the simple, original forms are to be found in other tongues.

(295) *English Words Ending in -OCK
and Their Foreign Relatives.*

English	MATT-ock	Hebrew	MAT-eh (staff)
"	PADD-ock	German	Schild-PATT (tortoise-shell)
"	CUST-ock	Russian	KUST (plant)

From these primitive suffixes many other endings developed in various tongues. *-AK* turned into *-AH*, or *-AS*, *-IK* into *-IS* or *-I*, *-UK* into *-US* or *-U*. In many other cases nouns remained at or returned to the primitive state where — as in Chinese — word and word-stem appear to be identical. This tendency in the Western European vernaculars, particularly English and French, has been stressed by such outstanding scholars as *A. Meillet*.

(296) *Extension of the Endings -AK, -EK, -IK, -OK, -UK.*

Slavic	SYR (cheese)	Swiss Patois	SER-ac (cheese)
English	GERM	Hungarian	GYERM-ek (child)
"	DAD	Alaskan	TAD-ak (father)
Sumerian	ID (water)	Californ.	ID-ik (water)
Latin	IGN-is (fire)	Greenland	IGN-ek (fire)
Latin	PIN-us (pine)	Alaskan	PIN-yuk (pine)
"	COEL-um (sky)	Chukchee	KELL-ak (sky)
Hebrew	YELED (child)	Sumerian	ILD-ak (offspring)
"	MAT-eh (staff)	English	MATT-ock
Greek	KHITON (coat)	Quiché	QUETON-ek (fur coat)
"	POTAM-os (river)	American	POTOM-ac
Italian	MART-e (Mars)	Assyrian	MARD-uk (Mars)
Spanish	NIN-o (child)	Eskimo	NAN-uk (son)

We could quote many thousands of similar examples thus proving that the identity of the vocabularies of our languages is in no way due to accidental coincidence, but is the result of original relationship. Thus the grammatical structure of the different tongues is related and stems from a common source.

The Primeval Tongue of all Mankind is no mere phantom, no empty dream, no futile attempt to square the circle. It is a reality. Although our modern and the historic languages appear entirely different, and — as a matter of fact — have become so diverse that we cannot understand one another without first studying our mutual tongues, beneath the surface numberless remnants have survived. Sometimes it seems as if we had only to stretch out our arms — as did *Strindberg* in his slumber — to seize the mysterious book which contains all the words of mankind. Again, however, it appears as if this were only a phantom, a mirage of the desert, luring the thirsty wanderer and vanishing as he approaches. We know of course that behind the similarity, the identity of numberless words in the different tongues, there must be some common pattern in whose likeness they were created. However, to reconstruct this primeval model, this lost Word, remains a very hard task.

Yet, mankind always felt that one evidence of its common descent lay in the secret of the origin of its tongues. Out of that dim consciousness as expressed in the mythological tales of many nations, the wish arose to come back to the original unity. As the Egyptian Pharaoh *Psamtik*, the German Emperor *Frederick II.*, and *King James of Scotland** attempted, by experimenting with newborn children, to rediscover that lost Primeval Speech, in the following ages scholars of different fields, the philosopher, *Leibniz,* the German clergyman, *Schleyer* in his *Volapük,* the Polish doctor, *Zamenhof* in his *Esperanto,* tried to re-establish the lost unity of speech by an artificial tie, an artificial common speech, a kind of Homunculus.

Yet it is with artificial tongues as with artificial limbs: they never can replace entirely our natural organs. It is true that such a mechanically formed language can render services up to a certain point, but it cannot take the place of the Lost Word, even in its decadent form. It can never fulfill the task we expect of it, because it underlies the same laws as the inherited human tongues. A deeper conception of what is called the Confusion of Tongues explains this tragedy on the basis of a moral failure of humanity. Why did the Primeval Tongue split? Why was the human family scattered around the earth and divided into races and nations? Because of their inner state, their spiritual and moral decay.

No artificial device will ever achieve what the Cosmic forces could not reach. When we look at our world, at our

*Compare James George Frazer, "Folklore in the Old Testament," Vol. I, p. 376.

epoch, at mankind in its present state, we find only division and separation. Whatever we do, whatever we create, will fall to pieces, if the basis for division is not eliminated from our midst.

We must become aware of our insufficiency, before we can overcome it. Unity of Speech in the Future presupposes the conscious unity of Mankind. It is an inner, not an outer process of evolution out of which that harmony for which we all long will be attained. It is a process of inner growth, inner purification, inner light which alone can lead us to the common source of all our existence.

LIST OF KEY-WORDS

(Romanic figures designate the *chart numbers*, those in Italics
the *pages*).

301